ipu

easy

Computer Basics

Windows® 7 Edition

Michael Miller

CONTENTS

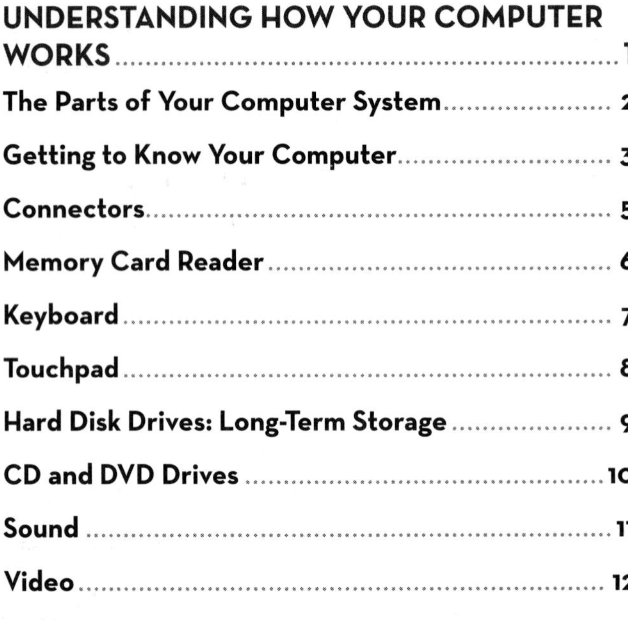

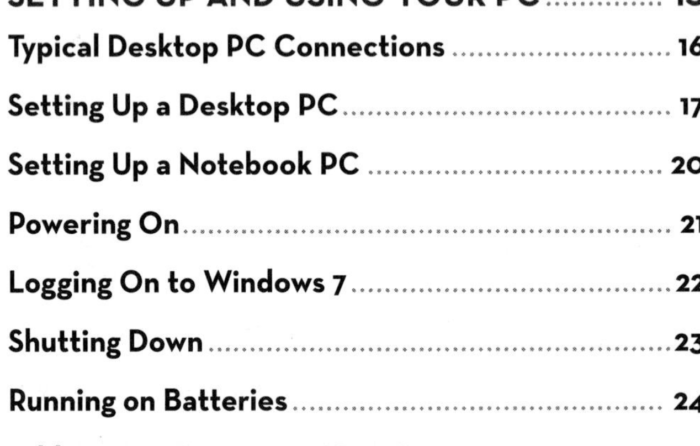

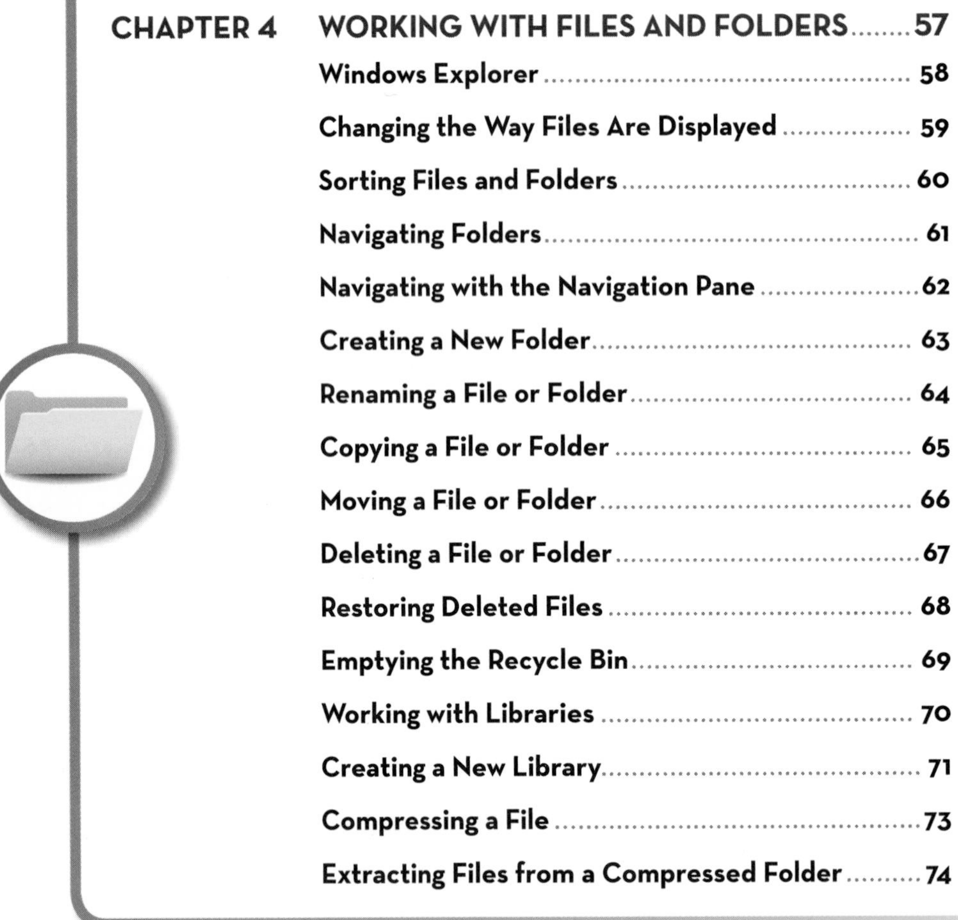

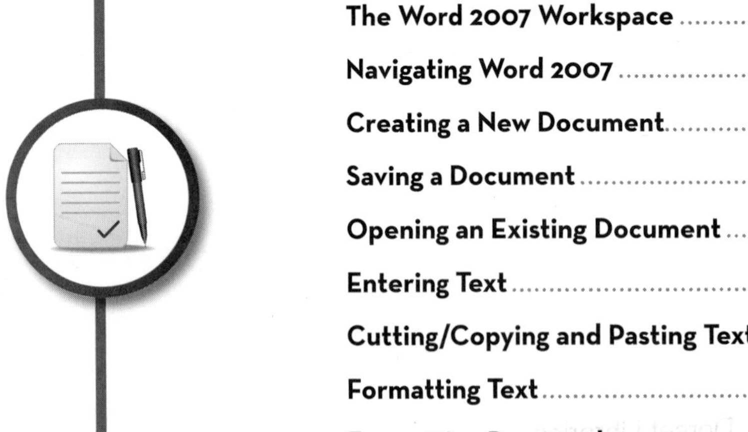

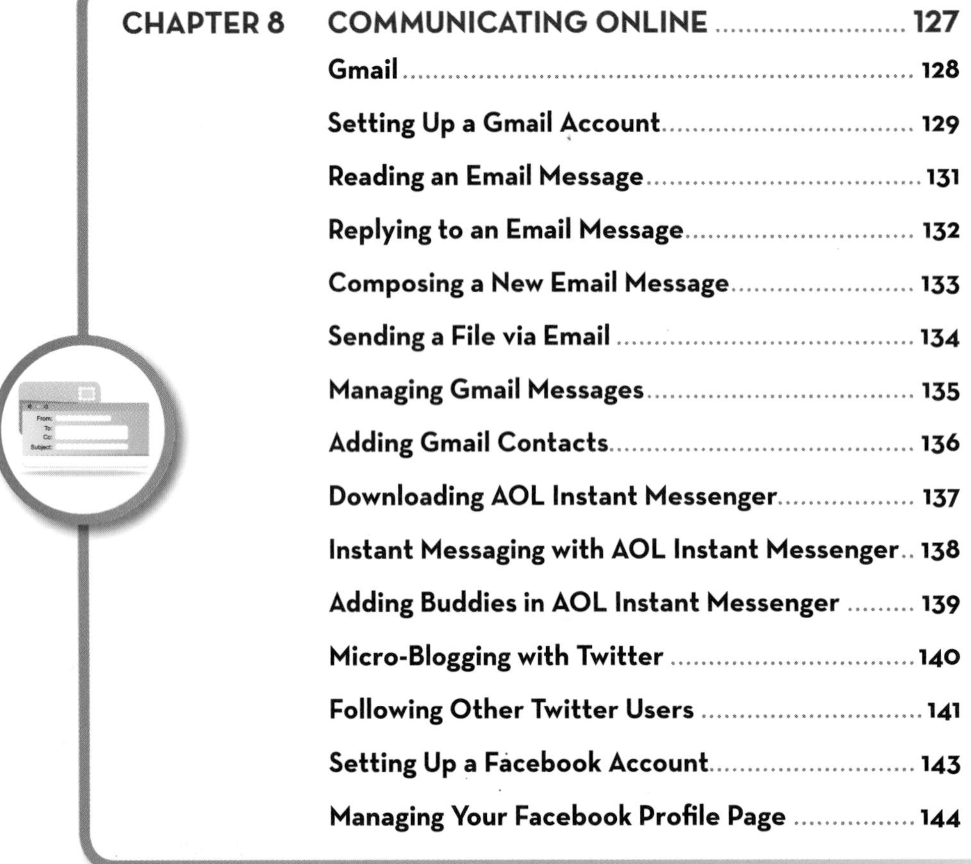

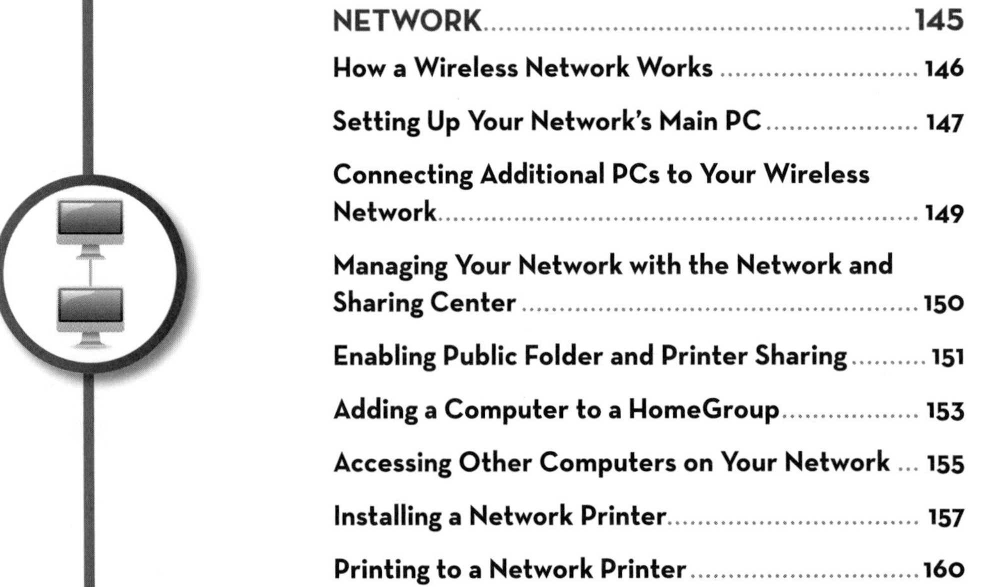

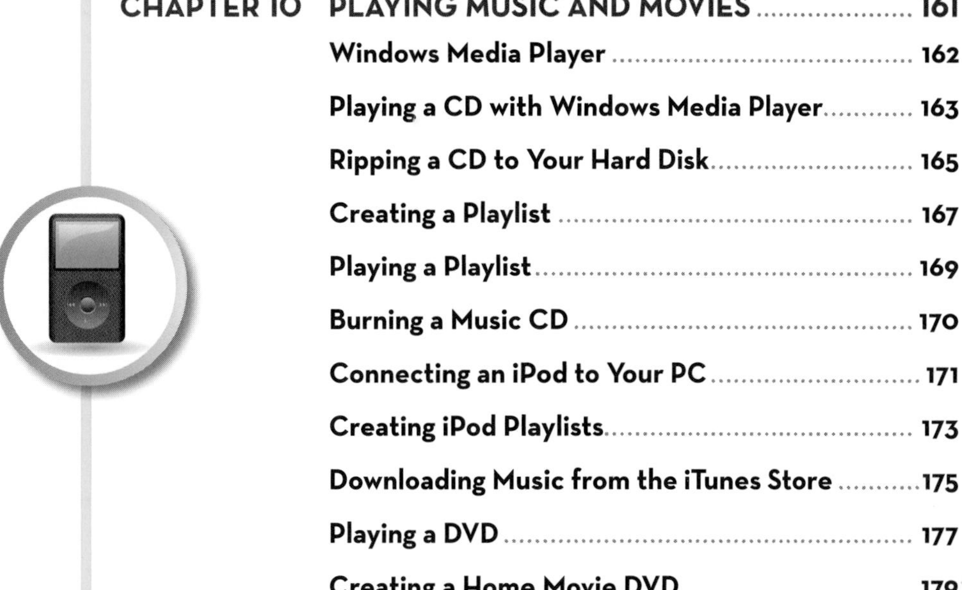

EASY COMPUTER BASICS, WINDOWS® 7 EDITION

ISBN-13: 978-0-7897-4227-8
ISBN-10: 0-7897-4227-6

U.K. ISBN-13: 978-0-7897-4232-2
U.K. ISBN-10: 0-7897-4232-2

Library of Congress Cataloging-in-Publication Data

Miller, Michael, 1958-
Easy computer basics : Windows 7 edition / Michael Miller.
p. cm.
Includes index.
ISBN 978-0-7897-4227-8
1. Microsoft Windows (Computer file) 2. Microcomputers. I. Title.
QA76.5M5314135 2009
004.165--dc22
2009023684

Printed in the United States of America

First Printing: September 2009

TRADEMARKS

All terms mentioned in this book that are known to be trademarks or service marks have been appropriately capitalized. Que Publishing cannot attest to the accuracy of this information. Use of a term in this book should not be regarded as affecting the validity of any trademark or service mark.

WARNING AND DISCLAIMER

Every effort has been made to make this book as complete and as accurate as possible, but no warranty or fitness is implied. The information provided is on an "as is" basis. The author and the publisher shall have neither liability nor responsibility to any person or entity with respect to any loss or damages arising from the information contained in this book.

BULK SALES

Que Publishing offers excellent discounts on this book when ordered in quantity for bulk purchases or special sales. For more information, please contact

U.S. Corporate and Government Sales
1-800-382-3419
corpsales@pearsontechgroup.com

For sales outside of the U.S., please contact

International Sales
international@pearson.com

Associate Publisher
Greg Wiegand

Acquisitions Editor
Michelle Newcomb

Development Editor
Charlotte Kughen

Managing Editor
Patrick Kanouse

Project Editor
Mandie Frank

Copy Editor
Karen Gill

Indexer
Heather McNeill

Proofreader
Water Crest Publishing

Technical Editor
Vince Averello

Publishing Coordinator
Cindy Teeters

Designer
Anne Jones

Compositor
Bronkella Publishing

ABOUT THE AUTHOR

Michael Miller is a successful and prolific author with a reputation for practical advice, technical accuracy, and an unerring empathy for the needs of his readers.

Mr. Miller has written more than 90 best-selling books over the past two decades. His books for Que include *Absolute Beginner's Guide to Computer Basics, Absolute Beginner's Guide to eBay, How Microsoft Windows Vista Works, Speed It Up: A Non-Technical Guide to Speeding Up Slow Computers, Your First Notebook PC,* and *Googlepedia: The Ultimate Google Resource*. He is known for his casual, easy-to-read writing style and his practical, real-world advice—as well as his ability to explain a variety of complex topics to an everyday audience.

You can email Mr. Miller directly at easycomputer@molehillgroup.com. His website is located at www.molehillgroup.com.

DEDICATION

To Sherry—life together is *easier.*

ACKNOWLEDGMENTS

Thanks to the usual suspects at Que, including but not limited to Greg Wiegand, Michelle Newcomb, Charlotte Kughen, Mandie Frank, Karen Gill, and technical editor Vince Averello.

WE WANT TO HEAR FROM YOU!

As the reader of this book, you are our most important critic and commentator. We value your opinion and want to know what we're doing right, what we could do better, what areas you'd like to see us publish in, and any other words of wisdom you're willing to pass our way.

As an associate publisher for Que Publishing, I welcome your comments. You can email or write me directly to let me know what you did or didn't like about this book—as well as what we can do to make our books better.

Please note that I cannot help you with technical problems related to the topic of this book. We do have a User Services group, however, where I will forward specific technical questions related to the book.

When you write, please be sure to include this book's title and author as well as your name, email address, and phone number. I will carefully review your comments and share them with the author and editors who worked on the book.

Email: feedback@quepublishing.com

Mail: Greg Wiegand
Associate Publisher
Que Publishing
800 East 96th Street
Indianapolis, IN 46240 USA

READER SERVICES

Visit our website and register this book at www.informit.com/title/9780789742278 for convenient access to any updates, downloads, or errata that might be available for this book.

IT'S AS EASY AS 1-2-3

Each part of this book is made up of a series of short, instructional lessons, designed to help you understand basic information.

1. Each step is fully illustrated to show you how it looks on screen.
2. Each task includes a series of quick, easy steps designed to guide you through the procedure.
3. Items that you select or click in menus, dialog boxes, tabs, and windows are shown in bold.

Tips, notes, and cautions give you a heads-up for any extra information you may need while working through the task.

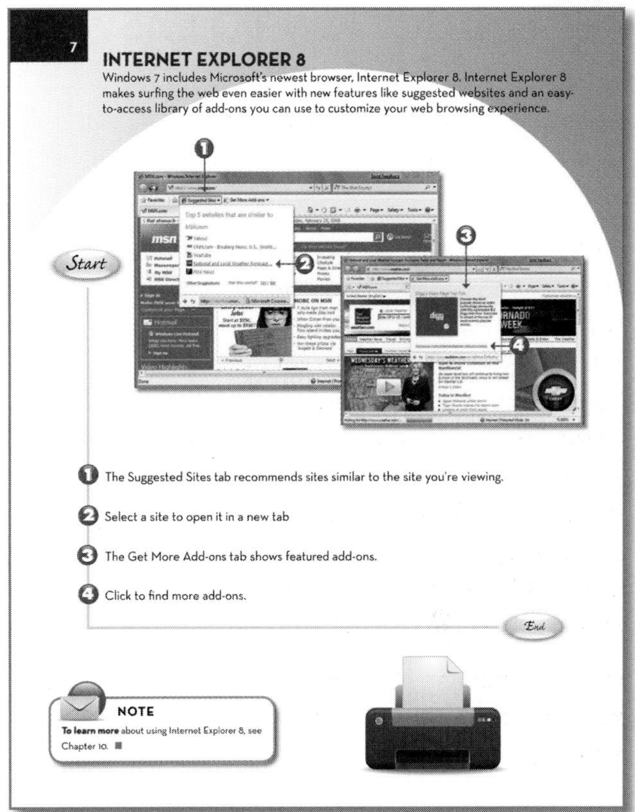

INTRODUCTION TO *EASY COMPUTER BASICS, WINDOWS 7 EDITION*

Computers don't have to be scary or difficult. Computers can be *easy*—if you know what to do.

That's where this book comes in. *Easy Computer Basics, Windows 7 Edition* is an illustrated, step-by-step guide to setting up and using your new computer. You'll learn how computers work, how to connect all the pieces and parts, and how to start using them. All you have to do is look at the pictures and follow the instructions. Pretty easy.

After you learn the basics, I'll show you how to do lots of useful stuff with your new PC. You'll learn how to use Microsoft Windows to copy and delete files; use Microsoft Word to write letters and memos; use Gmail to send and receive email messages; and use Internet Explorer to search for information on the Internet. We'll even cover some fun stuff, including listening to music, working with digital photographs, and using Facebook and Twitter.

If you're worried about how to keep your PC up and running, we'll cover some basic system maintenance, too. And, just to be safe, I'll show you how to protect your computer when you're online—against viruses, spam, spyware, and computer attacks. It's not hard to do.

To help you find the information you need, I've organized *Easy Computer Basics, Windows 7 Edition* into 13 chapters.

Chapter 1, "Understanding How Your Computer Works," describes all the pieces and parts of a typical notebook or desktop computer system. Read this section to find out all about hard drives, keyboards, speakers, and the like.

Chapter 2, "Setting Up and Using Your PC," shows you how to connect all the pieces and parts of a typical PC and get your new computer system up and running.

Chapter 3, "Using Microsoft Windows 7," introduces the backbone of your entire system—the Microsoft Windows 7 operating system—including how it works and how to use it.

Chapter 4, "Working with Files and Folders," shows you how to manage all the computer files you create—by moving, copying, renaming, and deleting them.

Chapter 5, "Using Microsoft Word," shows you how to use Microsoft's popular word processor to create letters and other documents.

Chapter 6, "Connecting to the Internet," is all about how to get online—both at home and on the road, via Wi-Fi hotspots.

Chapter 7, "Browsing the Web," shows you what to do when you get online. You'll learn how to use Internet Explorer to surf the Web, search for information, shop for items online, and view and upload YouTube videos.

Chapter 8, "Communicating Online," is all about using the Internet to talk to other users. You'll learn about email, instant messaging, Twitter, and Facebook.

Chapter 9, "Setting Up a Wireless Home Network," helps you connect all the computers in your house to a wireless network and share a broadband Internet connection.

Chapter 10, "Playing Music and Movies," shows you how to download and play digital music files, listen to CDs on your PC, burn your own audio CDs, copy songs from your PC to your Apple iPod, and watch DVDs on your computer screen.

Chapter 11, "Working with Digital Photos," helps you connect a digital camera to your PC and edit your digital photos using the Windows Photo Gallery program.

Chapter 12, "Protecting Your Computer," is all about stopping spam, viruses, spyware, phishing scams, and the like.

Chapter 13, "Taking Care of Your Computer," shows you how to keep your PC running smoothly, back up your important data, and recover from serious crashes.

And that's not all. At the back of the book, you'll find a glossary of common computer terms—so you can understand what all the techie types are talking about!

So, is using a computer really this easy? You bet—just follow the simple step-by-step instructions, and you'll be computing like a pro!

UNDERSTANDING HOW YOUR COMPUTER WORKS

Chances are you're reading this book because you have a new computer. At this point, you might not be totally sure what it is you've gotten yourself into. Just what is this mess of boxes and cables—how does it all go together, and how does it work?

We'll start by looking at the physical components of your system—the stuff we call computer *hardware*. A lot of different pieces and parts make up a typical computer system. You should note, however, that no two computer systems are identical because you can always add new components to your system—or disconnect other pieces you don't have any use for. And notebook computers are a bit different from desktop models, even though they do the same thing; the parts are just assembled a little differently.

THE PARTS OF YOUR COMPUTER SYSTEM

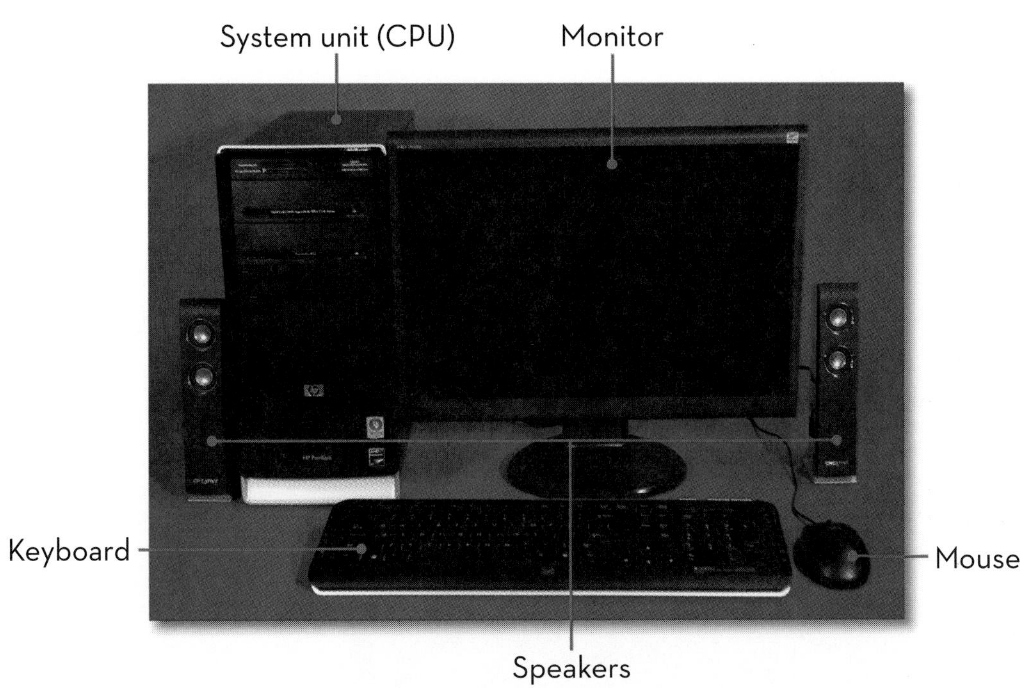

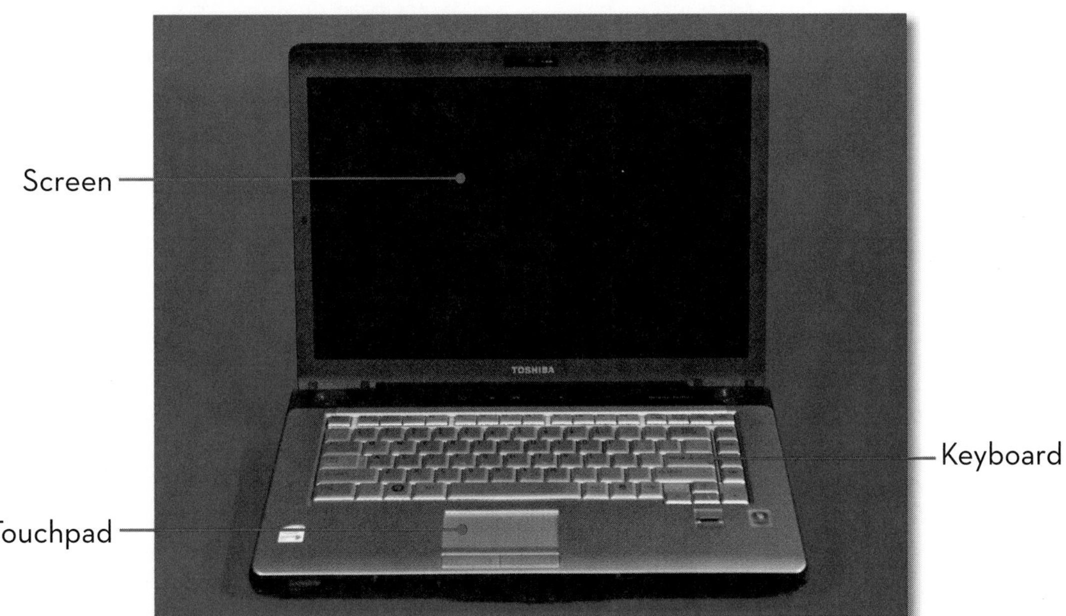

GETTING TO KNOW YOUR COMPUTER

Most new computers today are notebook models. A notebook or laptop PC differs from a desktop PC in that all the pieces and parts are combined into a single unit that you can take with you virtually anywhere. And since all components are built-in, you don't have to worry about making sure everything is connected!

Start

Modem (telephone) connector

USB ports

CD-ROM/ DVD drive

Power cable connection

End

NOTE

Connecting Ports Because not all components you plug into your system have the same type of connectors, you end up with an assortment of different jacks—called ports in the computer world. ■

NOTE

External Peripherals Even though a notebook PC has the keyboard, mouse, and monitor built-in, you can still connect external keyboards, mice, and monitors to the unit. This is convenient if you want to use a bigger keyboard or monitor or a real mouse (instead of the notebook's track pad). ■

Start

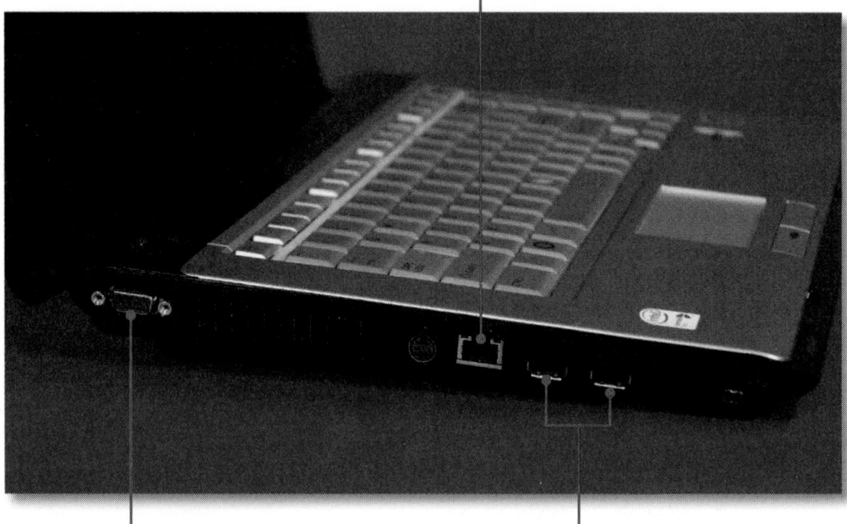

End

NOTE

Desktops and Laptops Most desktop computers differ from notebook units in that all the components are separate. The primary component of a desktop PC is the system unit, and to it you connect your PC's external monitor, keyboard, mouse, and speakers. (So-called "all in one" desktops have the monitor, system unit, and speakers in a single unit, however.) ■

NOTE

Desktop Front and Back On a desktop PC, most of the primary components connect to ports on the back of the system unit. The front of the system unit is where you insert CDs, DVDs, and other types of storage media. ■

CONNECTORS

Every component you plug into your computer has its own connector, and not all connectors are the same. This results in an assortment of jacks—called *ports* in the computer world. The USB port is probably the most common, used to connect all sorts of external peripherals, including printers, keyboards, mice, and disk drives.

Start

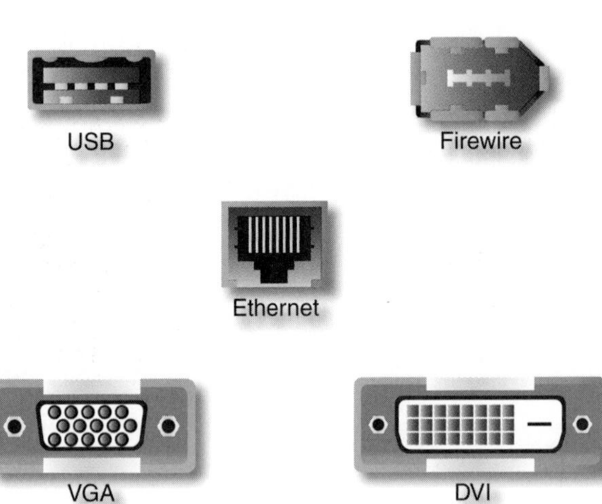

End

NOTE

Portable Devices Most portable devices that you connect to your computer, such as iPods and digital cameras, connect via USB. ■

MEMORY CARD READER

Most computers today include a set of memory card readers, typically grouped on the front or side of the unit. Memory cards store photos and movies recorded on digital cameras and camcorders. To read the contents of a memory card, simply insert the card into the proper slot of the memory card reader.

Start

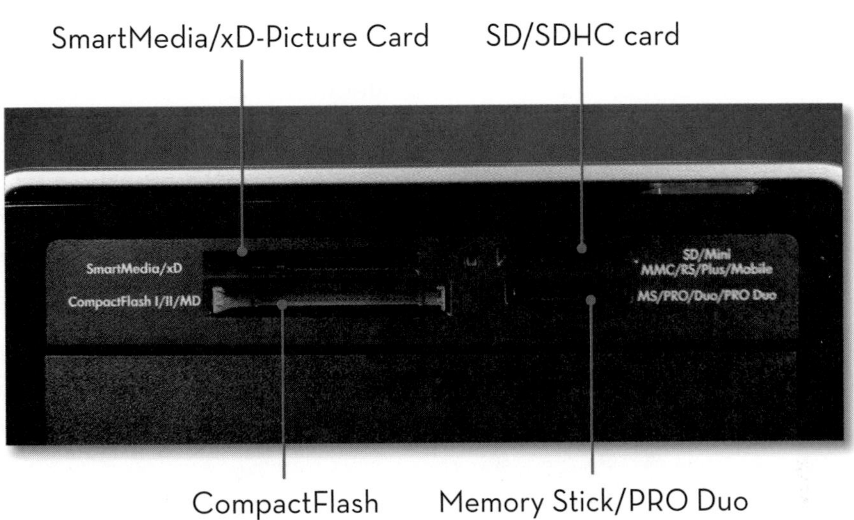

End

NOTE

Memory Card Formats Different portable devices use different types of memory cards—which is why your computer has so many memory card slots. The most popular memory cards today are the Secure Digital (SD), Secure Digital High Capacity (SDHC), CompactFlash (CF), Memory Stick, and xD-Picture Card formats. ■

KEYBOARD

A computer keyboard looks and functions just like a typewriter keyboard, except that computer keyboards have a few more keys (for navigation and special program functions). When you press a key on your keyboard, it sends an electronic signal to your system unit that tells your machine what you want it to do.

Start

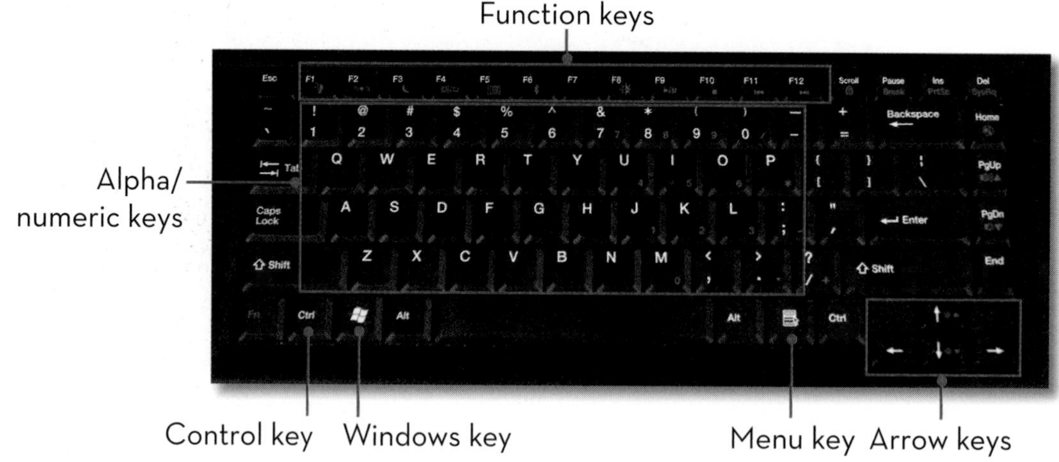

End

TIP

Numeric Keypad Because of the small form factor, notebook PC keyboards typically lack the separate numeric keypad found on desktop PC keyboards. If you need a numeric keypad with your notebook PC, you can connect an external keyboard—with built-in keypad—to your computer. ■

TIP

Wireless Keyboards If you want to cut the cord, consider a wireless keyboard or mouse. These wireless devices operate via radio frequency signals and let you work several feet away from your computer, with no cables necessary. ■

TOUCHPAD

On a desktop PC, you control your computer's onscreen pointer (called a *cursor*) with an external device called a *mouse*. On a notebook PC, you use a small *touchpad* instead. Move your finger around the touchpad to move the cursor, and then click the left and right buttons below the touchpad to initiate actions in your program.

Start

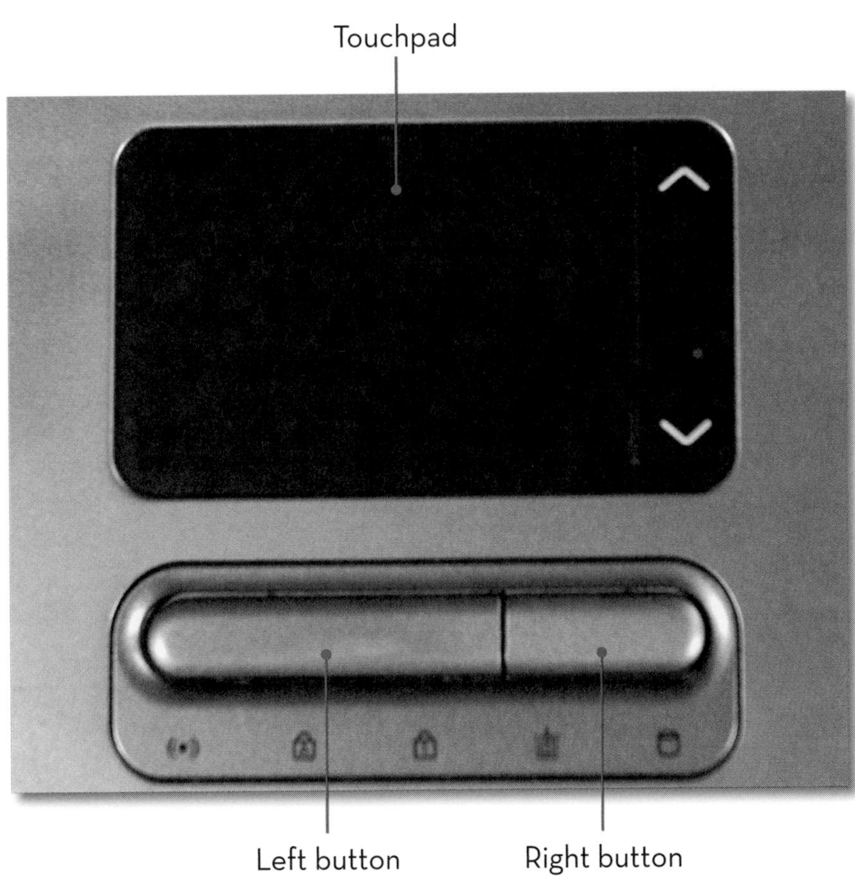

End

TIP

External Mice If you'd rather use a mouse than a touchpad, you can connect any external mouse to your notebook PC via the USB port. Some manufacturers sell so-called notebook mice that are smaller and more portable than normal models. ■

TIP

Mouse Options Most external mice offer more control options than built-in touchpads. For example, some mice include a scrollwheel you can use to quickly scroll through a web page or word processing document. ■

HARD DISK DRIVES: LONG-TERM STORAGE

The hard disk drive inside your computer stores all your important data—up to 1 terabyte (TB) or more, depending on your computer. A hard disk consists of metallic platters that store data magnetically. Special read/write heads realign magnetic particles on the platters, much like a recording head records data onto magnetic recording tape.

Start

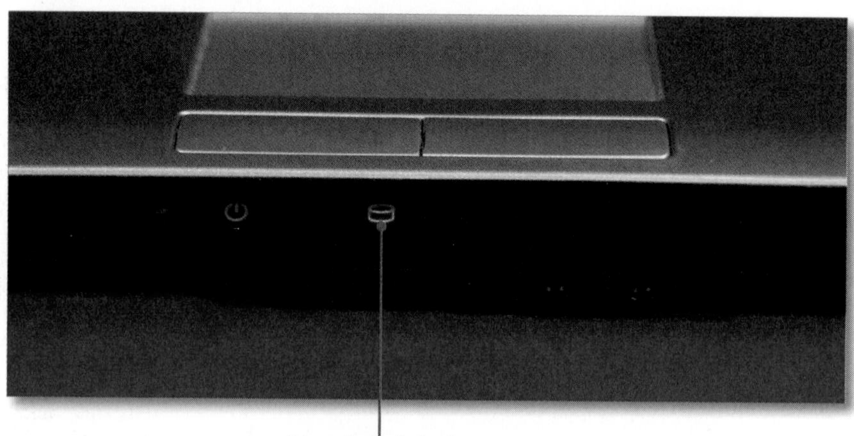

Hard disk light

End

TIP

Formatting the Drive Before data can be stored on a hard disk, the disk must first be formatted. When you format a hard disk, your computer prepares each track and sector of the disk to accept and store data magnetically. (Most new hard disks, such as the one in your new PC, come preformatted.) ■

CD AND DVD DRIVES

Computer or data CDs and DVDs look just like the compact discs and movie DVDs you play on your home audio/video system. Data is encoded in microscopic pits below the disc's surface and is read from the disc via a drive that uses a consumer-grade laser. The laser beam follows the tracks of the disc and reads the pits, translating the data into a form your computer can understand.

Start

Disc tray

End

NOTE

DVD Versus CD Most new PCs come with combination CD/DVD drives that can read and write both CDs and DVDs. The advantage of a data DVD over a data CD is that a DVD disc can hold much more data—4.7 gigabytes (GB) on a DVD versus 700 megabytes (MB) for a typical CD. ■

NOTE

Music and Movies A computer CD drive can play back both data and commercial music CDs. A computer DVD drive can play back both data and commercial movie DVDs. ■

SOUND

Most notebook and desktop computers today come with right and left speakers for stereo sound. Sound systems for desktop PCs can include a separate subwoofer for better bass. All speaker systems are driven by a sound card or chipset installed inside the computer.

Start

End

TIP

External Speakers If the speakers in a notebook PC are too small for your taste, you can connect a set of larger external USB speakers instead. ■

NOTE

Surround Sound So-called 5.1 surround sound speaker systems come with five satellite speakers (three front and two rear) and the ".1" subwoofer—great for listening to movie soundtracks or playing explosive-laden video games. ■

VIDEO

Your computer electronically transmits words and pictures to the computer screen built into your notebook, or to a separate video monitor on a desktop system. These images are created by a *video card* installed inside the computer. Settings in Windows tell the video card how to display the images you see on the screen.

Start

End

NOTE

CRT Versus LCD Many older computer systems used traditional cathode ray tube (CRT) monitors. Newer flat-screen monitors use an LCD display instead, which takes up less desk space.

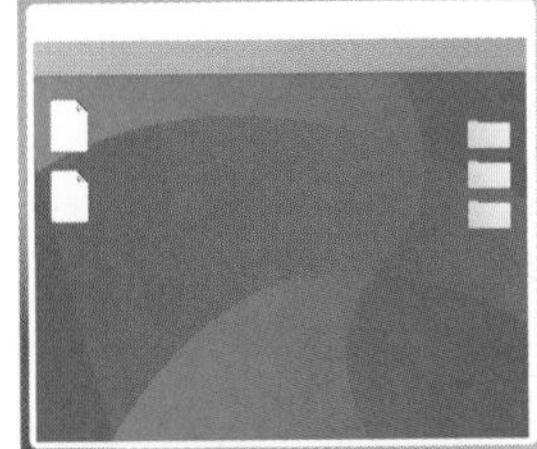

PRINTERS

To create a hard copy of your work, you must add a printer to your system. The two most common types are *laser* printers and *inkjet* printers. Laser printers work much like copy machines, applying toner (powdered ink) to paper by using a small laser. Inkjet printers shoot jets of ink onto the paper's surface to create the printed image.

Start

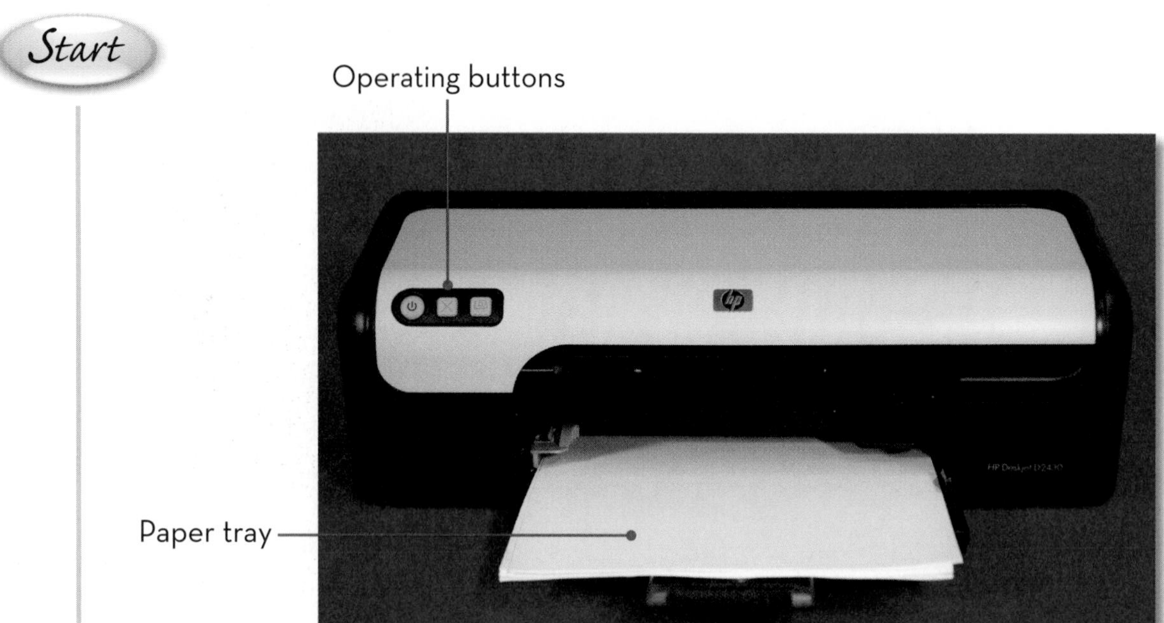

End

TIP

Black and White Versus Color Black-and-white printers are faster than color printers and better if you're printing memos, letters, and other single-color documents. Color printers are essential if you want to print pictures taken with a digital camera.

SCANNERS

You can create a digital copy of any photo or document by scanning it into your computer as a digital file. To do this, you use a peripheral called a *scanner*, which uses an image sensor to scan and digitize the elements of the document. These elements are then converted into the appropriate file format on your computer.

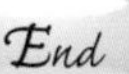

NOTE

Flatbed Scanners Most consumer scanners are so-called flatbed scanners. The item you wish to scan is placed on a flat glass plate (the "bed"). The image sensor moves beneath the glass to scan the document. ■

NOTE

Different Scans Most scanners can scan black-and-white text documents, color documents, and full-color photographs. ■

SETTING UP AND USING YOUR PC

When you first get a new PC, you have to get everything set up, connected, and ready to run. If you're using a desktop PC, setup involves plugging in all the external devices—your monitor, speakers, keyboard, and such. If you're using a notebook PC, the task is a bit easier, as most of the major components are built into the computer itself.

Whichever type of PC you own, start by positioning it so that you easily can access all the connections on the unit. You'll need to carefully run the cables from each of the external peripherals to the main unit, without stretching the cables or pulling anything out of place. And remember, when you plug in a cable, you should make sure that it's *firmly* connected—both to the computer and to the specific piece of hardware. Loose cables can cause all sorts of weird problems, so be sure they're plugged in really well.

TYPICAL DESKTOP PC CONNECTIONS

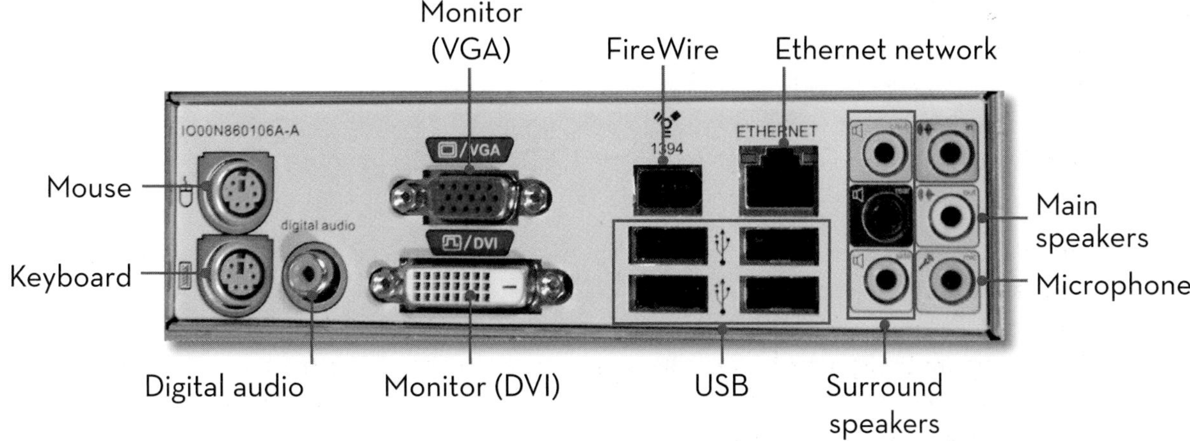

SETTING UP A DESKTOP PC

You need to connect all the pieces and parts to your computer's system unit before powering it on. Once all your peripherals are connected, you can then connect your system unit to a power source. Just make sure the power source is turned off before you connect!

Start

1. Connect the green mouse cable to the green mouse port on the back of your system unit.

2. Connect the purple keyboard cable to the purple keyboard port on the back of your system unit.

3. Connect the blue monitor cable to the blue monitor port on the back of your system unit; make sure the other end is connected to your video monitor.

Continued

NOTE

Mice and Keyboards Most mice and keyboards connect to dedicated mouse and keyboard ports on your system unit. Know, however, that many new mice and keyboards connect via USB ports, so you should use whatever connection is appropriate. ■

TIP

Digital Connections Some newer LCD monitors use a digital video interface (DVI) connection instead of the older VGA-type connection. If you have a choice, a DVI connection delivers a crisper picture than the older analog connection—although a DVI cable is a bit more expensive than a VGA cable. ■

4 Connect the green phono cable from your main external speaker to the audio out or sound out connector on your system unit; connect the other end of the cable to the speaker.

5 Connect one end of your printer's USB cable to a USB port on the back of your system unit; connect the other end of the cable to your printer.

Continued

TIP

Your Connection Might Vary Not all speaker systems connect the same way. For example, many systems run the main cable to one speaker (such as the subwoofer) and then connect that speaker to the other speakers in the systems. Make sure you read your manufacturer's instructions before you connect your speaker system. ■

TIP

Connect by Color Most PC manufacturers color-code the cables and connectors to make the connection even easier—just plug the blue cable into the blue connector and so on. ■

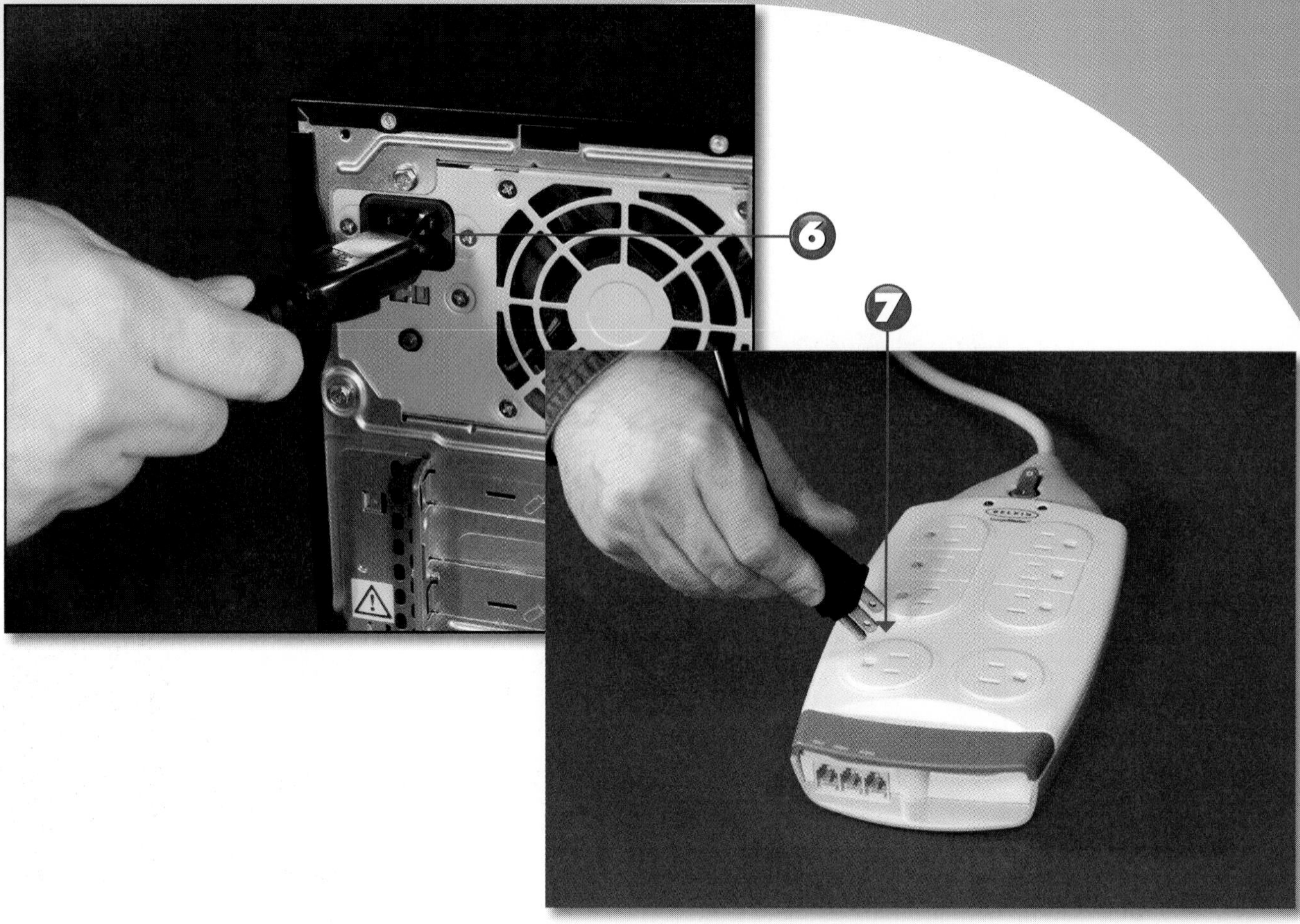

6 Connect one end of your computer's power cable to the power connector on the back of your system unit; connect the other end of the power cable to a power source.

7 Connect your printer, speakers, and other powered external peripherals to an appropriate power source.

End

TIP

Use a Surge Suppressor For extra protection, connect the power cable on your system unit to a surge suppressor rather than directly into an electrical outlet. This protects your PC from power-line surges that can damage its delicate internal parts. ■

SETTING UP A NOTEBOOK PC

Setting up a notebook PC is much simpler than setting up a desktop model. That's because almost everything is built into the notebook—except external peripherals, such a printer.

Start

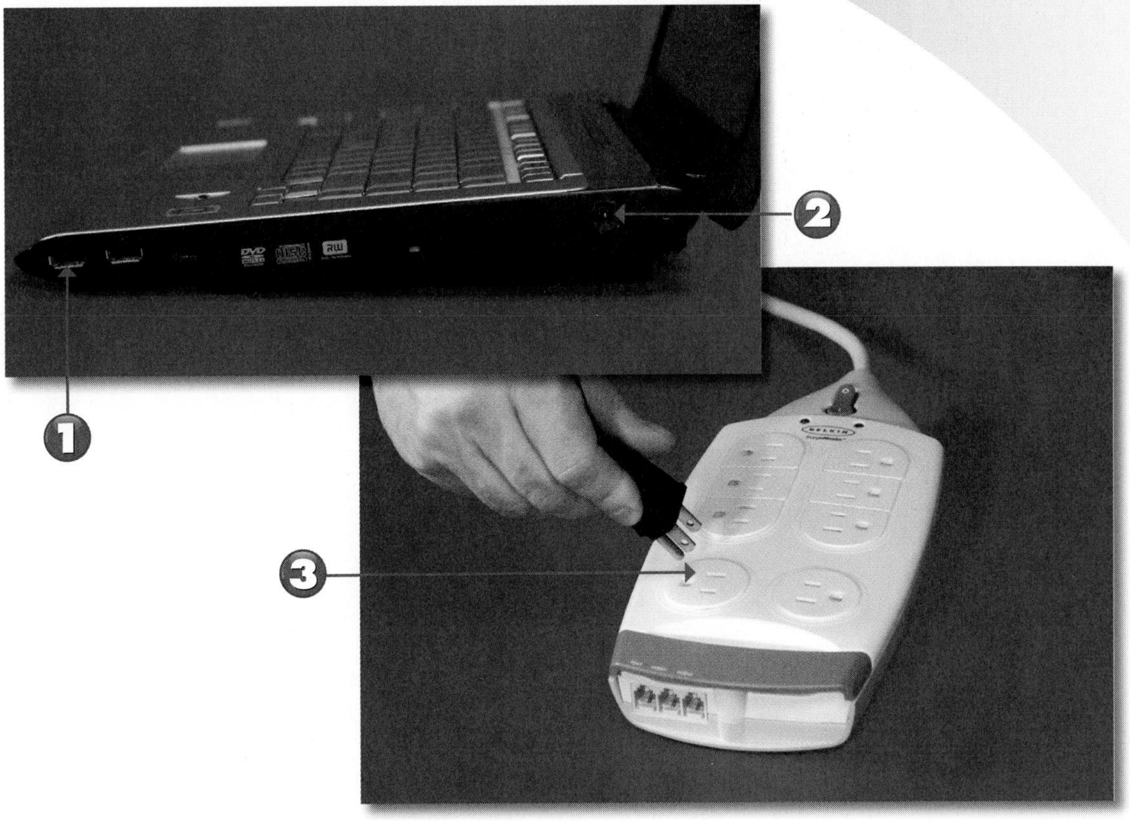

1. Connect one end of your printer's USB cable to a USB port on your PC; connect the other end of the cable to your printer.
2. Connect one end of your computer's power cable to the power connector on the side or back of your notebook; connect the other end of the power cable to a power source.
3. Connect your printer, speakers, and other powered external peripherals to an appropriate power source.

End

TIP

External Peripherals If you're using an external mouse or keyboard, connect it to a USB port on your notebook. If you're using an external monitor, connect it to your notebook's external video port. ■

POWERING ON

Now that you have everything connected, sit back and rest for a minute. Next up is the big step—turning it all on!

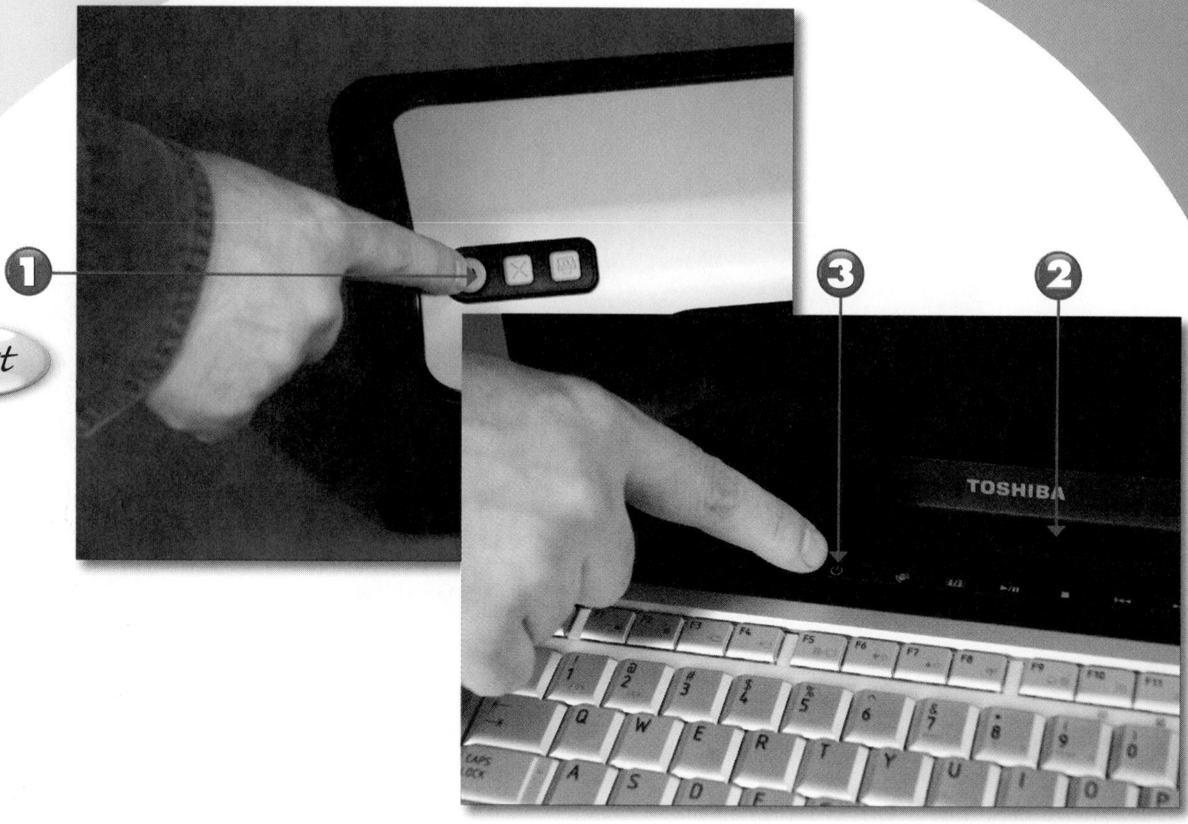

Start

1. Turn on your printer, monitor (for a desktop PC), and other powered external peripherals.
2. If you're using a notebook PC, open the notebook's case so that you can see the screen and access the keyboard.
3. Press the power or "on" button on your computer.

End

NOTE

Booting Up Technical types call the procedure of starting up a computer booting or booting up the system. Restarting a system (turning it off and then back on) is called rebooting. ■

CAUTION

Go in Order Your computer is the last thing you turn on in your system. That's because when it powers on, it has to sense all the other components—which it can do only if the other components are plugged in and turned on. ■

LOGGING ON TO WINDOWS 7

Windows 7 launches automatically as your computer starts up. After you get past the Windows Welcome screen, you're taken directly to the Windows desktop, and your system is ready to run.

Start

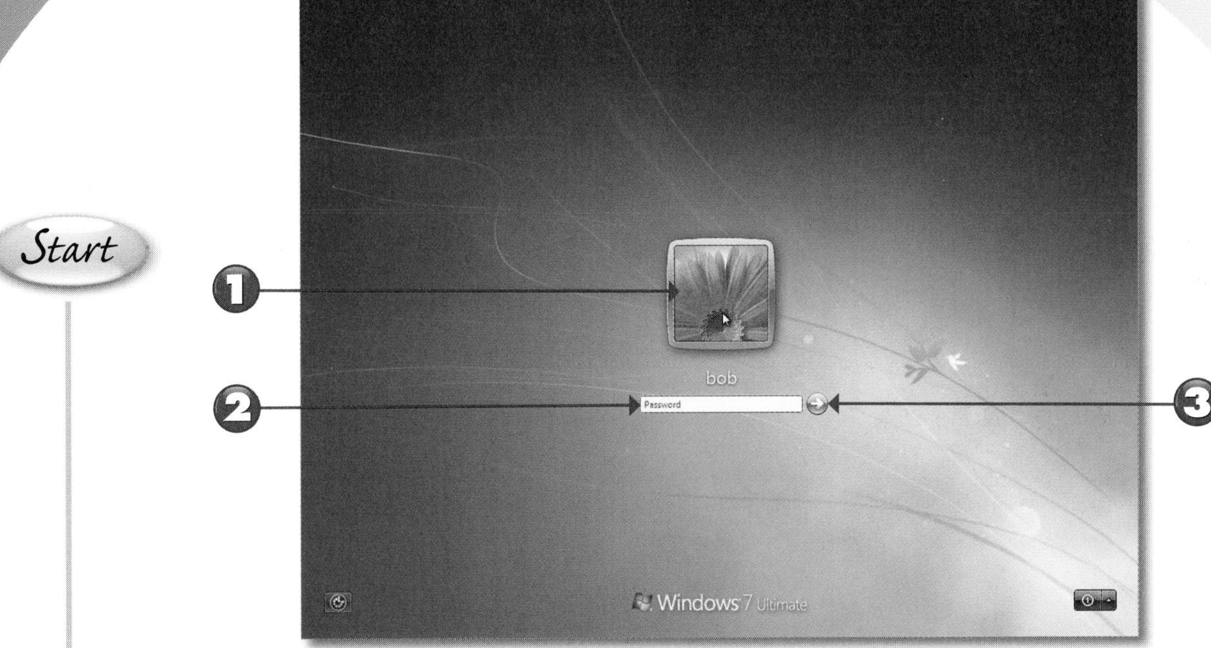

1. When you start your PC, you see the Windows Welcome screen; click your username or picture.
2. Enter your password (if necessary).
3. Press the **Enter** key on your keyboard or click the right arrow.

End

TIP

Single-User Systems If you have only a single user on your PC and that user doesn't have a password assigned, Windows moves past the Welcome screen with no action necessary on your part. ■

TIP

Starting Up for the First Time The first time you start your new PC, you're asked to perform some basic setup operations, including activating and registering Windows and configuring your system for your personal use. ■

SHUTTING DOWN

When you want to turn off your computer, you do it through Windows. In fact, you don't want to turn off your computer any other way—you *always* want to turn things off through the official Windows procedure.

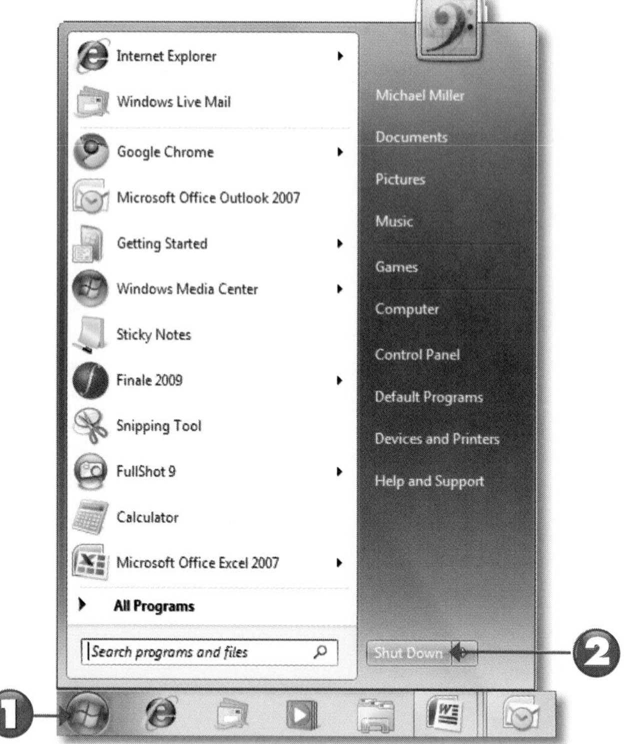

1. Click the **Start** button to display the Start menu.
2. Click the **Shut Down** button at the lower right.

End

CAUTION

Always Use Windows to Shut Down Do not turn off your computer without shutting down Windows. You could lose data and settings that are temporarily stored in your system's memory. ■

TIP

Sleep Mode Windows includes a special Sleep mode that keeps your computer running in a low-power state, ready to start up quickly when you turn it on again. To enter Sleep mode, click the right arrow next to the Shut Down button and select Sleep. To "wake up" your PC, simply press the computer's power button. ■

RUNNING ON BATTERIES

Most notebook PC batteries last for two hours or more before you need to plug into a power outlet and recharge. The battery icon in the Windows taskbar notification area (system tray) tells you how much battery power is left—and lets you select an alternate power plan.

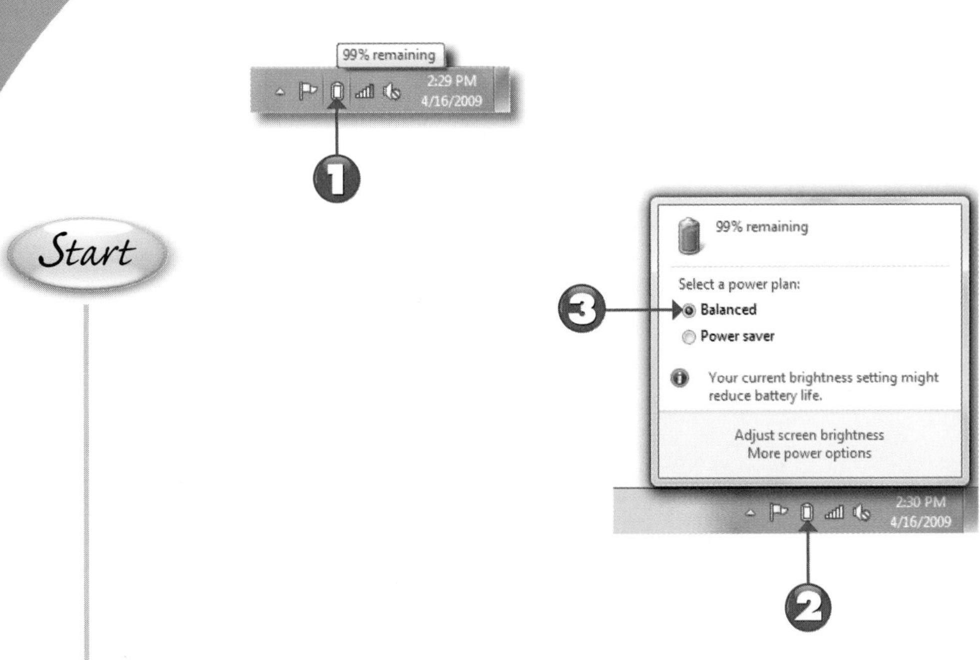

1. To view the remaining battery life, hover your cursor over the battery icon.
2. To select a different power plan, click the battery icon.
3. Select a new power plan from the pop-up menu.

End

NOTE

Power Plans A power plan combines different power-saving features to help you get more life out of each battery charge. For example, the Power Saver plan reduces screen brightness, turns off the display after three minutes of inactivity, and puts the computer to sleep if you haven't used it in 15 minutes. ■

ADDING NEW DEVICES TO YOUR SYSTEM

At some point in the future, you might want to expand your system—by adding a second printer, a scanner, a webcam, or something equally new and exciting. Most of these peripherals are external and connect to your PC using a USB cable. When you're connecting a USB device, not only do you not have to open your PC's case, but you also don't even have to turn off your system when you add the new device.

Start

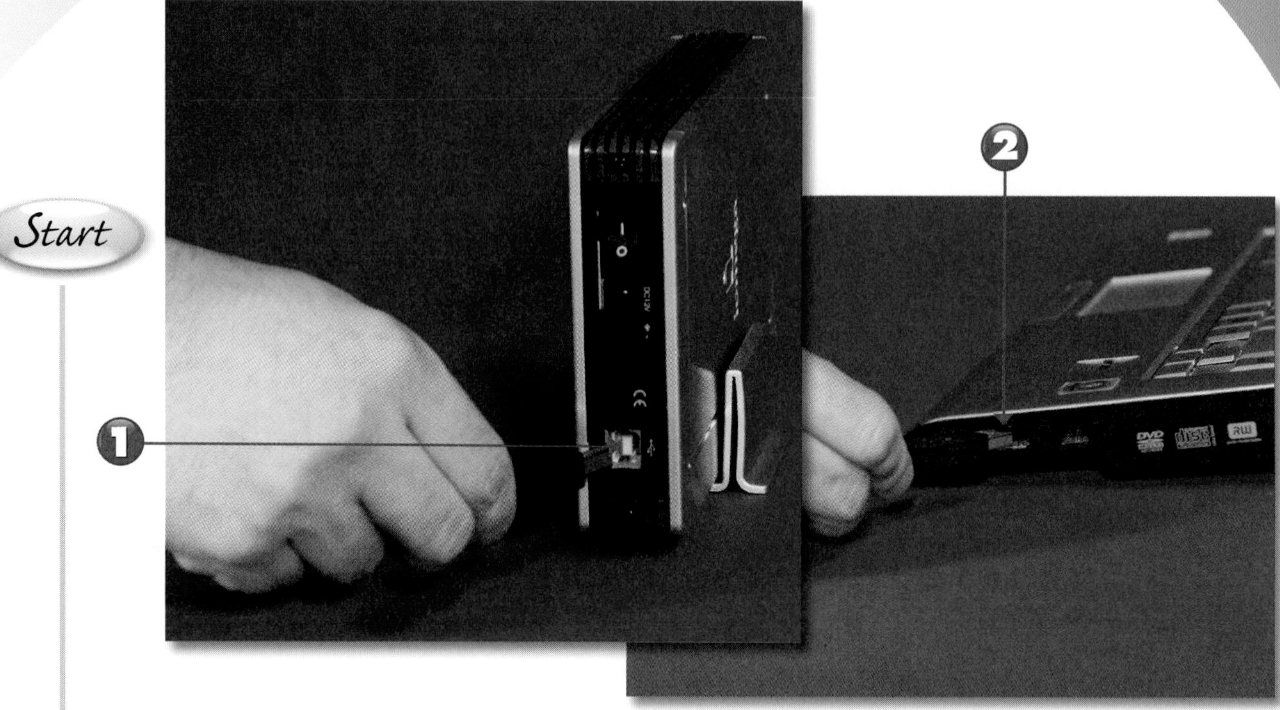

1. Connect one end of the USB cable to your new device.
2. Connect the other end of the cable to a free USB port on your PC.

Continued

TIP

Follow Directions As easy as most USB devices are to connect, you should still read the device's instructions and follow the manufacturer's directions for installation. ■

NOTE

FireWire Connections Some external devices, such as fast hard drives and video cameras, connect via FireWire, a slightly faster connection than USB. Connecting a device via FireWire is similar to connecting it via USB; just connect to your PC's FireWire port. ■

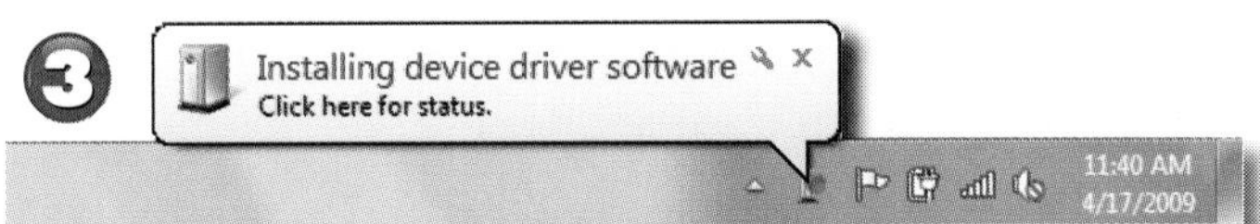

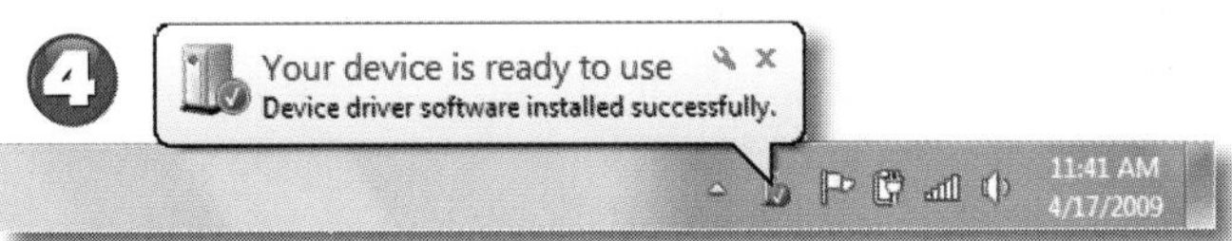

3. Windows should automatically recognize the new peripheral and install the necessary drivers.

4. An onscreen message will notify you when the installation is complete.

End

CAUTION

Install Before Connecting? Windows normally detects a new USB device when you connect it and then installs the driver automatically. However, some devices require you to install the driver before connecting the device. Again—make sure you read the directions before you install! ■

TIP

USB Hubs If you connect too many USB devices, you can run out of USB connectors on your PC. If that happens, buy an add-on USB hub, which lets you plug multiple USB peripherals into a single USB port. ■

USING MICROSOFT WINDOWS 7

Microsoft Windows is a piece of software called an *operating system*. An operating system does what its name implies—it operates your computer system, working in the background every time you turn on your PC. The *desktop* that fills your screen is part of Windows, as is the taskbar at the bottom of the screen and the big menu that pops up when you click the Start button.

Windows 7 is the latest version of the Microsoft Windows operating system, the successor to Windows Vista and Windows XP. It improves on both those previous versions of Windows, while maintaining the basic operating functions.

EXPLORING THE WINDOWS 7 DESKTOP

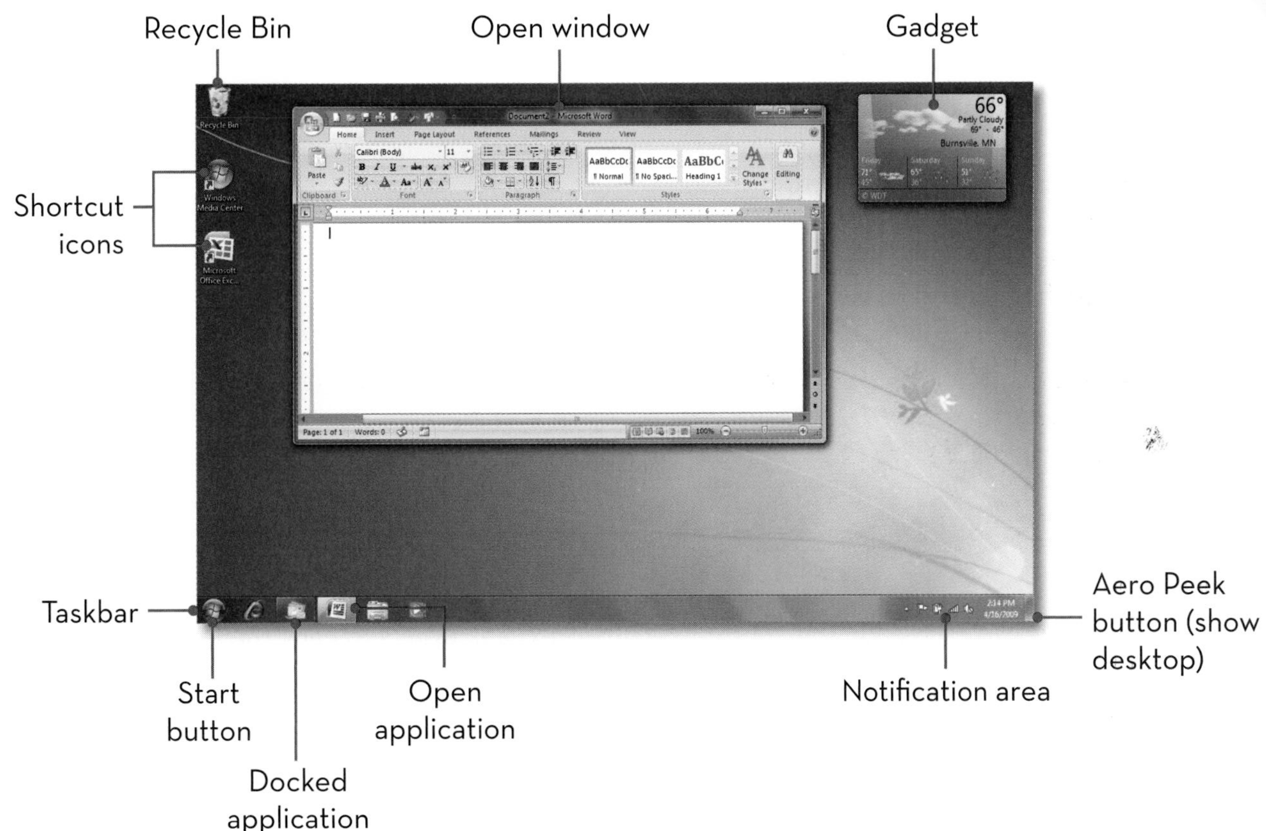

USING THE MOUSE

To use Windows efficiently, you must master a few simple operations, all of which you perform with your mouse. Most mouse operations include *pointing* and *clicking*. Normal clicking uses the left mouse button; however, some operations require that you click the right mouse button instead.

1. To single-click, position the cursor over the onscreen item and click the left mouse or touchpad button.
2. To double-click, position the cursor over the onscreen item and click the left mouse or touchpad button twice in rapid succession.

Continued

TIP

Click to Select Pointing and clicking is an effective way to select icons, menu items, directories, and files. ■

TIP

Hovering Another common mouse operation is hovering, where you hold the cursor over an onscreen item without pressing either of the mouse buttons. For example, when you hover your cursor over an icon or menu item, Windows displays a ToolTip that tells you a little about the selected item. ■

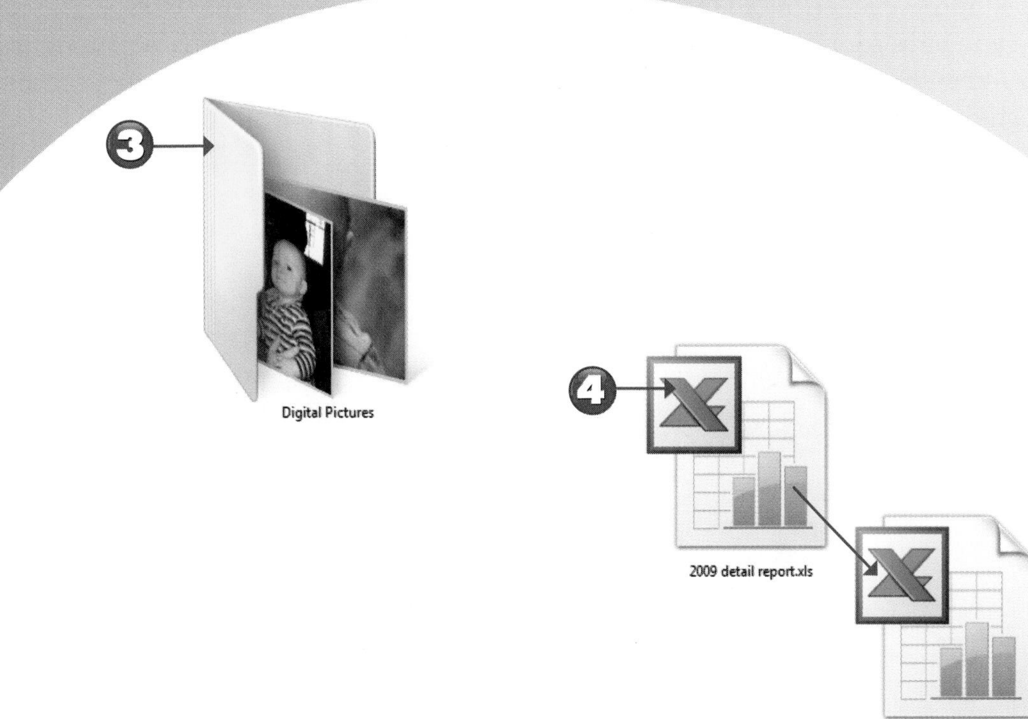

3. To right-click, position the cursor over the onscreen item and then click the *right* mouse button.
4. To drag and drop an item from one location to another, position the cursor over the item, click and hold the left mouse button, drag the item to a new position, and then release the mouse button.

End

TIP

Pop-Up Menus Many items in Windows feature a context-sensitive pop-up menu or Jump List. You access this menu or list by right-clicking the item. (When in doubt, right-click the item and see what pops up!) ■

TIP

Moving Files You can use dragging and dropping to move files from one folder to another or to delete files by dragging them onto the Recycle Bin icon. ■

SCROLLING A WINDOW

Many windows contain more information than can be displayed in the window at once. When you have a long document or web page, only the first part of the document or page is displayed in the window. To view the rest of the document or page, you have to scroll down through the window, using the various parts of the scrollbar.

Start

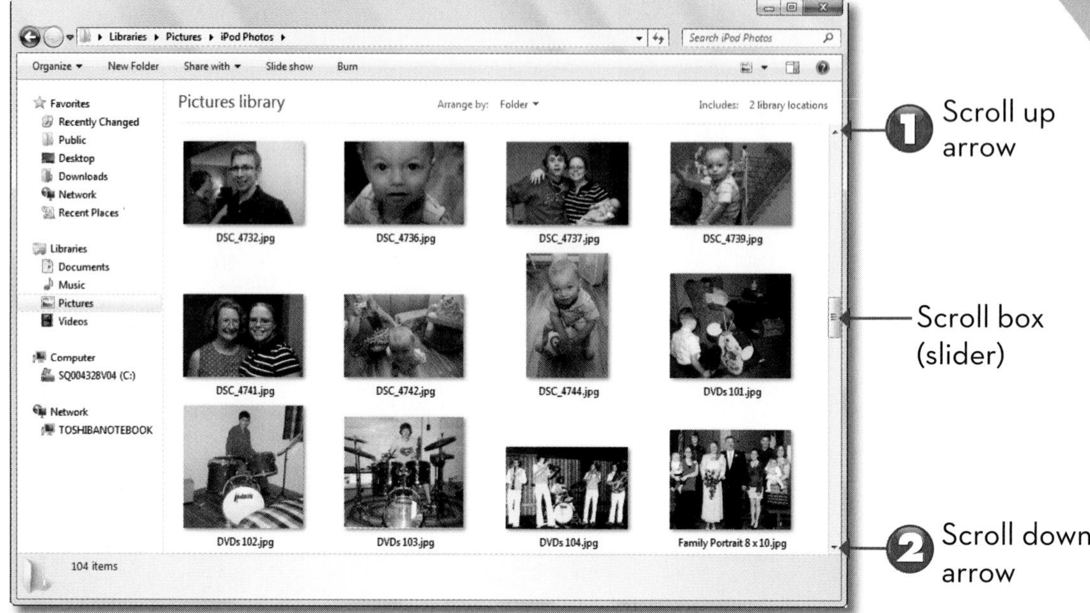

1. Click the up arrow on the window's scrollbar to scroll up one line at a time.

2. Click the down arrow on the window's scrollbar to scroll down one line at a time.

TIP

Other Ways to Scroll To move to a specific place in a long document, use your mouse to grab the scroll box (also called a slider) and drag it to a new position. You can also click the scrollbar between the scroll box and the end arrow, which scrolls you one screen at a time. ■

MAXIMIZING, MINIMIZING, AND CLOSING A WINDOW

After you've opened a window, you can maximize it to display full screen. You can also minimize it so that it disappears from the desktop and resides as a button on the Windows taskbar, and you can close it completely.

Start

1. To maximize the window, click the **Maximize** button.
2. To minimize the window, click the **Minimize** button.
3. To close the window completely, click the **Close** button.

End

TIP

Restoring a Window If a window is already maximized, the Maximize button changes to a Restore Down button. When you click the Restore Down button, the window resumes its previous (premaximized) dimensions. ■

USING AERO SNAPS

Windows 7 adds some new ways to manage open windows on your desktop, collectively called Aero Snaps. Aero Snaps let you maximize windows and stack multiple windows side by side with just a few drags of the mouse.

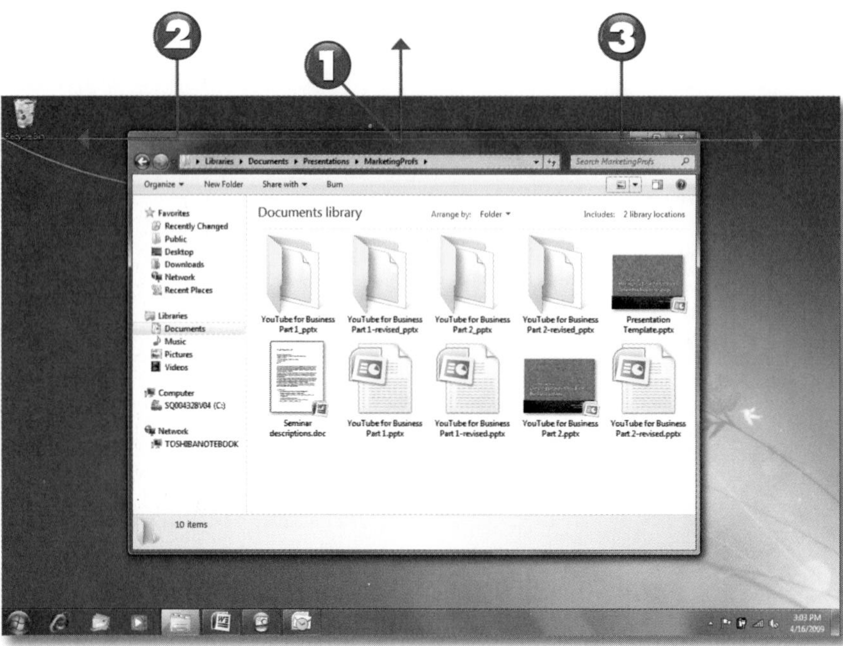

Start

1. To maximize a window, click the window's title bar and drag it to the top edge of the screen, or press **Windows + up arrow**.

2. To snap a window to the left side of the screen, click the window's title bar and drag it to the left edge of the screen, or press **Windows + left arrow**.

3. To snap a window to the right side of the screen, click the window's title bar and drag it to the right edge of the screen, or press **Windows + right arrow**.

End

TIP

Restoring a Maximized Window To restore a maximized window, click the window's title bar and drag it down from the top of the screen, or press Windows + down arrow. ■

USING THE WINDOWS START MENU

All the software programs and utilities on your computer are accessed via Windows's Start menu, which consists of two columns of icons. Your most frequently used programs are listed in the left column; basic Windows utilities and folders are listed in the right column. To open a specific program or folder, just click the menu icon.

Start

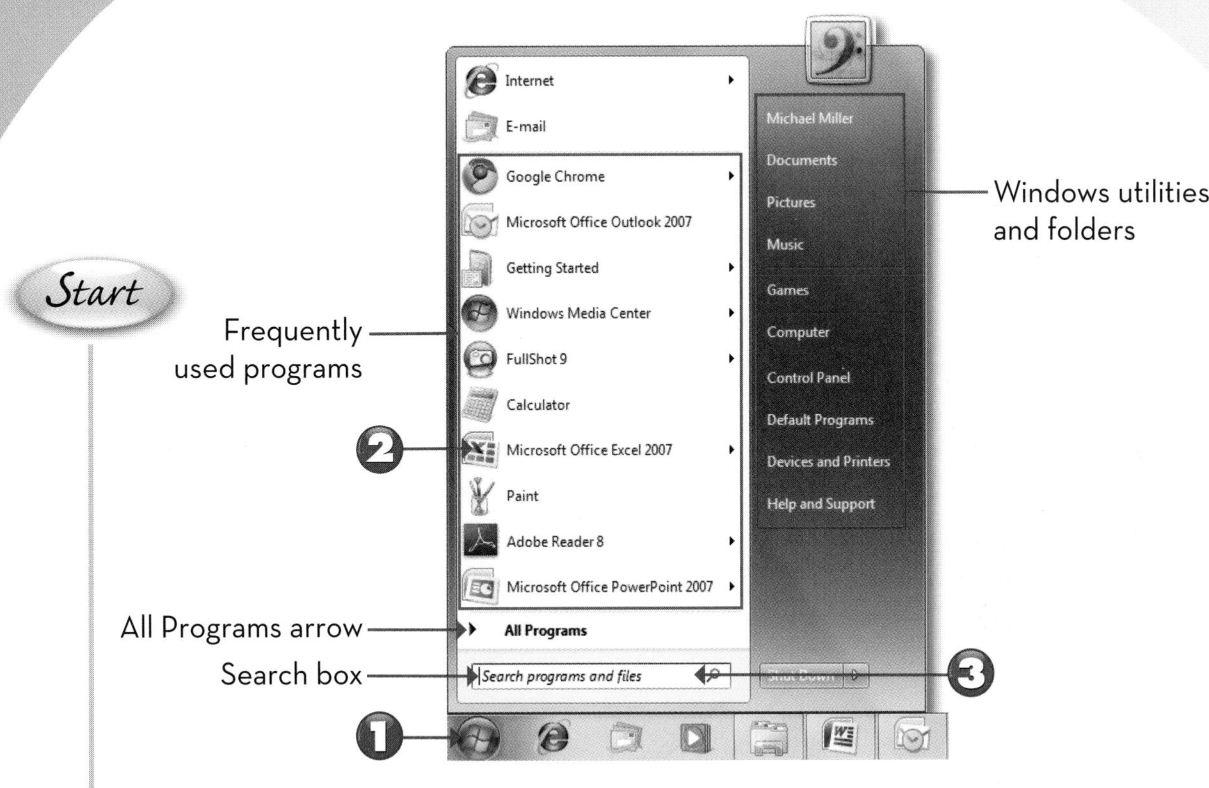

1. Click the round **Start** button to open the Start menu.
2. Click any menu item to launch a program or open a folder.
3. Alternatively, you can enter a program name into the **Search** box to search for that program.

End

OPENING A PROGRAM

To view all the programs installed on your PC, open the **Start** menu and click the **All Programs** arrow. This displays a new menu called the Programs menu. From here, you can access various programs, organized by type and title or manufacturer.

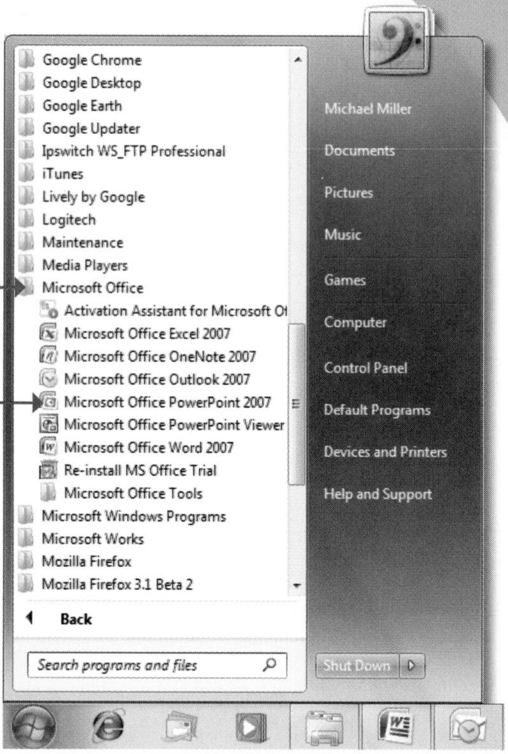

1. Click the **Start** button to display the Start menu.
2. Click the **All Programs** icon to display the Programs menu.
3. Click any folder to expand that item and show its contents
4. Click the icon for the program you want to launch.

TIP

More Programs in the Folder Most programs on the Programs menu are stored in folders. Click any folder to expand it and see the programs stored within. ■

TIP

Recently Opened Documents To view a list of recently opened documents for any application, click the right arrow next to the application's icon in the Programs menu. ■

DISPLAYING AND PEEKING AT THE DESKTOP

What do you do if you have a lot of windows open but need to view or access an item residing on the desktop below? Windows 7 lets you peek at the desktop below all your windows (called Aero Peek) or quickly minimize all windows to access desktop items.

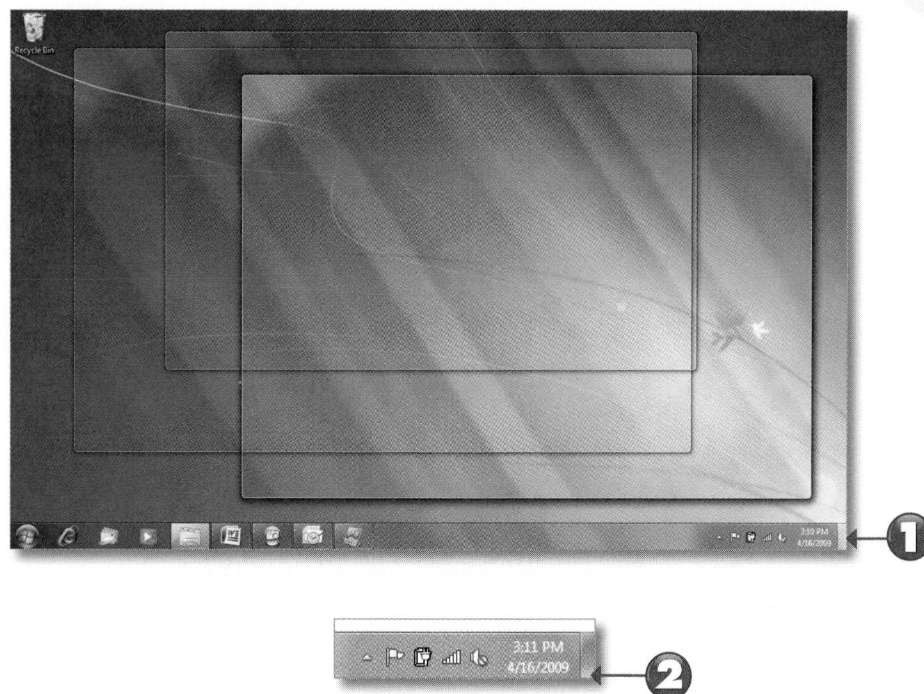

Start

1. To peek at the desktop below all open windows, hover your cursor over the **Show Desktop** button at the far right of the taskbar.

2. To quickly minimize all windows and show a clear desktop, click the **Show Desktop** button at the far right of the taskbar.

End

TIP

Aero Peek When you preview the desktop with Aero Peek, all open windows are shown as translucent window outlines. ■

SWITCHING BETWEEN PROGRAMS

After you've launched a few programs, you can easily switch between one open program and another. In fact, Windows 7 offers several ways to switch programs, including Windows Flip, Flip 3D, and new taskbar thumbnails.

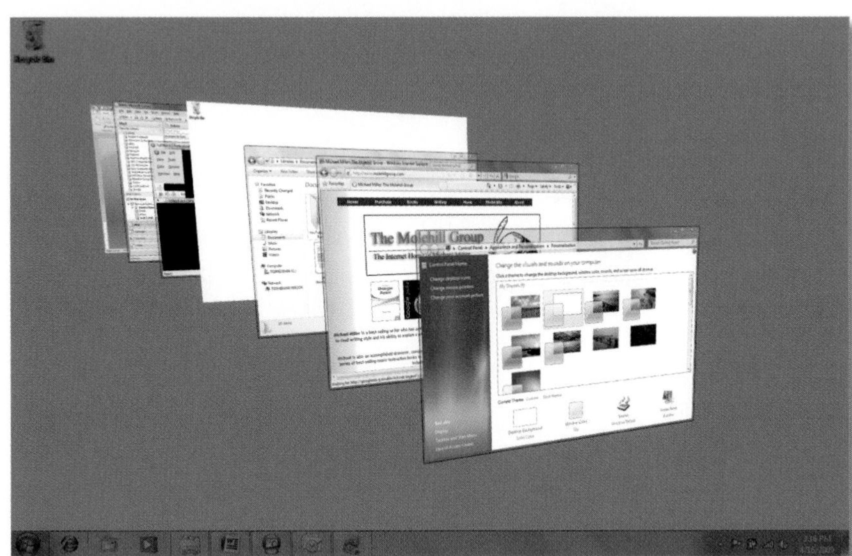

Start

1. To display thumbnails of all open programs (Windows Flip), press **Alt + Tab**; repeat to cycle through and select a program.
2. To display a three-dimensional stack of all open programs (Flip 3D), press **Windows + Tab**; repeat to cycle through and select a program.

Continued

NOTE

Flip 3D The Flip 3D feature is not available in the Home Basic version of Windows 7, or if your hardware isn't capable of running Windows 7's Aero interface.

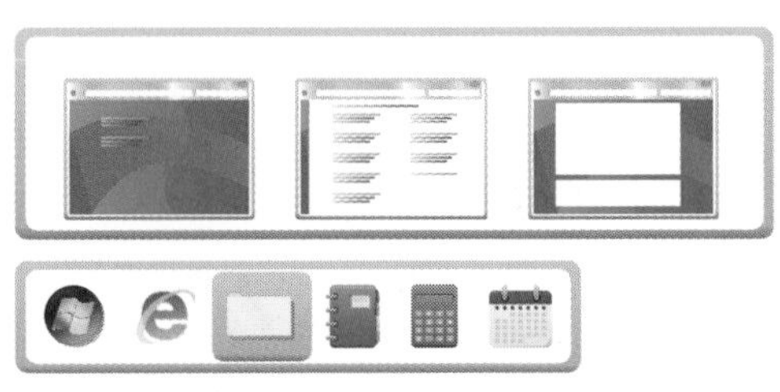

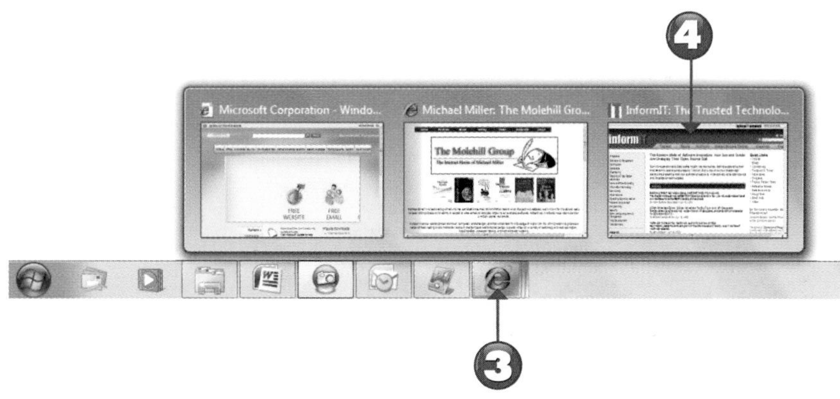

3 When a program or document is open, an icon for that item appears in the Windows taskbar. Hover over that icon to view a thumbnail preview of all open documents for that application.

4 To switch to an open document from the taskbar, hover over the icon for that item and then click the thumbnail for that document.

End

NOTE

Multiple Documents If multiple documents or pages for an application are open, multiple thumbnails will appear when you hover over that application's icon in the taskbar. ■

MANAGING THE WINDOWS TASKBAR

The taskbar is that area at the bottom of the Windows desktop, and it's completely revised for Windows 7. In Windows 7, icons on the taskbar can represent frequently used programs, open programs, or open documents.

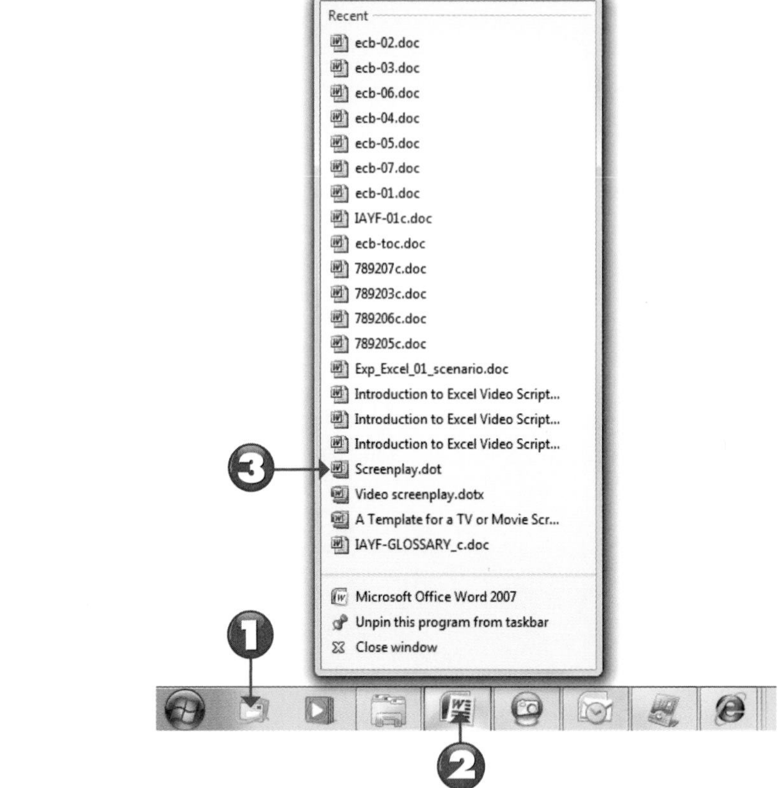

Start

1. To open an application from the taskbar, click the application's icon.
2. To view a list of recently opened documents for an application, right-click the application's icon to display a Jump List, and then select an item.
3. To open a new blank document for an already-open application, right-click the application's icon to display the Jump List, and then click the application item.

Continued

TIP

Taskbar Icons A taskbar icon with a plain background represents an unopened application. A taskbar icon with a see-through border represents a running application. A taskbar icon with a shaded background represents the highlighted or topmost window on your desktop. ■

TIP

Multiple Documents An application with multiple documents open is represented by a "stacked" taskbar icon. ■

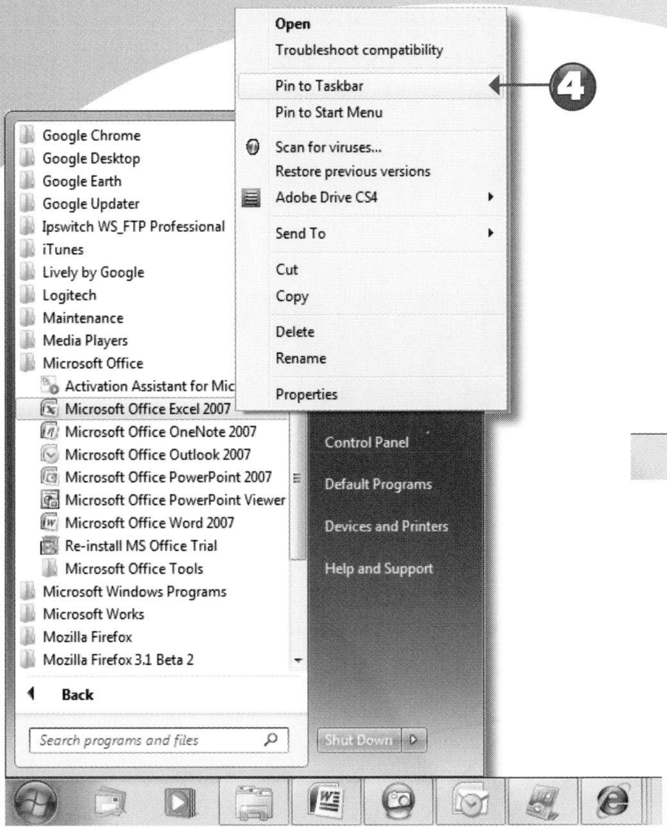

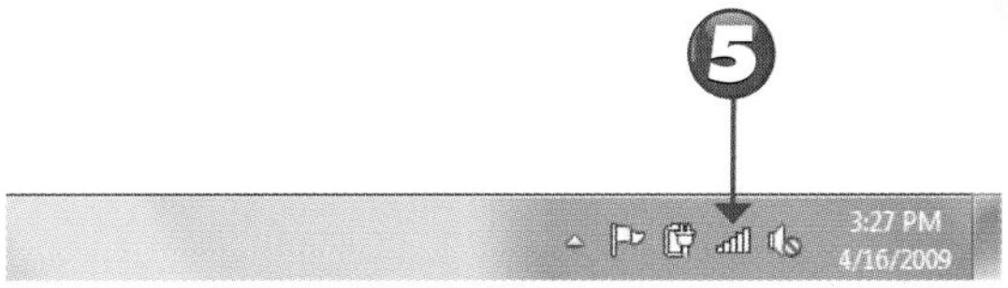

4 To add an application icon to the taskbar, navigate to that program from the Windows Start menu, and then right-click the item and click **Pin to Taskbar**.

5 The far-right side of the taskbar is called the notification area, and it displays icons for essential Windows operations. To view more details about any item displayed in this area, click that item's icon.

End

NOTE

Notification Area The notification area is sometimes called the system tray. ■

TIP

Hidden Icons Some notification area items are hidden by default. To see hidden items, click the up arrow to the left of the notification area. ■

WORKING WITH GADGETS

Windows 7 lets you add small utilities, called *gadgets*, to your desktop. Microsoft offers many different gadgets, each of which typically performs a single purpose. For example, the Weather gadget displays weather updates for your location; the Clock gadget displays the current time.

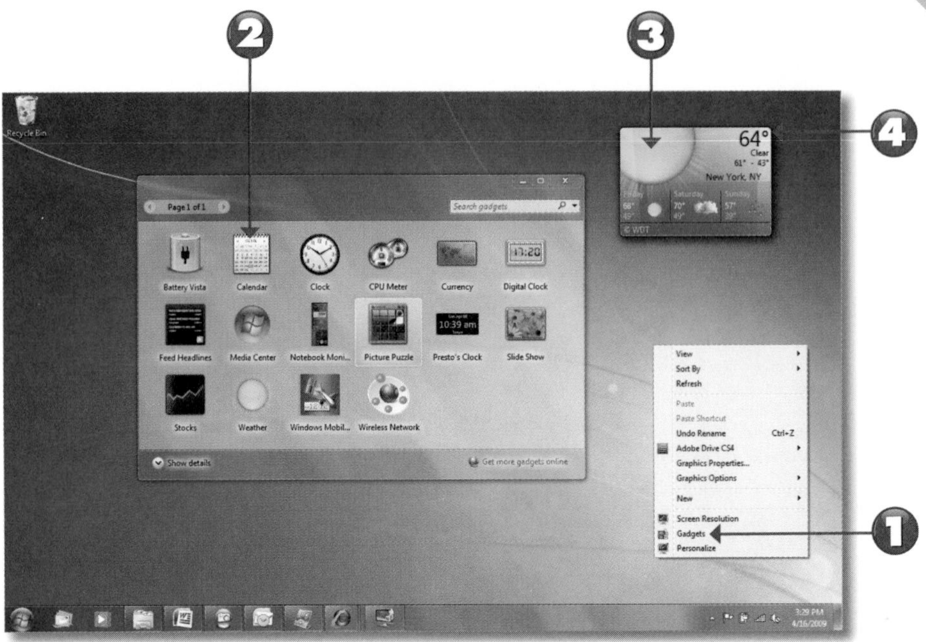

Start

1. To add a gadget to your desktop, right-click the desktop and then click **Gadgets**.
2. When the Gadgets window appears, double-click the gadget you wish to add—or click **Get More Gadgets Online** for a larger selection.
3. To move a gadget, click and drag the gadget with your mouse to a new location.
4. To close a gadget, hover over the gadget and then click the **X**.

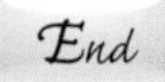

TIP

Configuring Gadgets To configure a gadget, right-click the gadget and then select Options. ■

NOTE

Goodbye, Sidebar In Windows Vista, gadgets were docked to a sidebar that appeared on the right side of the desktop. Windows 7 does away with the sidebar but lets you add gadgets directly to the desktop. ■

MANAGING DRIVES WITH COMPUTER EXPLORER

Windows's Computer Explorer folder lets you access each major component of your system and perform basic maintenance functions. For example, you can use Computer Explorer to "open" the contents of your hard disk and then copy, move, and delete individual files.

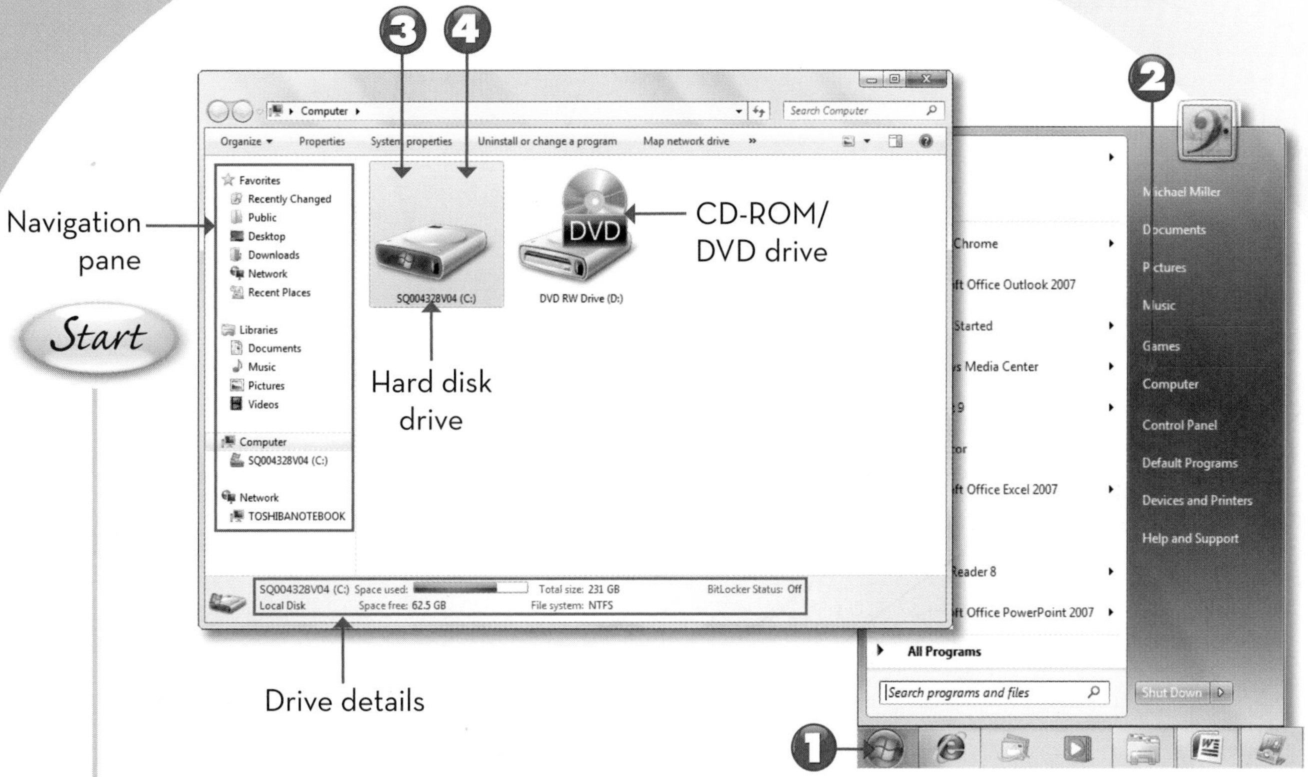

Navigation pane

CD-ROM/ DVD drive

Hard disk drive

Drive details

Start

1. Click the **Start** button to display the Start menu.
2. Click **Computer**.
3. Click any icon to view details about the drive at the bottom of the window.
4. Double-click any icon to view its contents.

End

TIP

View Drive Contents To view the contents of a specific drive, double-click the drive's icon. You'll see a list of folders and files located on that drive; to view the contents of any folder, double-click the icon for that folder. ■

TIP

Tree View Computer Explorer features a Navigation pane that contains an item labeled "Computer," along with the hard drives on your PC. Click to expand any drive and display a "tree" view of all the folders and subfolders on that drive. Click any item to view its contents in the main folder window. ■

USING MENUS

Many Windows programs use a set of pull-down menus to store all the commands and operations you can perform. The menus are aligned across the top of the window, just below the title bar, in what is called a *menu bar*. You open (or pull down) a menu by clicking the menu's name; you select a menu item by clicking it with your mouse.

Start

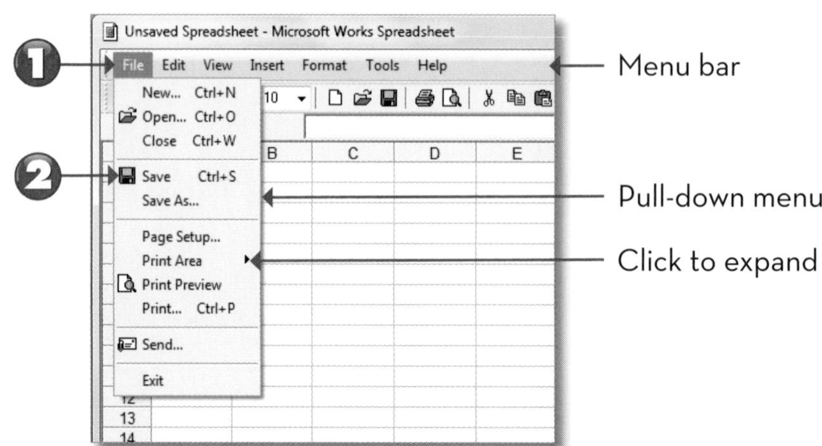

1. Click the menu's name to pull down the menu.
2. Click the menu item to select it.

End

TIP

Not All Items Are Available If an item in a menu, toolbar, or dialog box is dimmed (or grayed), that means it isn't available for the current task. ■

USING TOOLBARS AND RIBBONS

Some Windows programs put the most frequently used operations on one or more *toolbars* or *ribbons*, typically located just below the menu bar. A toolbar looks like a row of buttons, each with a small picture (called an *icon*) and maybe a bit of text. You activate the associated command or operation by clicking the button with your mouse.

Start

1. Click a tab to select that particular ribbon.

2. Click a ribbon/toolbar button to select that operation.

End

TIP

Long Toolbars If the toolbar is too long to display fully on your screen, you'll see a right arrow at the far-right side of the toolbar. Click this arrow to display the buttons that aren't currently visible. ■

NOTE

Ribbons The ribbon interface is found in newer applications. Most older applications use toolbars instead. ■

MANAGING WINDOWS WITH THE CONTROL PANEL

The Windows Control Panel is used to manage most (but not all) of Windows's configuration settings. The Control Panel contains links to individual utilities that let you adjust and configure various system properties.

Start

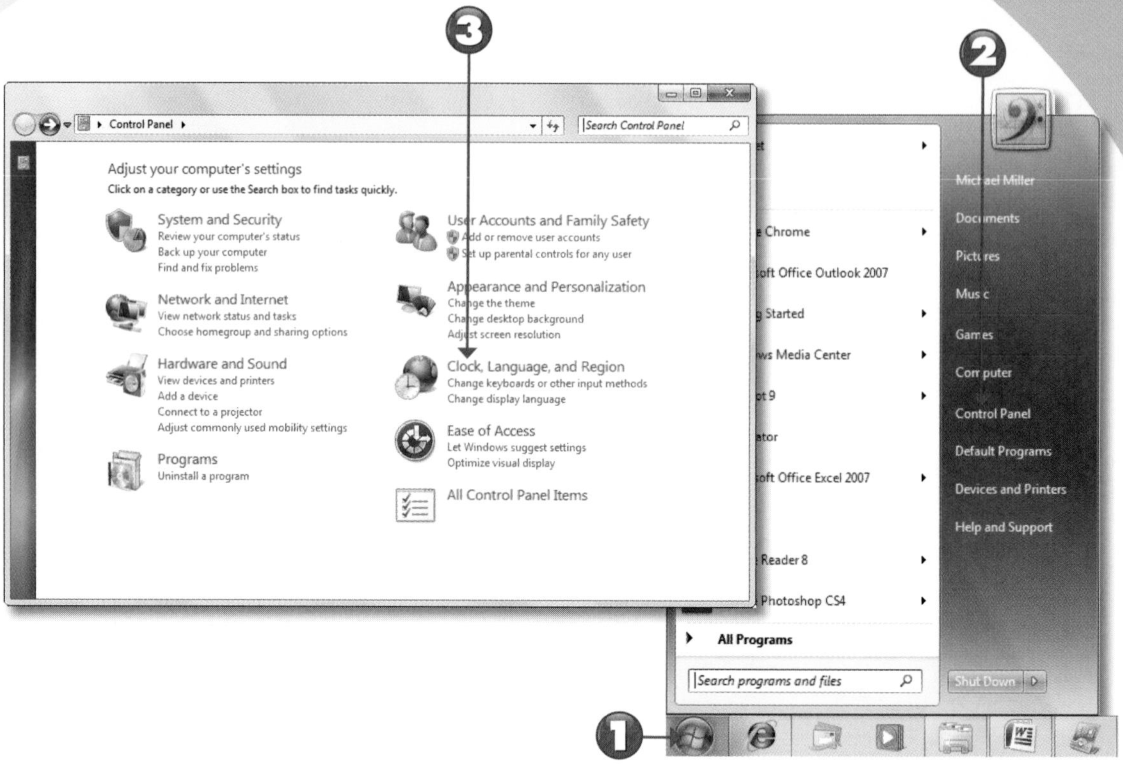

1. Click the **Start** button to display the Start menu.
2. Click **Control Panel** to open the Control Panel.
3. Click the heading or link for the category you want to configure.

Continued

TIP

Control Panel Categories Individual settings within the Control Panel are organized by major category—System and Security, Network and Internet, and so on. You first have to select a specific category to access all its related settings. ■

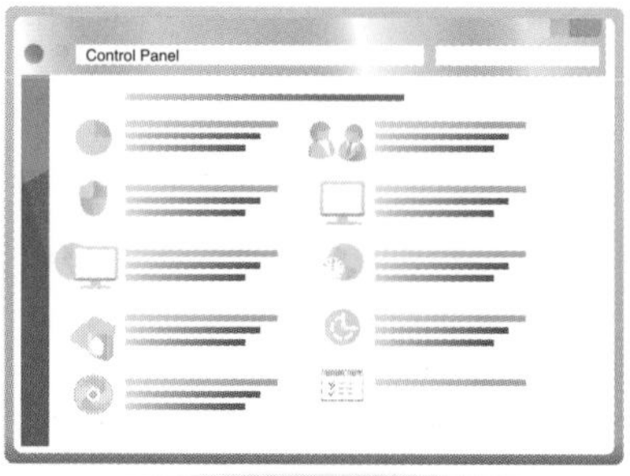

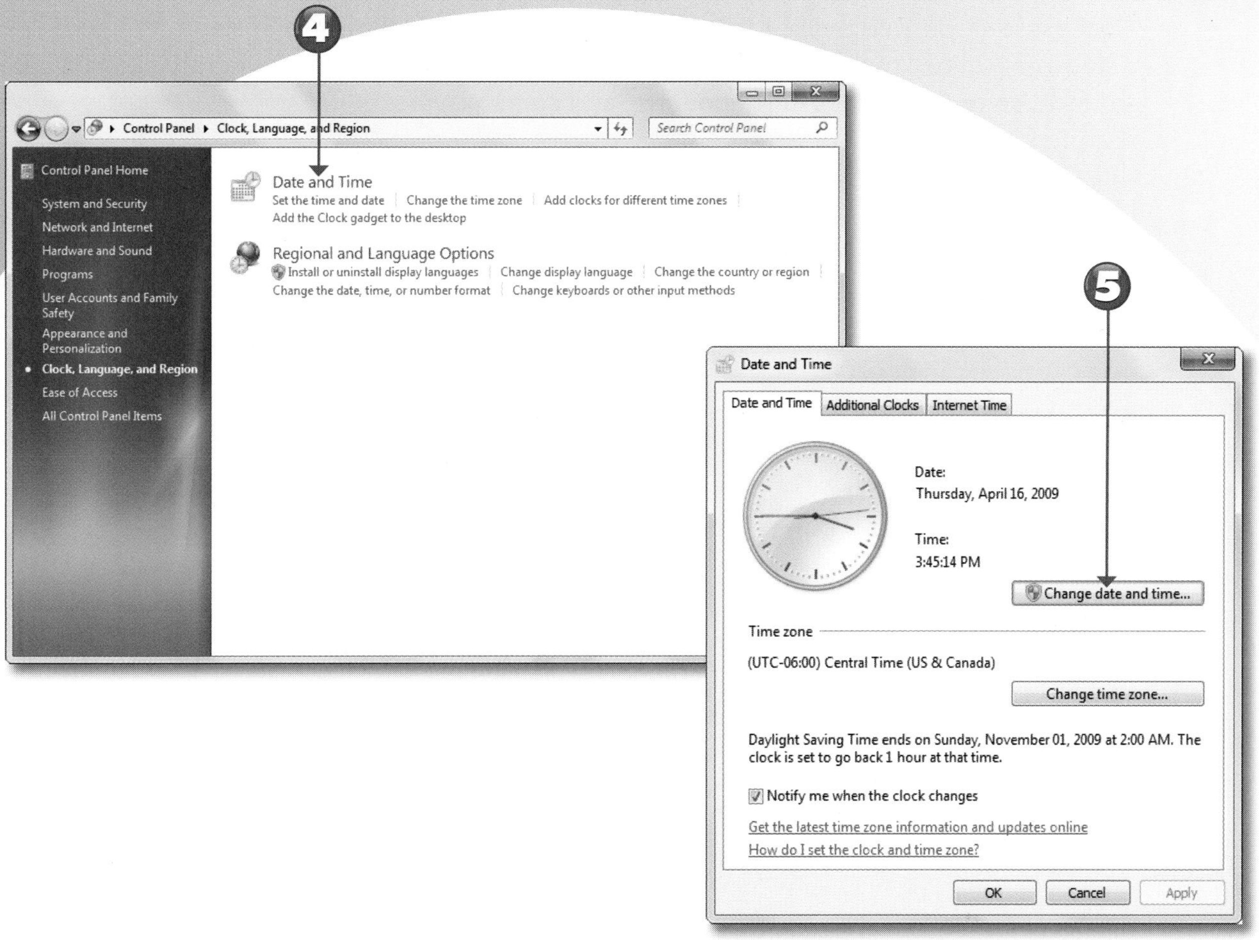

4 Click the task you want to perform.

5 Configure the settings for that task using the selected utility's dialog box.

End

TIP

Configuring Individual Settings When you open a configuration utility, you'll see a dialog box for that particular item. You can then change the individual settings within that dialog box; click the OK button to register your new settings. ■

CHANGING DESKTOP THEMES

Most users like to personalize the look of the Windows desktop. To this end, Windows 7 includes a number of preconfigured desktop *themes*, comprised of selected desktop backgrounds, color schemes, sound schemes, and screensavers.

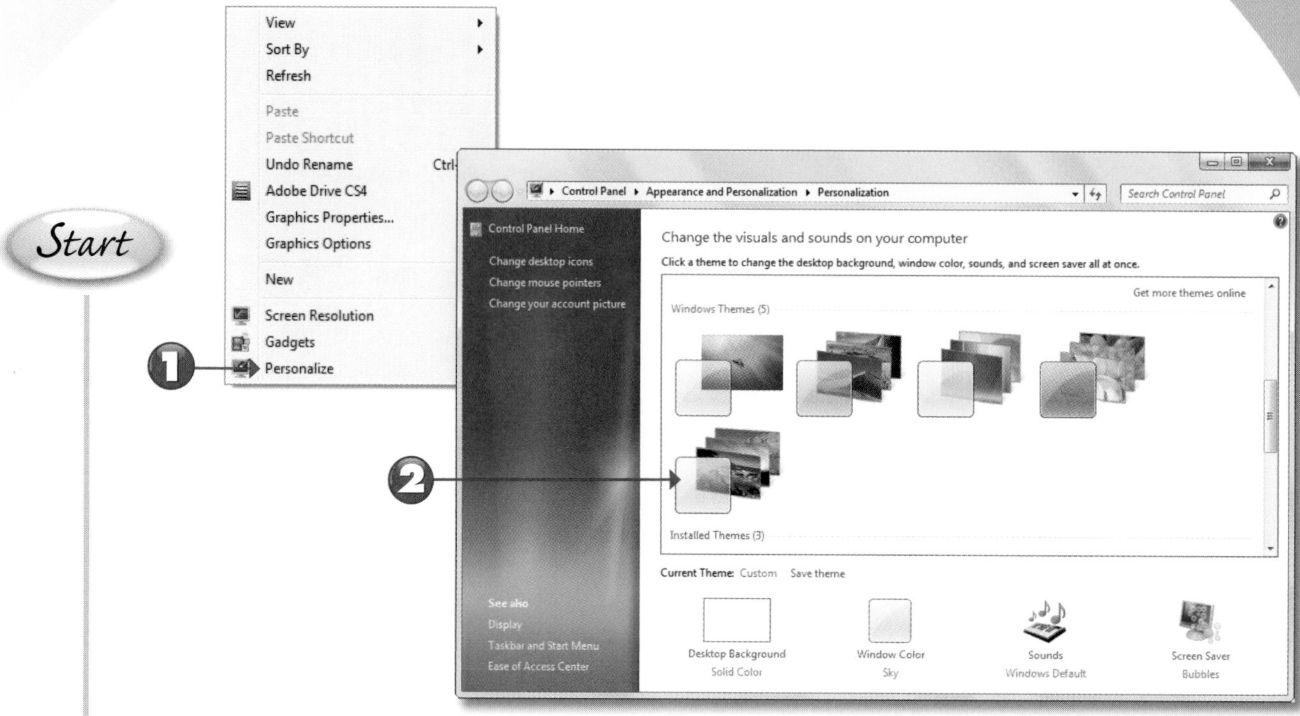

1. Right-click anywhere on the desktop and click **Personalize**.

2. Click the new theme you want to apply.

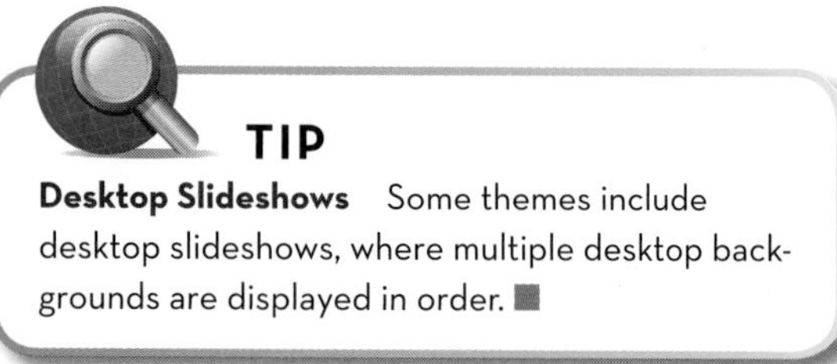

TIP

Desktop Slideshows Some themes include desktop slideshows, where multiple desktop backgrounds are displayed in order. ■

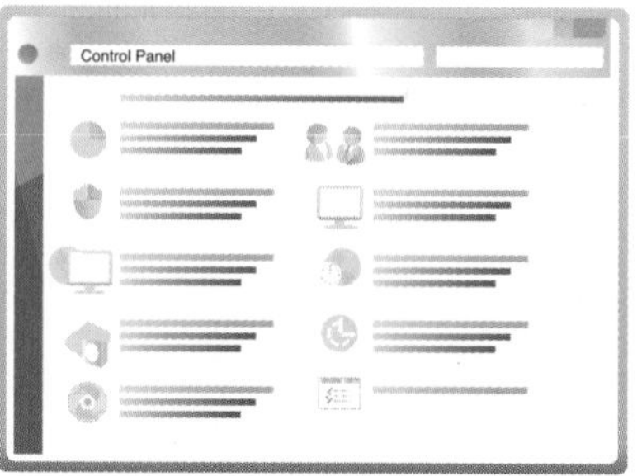

CHANGING THE COLOR SCHEME

The default Windows 7 desktop uses a predefined combination of colors and transparencies. If you don't like the way this looks, you can choose from several other color schemes.

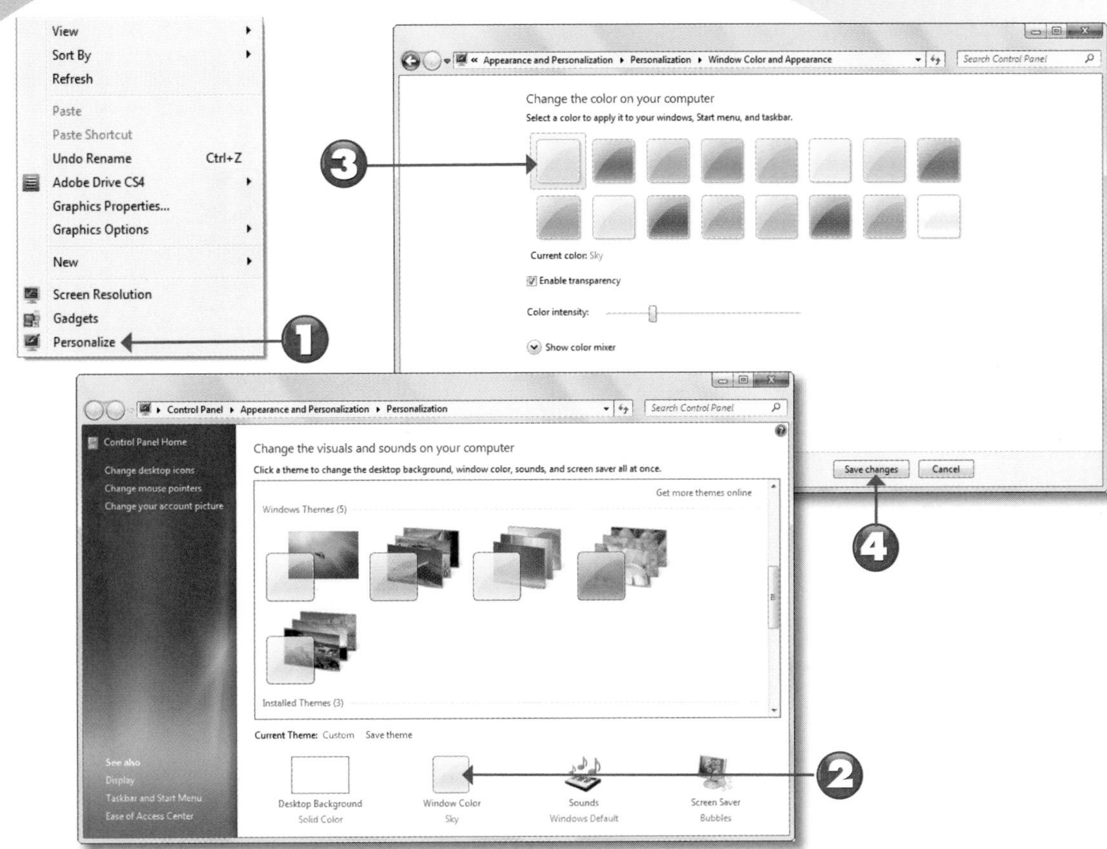

Start

1. Right-click anywhere on the desktop and click **Personalize**.
2. Click **Window Color** at the bottom of the window.
3. Click any of the default color schemes.
4. Click **Save Changes**.

End

TIP

Change the Transparency To change the degree of transparency in Windows 7's windows and dialog boxes, adjust the Color Intensity slider. Or, to turn off the transparency completely, uncheck the Enable Transparency option. ■

USING A SCREENSAVER

Screensavers display moving designs on your computer screen when you haven't typed or moved the mouse for a while. This provides some small degree of entertainment if you're bored at your desk.

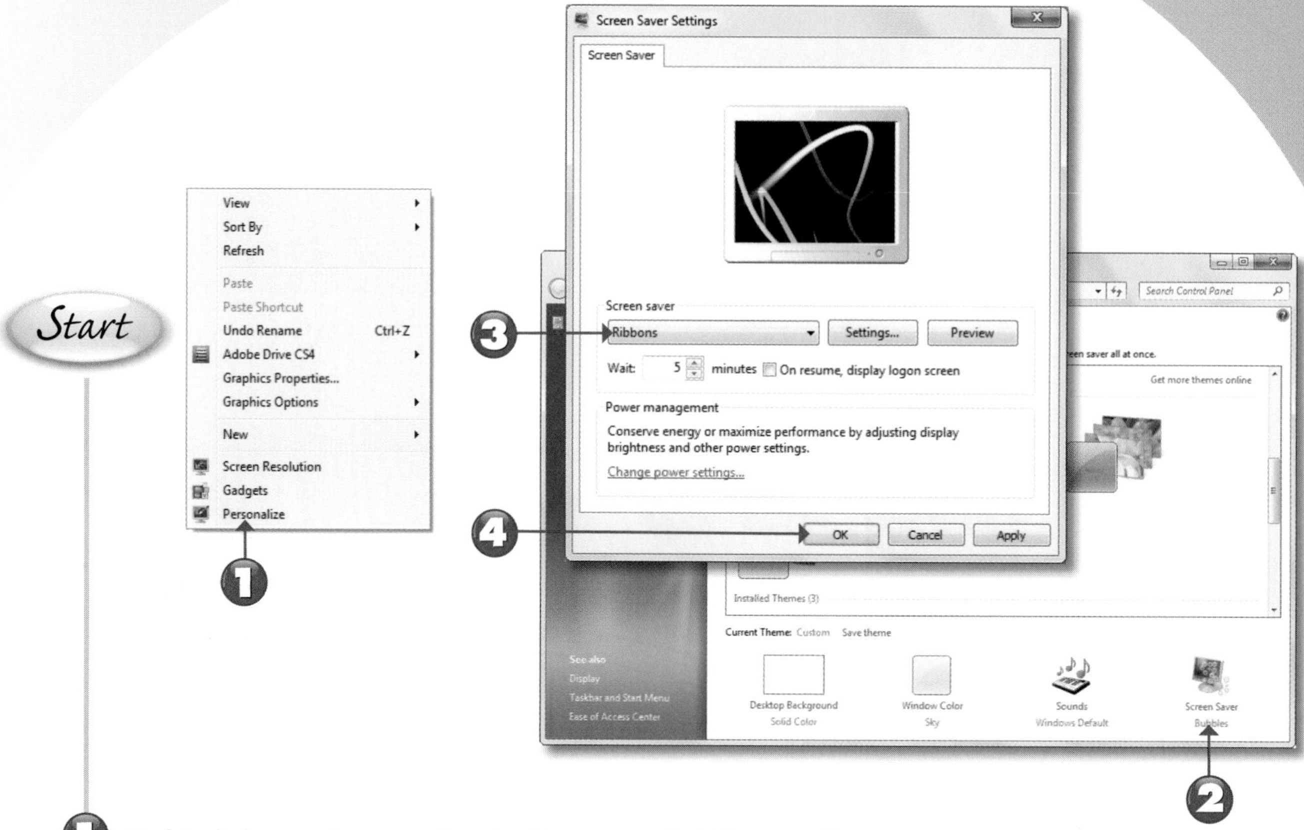

1. Right-click anywhere on the desktop and click **Personalize**.
2. Click **Screen Saver** at the bottom of the window.
3. Select a screensaver from the Screen Saver drop-down list.
4. Click **OK** when you're done.

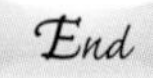

TIP

How Long to Wait? To determine the number of minutes you want the screen to be idle before the screensaver activates, select a new value from the Wait list. ■

TIP

Configure the Screensaver Click the Settings button to configure settings specific to an individual screensaver (if available). ■

PERSONALIZING THE DESKTOP BACKGROUND

Windows also lets you change just the desktop background, without changing the entire theme. Windows 7 includes a number of built-in desktop wallpapers; you can also choose your own photo or graphic for your desktop background.

Start

1. Right-click anywhere on the desktop and click **Personalize**.
2. Click **Desktop Background** at the bottom of the window.
3. When the next window opens, select one of Windows's built-in backgrounds from the list.
4. Click **Save Changes**.

TIP

Position Your Picture To determine how the image file is displayed on your desktop, select one of the options from the Picture Position list: Fill, Fit, Stretch, Tile, or Center. ■

TIP

Choose a Custom Background To use a picture of your own for your desktop background, click the Browse button next to the Picture Location list, and then select the picture you want from your computer's hard disk. ■

CREATING A DESKTOP SLIDESHOW

New to Windows 7 is the capability of having multiple desktop backgrounds, displayed one after another in a desktop slideshow. It's a great way to view all your favorite photos—without having to manually switch backgrounds.

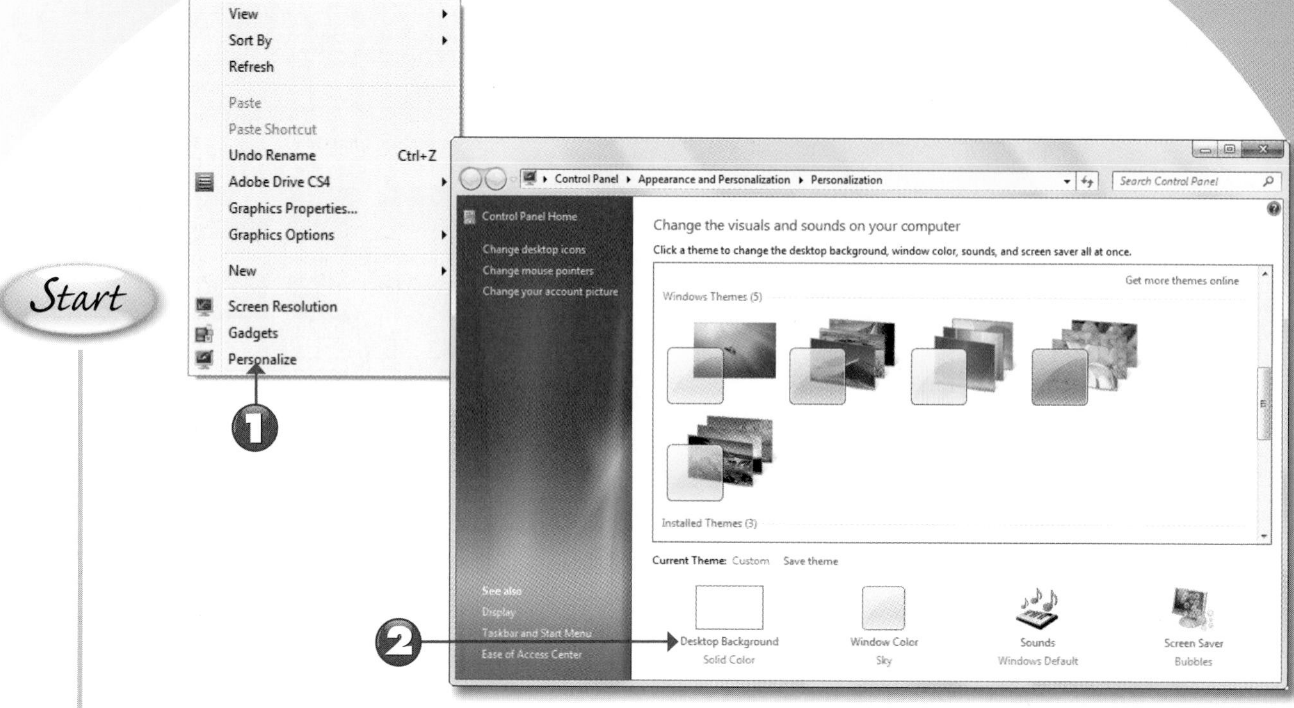

1. Right-click anywhere on the desktop and click **Personalize**.

2. Click **Desktop Background** at the bottom of the window.

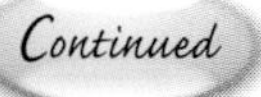

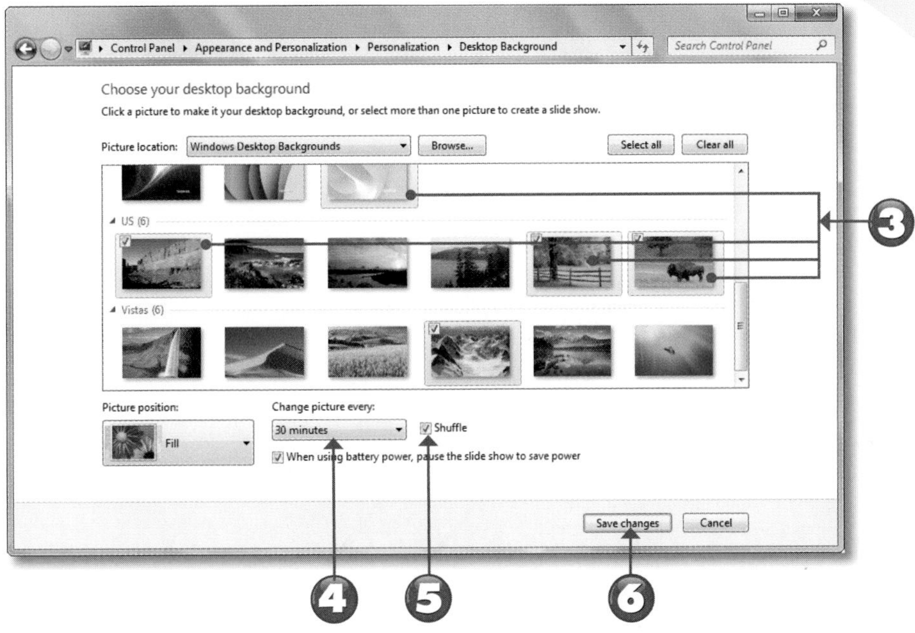

3. When the next window opens, hold down the **Ctrl** key and click the background images you want to include in the slideshow.

4. To determine how long each background displays, select a value from the **Change Picture Every** list.

5. To display background images in a random order, click the **Shuffle** option.

6. Click **Save Changes**.

End

TIP

Choose Your Own Images To include your own photos in the desktop slideshow, click the Browse button next to the Picture Location list, and then select the pictures you want from your computer's hard disk.

SETTING UP ADDITIONAL USERS

If you have multiple people using your PC, you should assign each user in your household his or her own password-protected user account. Anyone trying to access another user's account and files without the password will then be denied access.

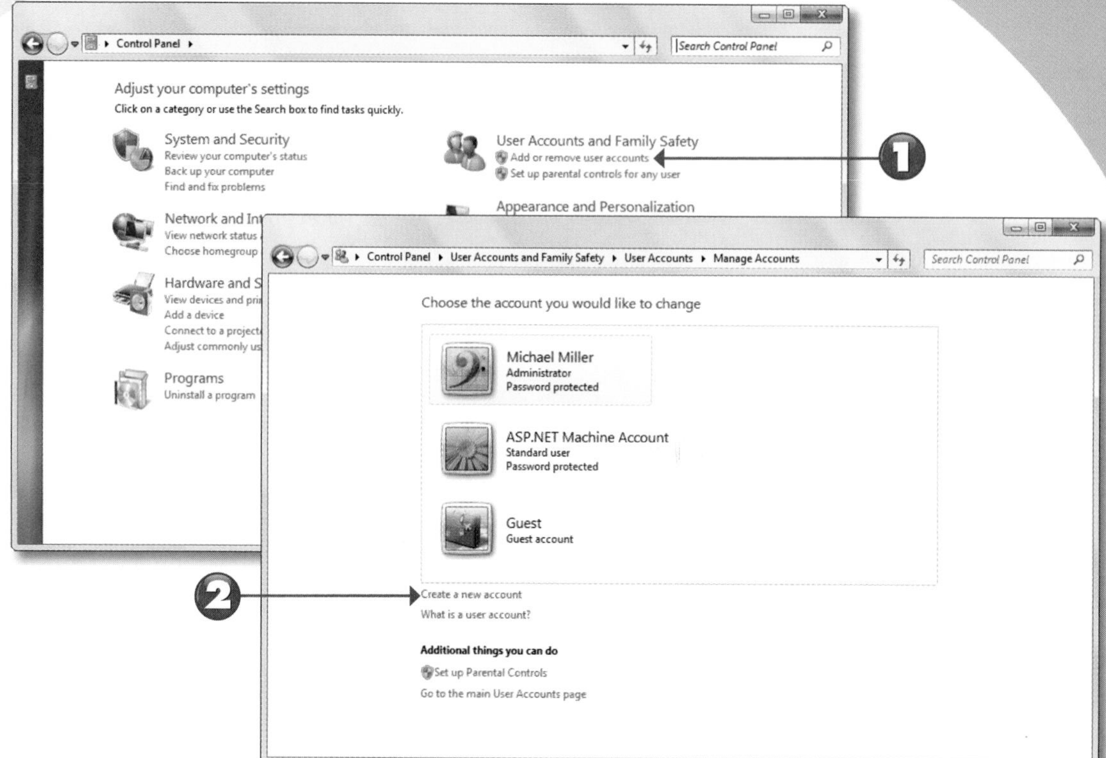

1. From the Windows Control Panel, click **Add or remove user accounts** from the User Accounts and Family Safety section.

2. Click **Create a new account**.

Continued

TIP

Different Users You can create two types of user accounts—Standard user or Administrator. You should set yourself up as an administrator because only this account can make system-wide changes to your PC. ■

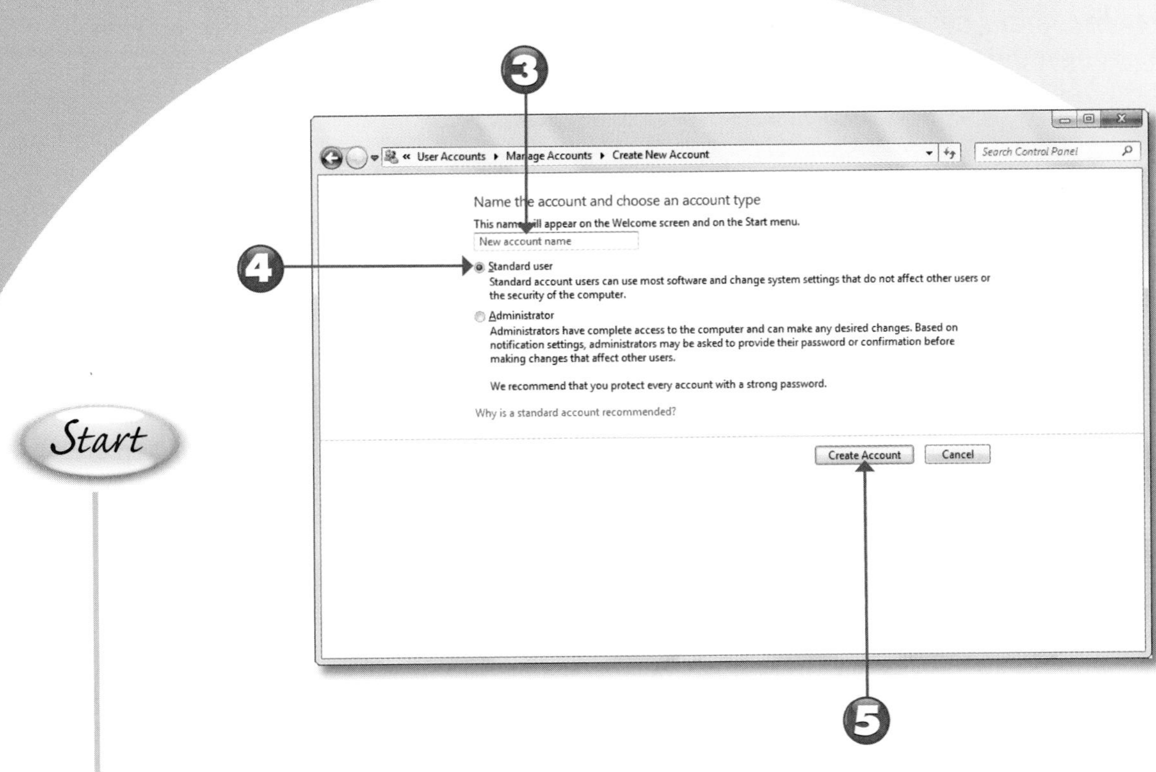

3 Enter a name for the account.

4 Select the type of account to create: **Standard user** or **Administrator**.

5 Click the **Create Account** button. Windows 7 now creates the new account and randomly assigns a picture that will appear next to the username.

End

TIP

Change Your Picture You can change an account picture by returning to the Manage Accounts window, selecting the account, and then selecting the Change the Picture option. ■

TIP

Create a Password By default, no password is assigned to the new account. You can assign a password by returning to the Manage Accounts window, selecting the account, and then selecting the Create a Password option. ■

DOWNLOADING WINDOWS LIVE APPLICATIONS

Microsoft makes additional Windows applications available for free download from **download.live.com**. These applications include Family Safety (parental controls), Mail (email), Messenger (instant messaging), Movie Maker (digital video editing), Photo Gallery (digital photo editing), Toolbar (for Internet Explorer), and Writer (blogging).

1. From Internet Explorer, go to **download.live.com**.
2. Click the link for the application you want to download.
3. Click **Download**.

NOTE

Built-In Applications Many of these now-optional applications used to be built into previous versions of Windows, and have been "unbundled" in Windows 7. ■

GETTING HELP IN WINDOWS

When you can't figure out how to perform a particular task, it's time to ask for help. In Windows 7, this is done through the Windows Help and Support Center.

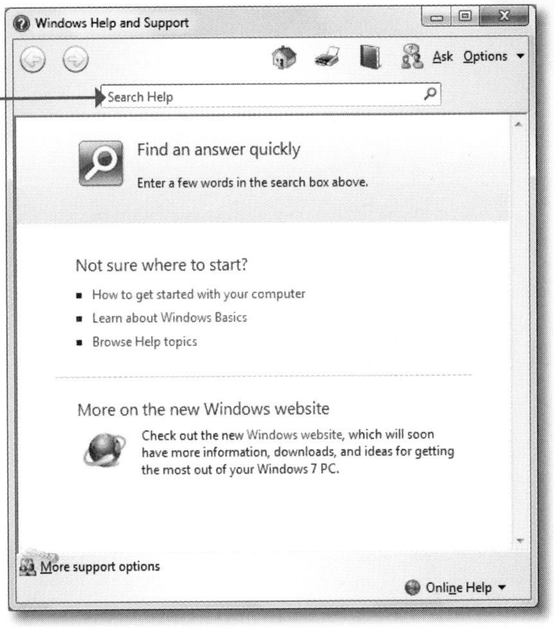

Start

1. Click the **Start** button to display the Start menu.

2. Click **Help and Support**.

3. Enter your query into the Search Help box at the top of the next dialog box, and then press **Enter**.

End

TIP

Browse for Help You can also browse the topics in Windows' Help system. Click the Browse Help icon at the top of the dialog box, and then click the appropriate topic below. ■

TIP

More on the Web More help information is available on Microsoft's website, www.microsoft.com. ■

WORKING WITH FILES AND FOLDERS

All the data for documents and programs on your computer is stored in electronic files. These files are then arranged into a series of folders and subfolders—just as you'd arrange paper files in a series of file folders in a filing cabinet.

In Windows 7, you use Windows Explorer to view and manage the folders and files on your system. You open Windows Explorer by clicking the Windows Explorer button on the Windows taskbar.

WINDOWS EXPLORER

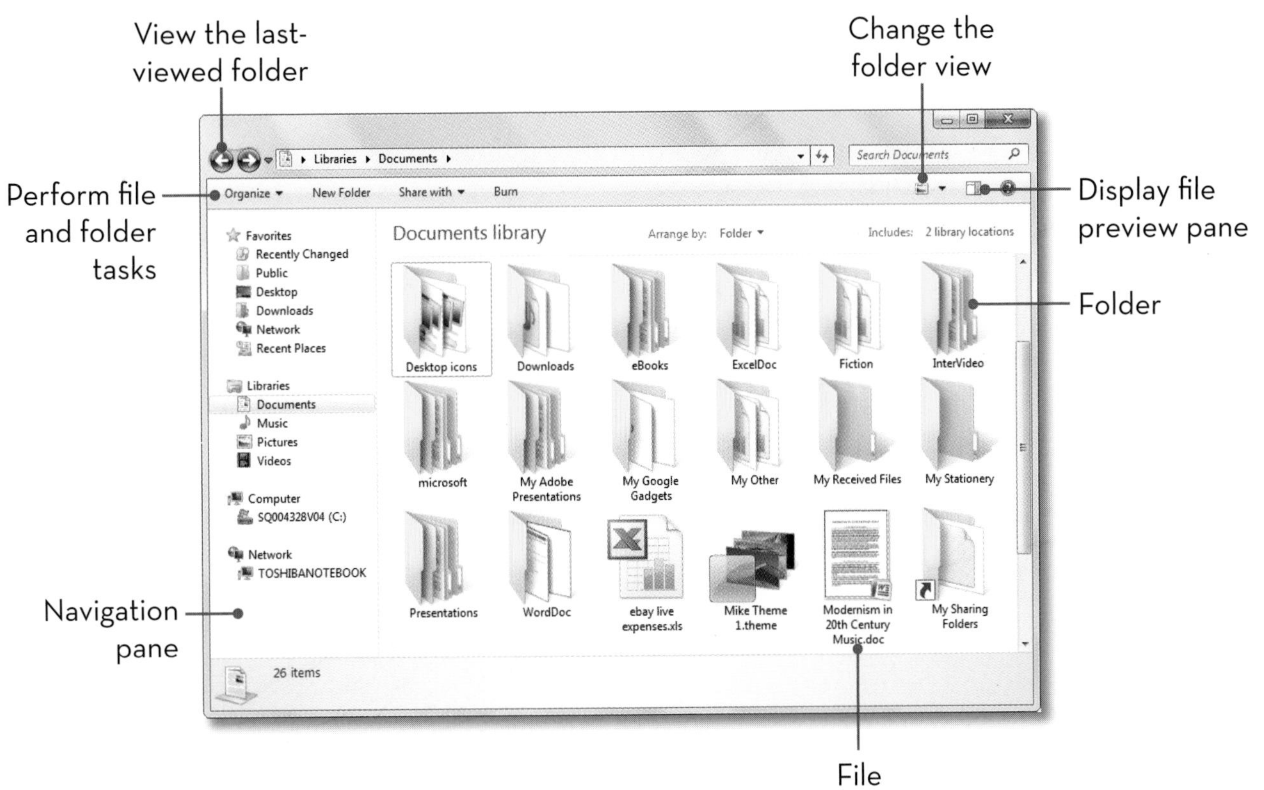

CHANGING THE WAY FILES ARE DISPLAYED

You can choose to view the contents of a folder in a variety of ways. The icon views are nice in that they show a small thumbnail preview of any selected file.

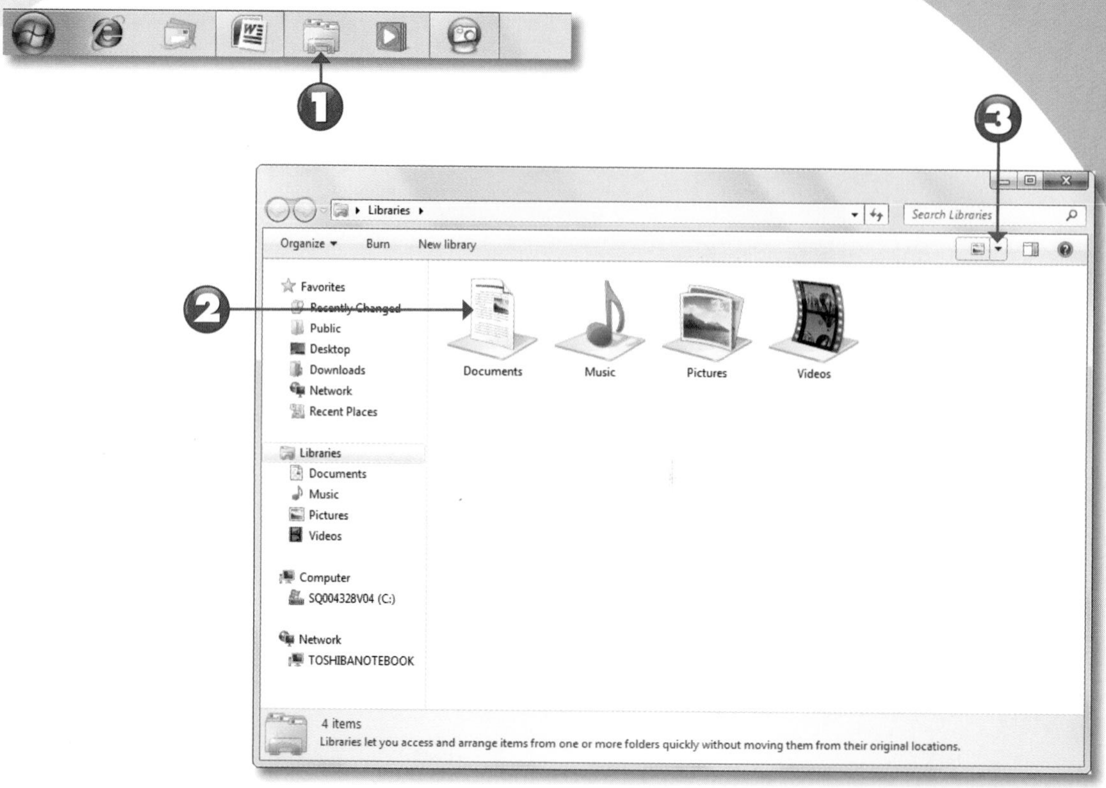

Start

1. Click the **Windows Explorer** button on the Windows taskbar.

2. Your documents are organized into Documents, Music, Pictures, and Videos folders. Double-click any folder to view the folder's contents.

3. Click the down arrow next to the **Views** button on the toolbar, and then move the slider to select from the **Content**, **Tiles**, **Details**, **List, Small Icons**, **Medium Icons**, **Large Icons**, and **Extra Large Icons** views.

TIP

Which View Is Best? Any of the larger icon views are best for working with graphics files. Details view is best if you're looking for files by date or size. ■

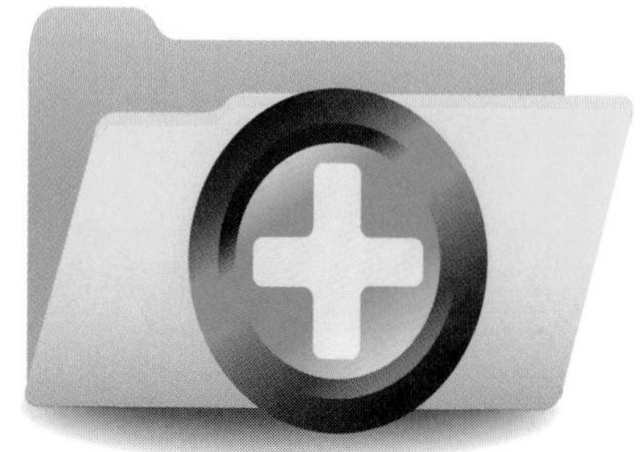

SORTING FILES AND FOLDERS

When viewing files in Windows Explorer, you can sort your files and folders in a number of ways. To view your files in alphabetical order, choose to sort by **Name**. To see all similar files grouped together, choose to sort by **Item Type**. To sort your files by the date and time they were last edited, select **Date modified**.

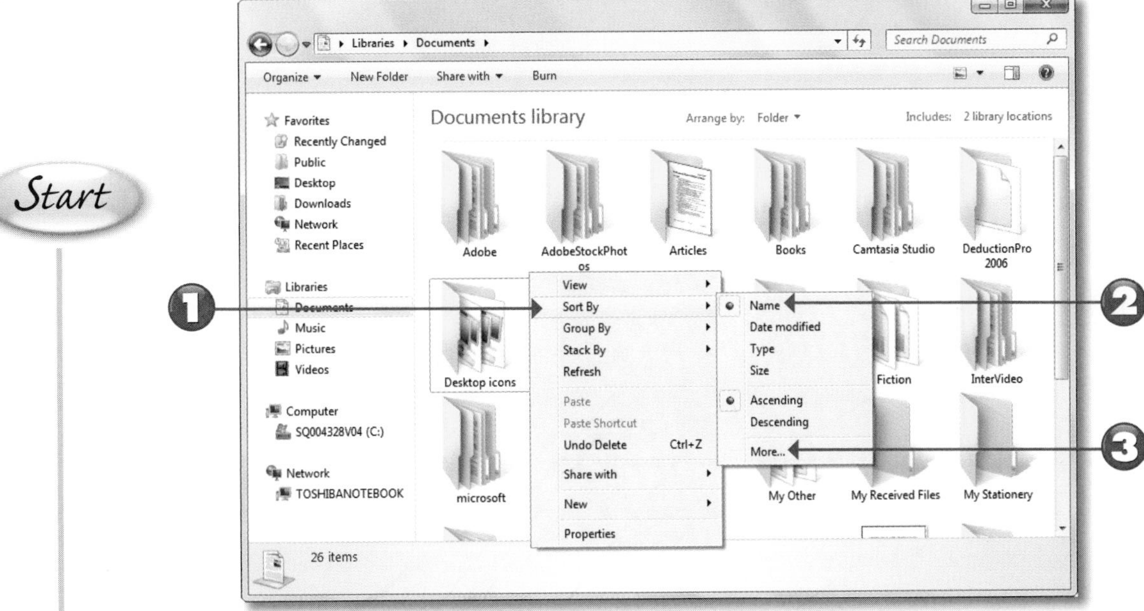

1. Right-click any open space within Windows Explorer and select **Sort By**.
2. Choose to sort by **Name**, **Date modified**, **Type**, or **Size**.
3. To view more sorting options, click **More**.

End

TIP

More Sorting Options When you opt to view More sorting options, you can sort by dozens of different parameters, all of which change based on what type of file you're viewing. For example, if you're viewing music files, you can sort by Album, Artists, Bit Rate, Composers, Genre, and the like. ■

NAVIGATING FOLDERS

You can navigate through the folders and subfolders in Windows Explorer in several ways.

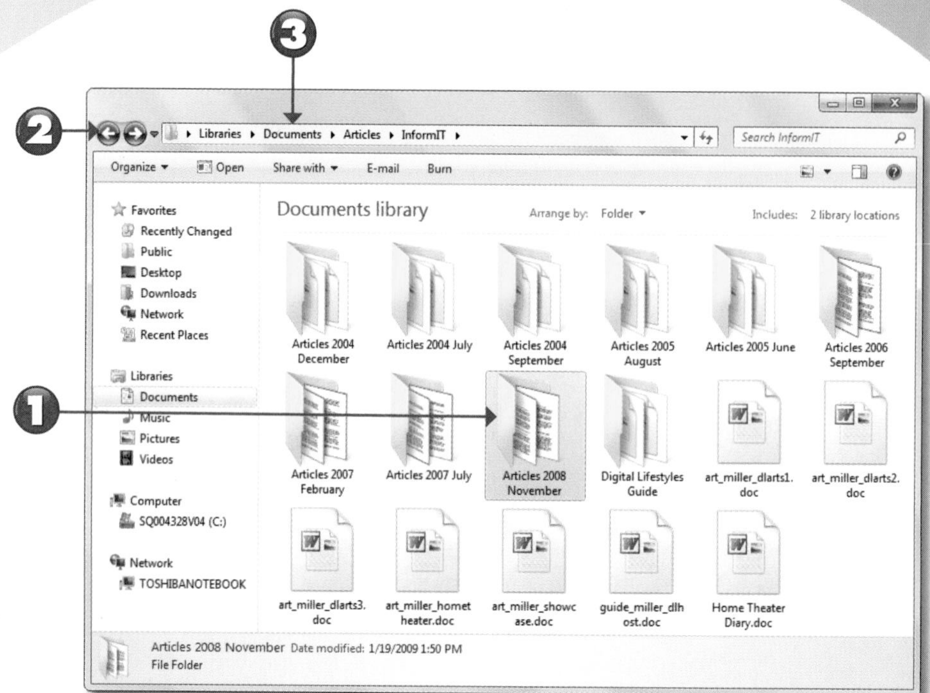

Start

1. To view the contents of a disk or folder, double-click an icon.
2. To move back to the disk or folder previously selected, click the **Back** button on the toolbar.
3. To move up the hierarchy of folders and subfolders to the next highest item, click that item in the address box at the top of the window.

End

TIP

Moving Forward If you've moved back through multiple disks or folders, you can move forward to the next folder by clicking the Forward button. ■

TIP

Breadcrumbs The list of folders and subfolders in Windows Explorer's address box presents a "bread-crumb" approach to navigation. You can view even earlier folders by clicking the left arrow next to the folder icon in the address box; this displays a pull-down menu of the recently visited and most popular items. ■

NAVIGATING WITH THE NAVIGATION PANE

Another way to navigate your files and folders is to use the Navigation pane. This pane, on the left side of the Windows Explorer window, displays both favorite links and a hierarchical folder tree.

Start

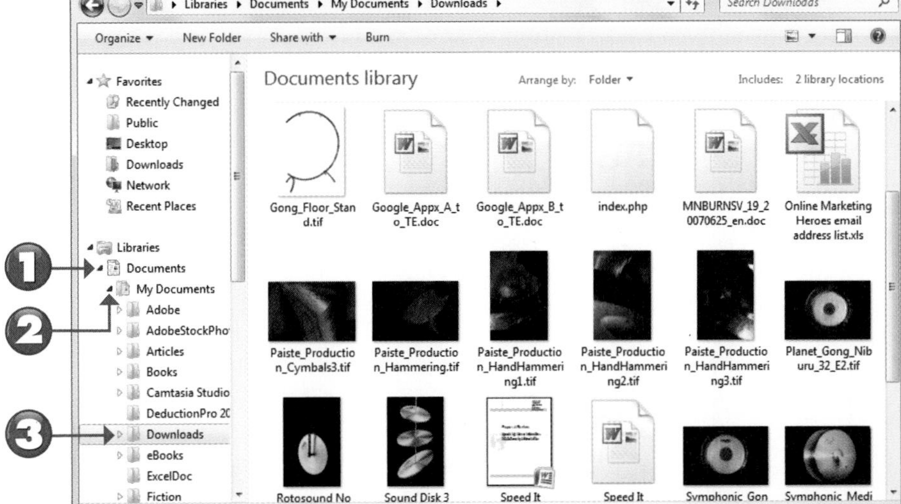

1. Click an icon in the **Favorites** or **Libraries** section to open the contents of the selected item.
2. Click the arrow icon next to any folder to display all the subfolders it contains.
3. Click a folder to display its contents in the main Windows Explorer window.

End

NOTE

Favorites Windows 7's Favorites include the following actual and virtual folders: Recently Changed, Public, Desktop, Downloads, Network, and Recent Places. ■

NOTE

Computer To navigate all the drives and folders on your computer, click the Computer folder in the Navigation pane. ■

CREATING A NEW FOLDER

The more files you create, the harder it is to organize and find things on your hard disk. When the number of files you have becomes unmanageable, you need to create more folders—and subfolders—to better categorize your files.

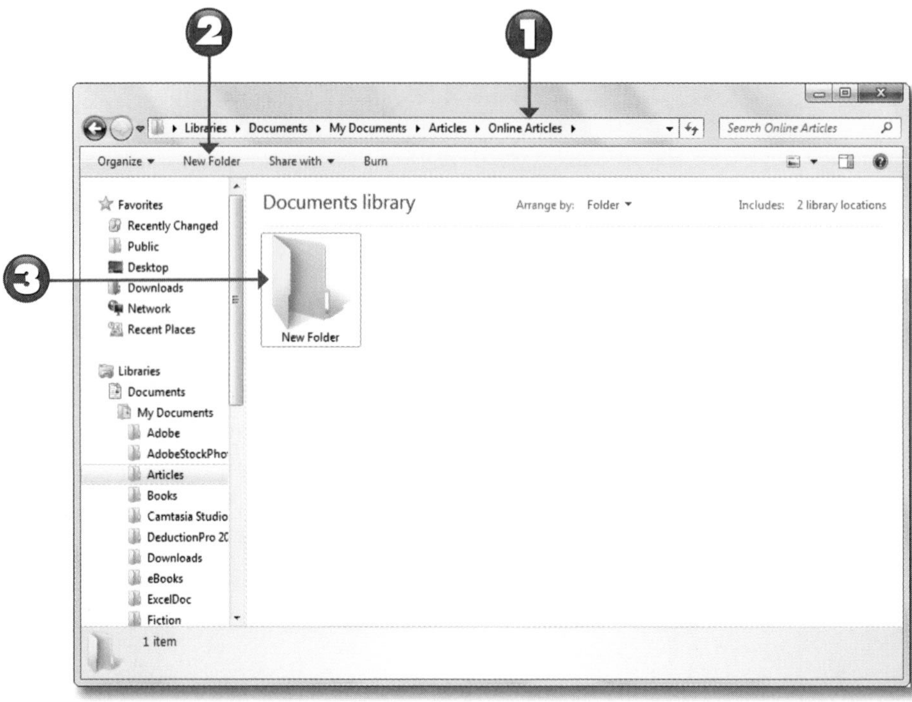

Start

1. Navigate to the drive or folder where you want to place the new folder.
2. Click the **New Folder** button on the Windows Explorer toolbar.
3. A new, empty folder now appears with the filename “New Folder” highlighted. Type a name for your folder and press **Enter**.

End

CAUTION

Illegal Characters Folder names and filenames can include up to 255 characters—including many special characters. You *can't*, however, use the following “illegal” characters: \ / : * ? “ < > |. ■

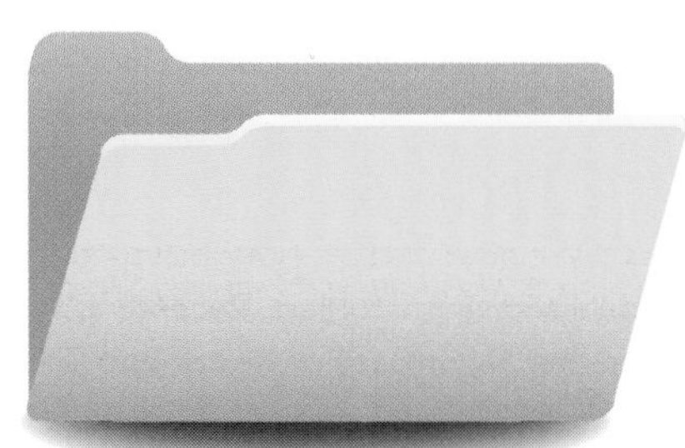

RENAMING A FILE OR FOLDER

When you create a new file or folder, it helps to give it a name that describes its contents. Sometimes, however, you might need to change a file's name. Fortunately, Windows makes renaming an item relatively easy.

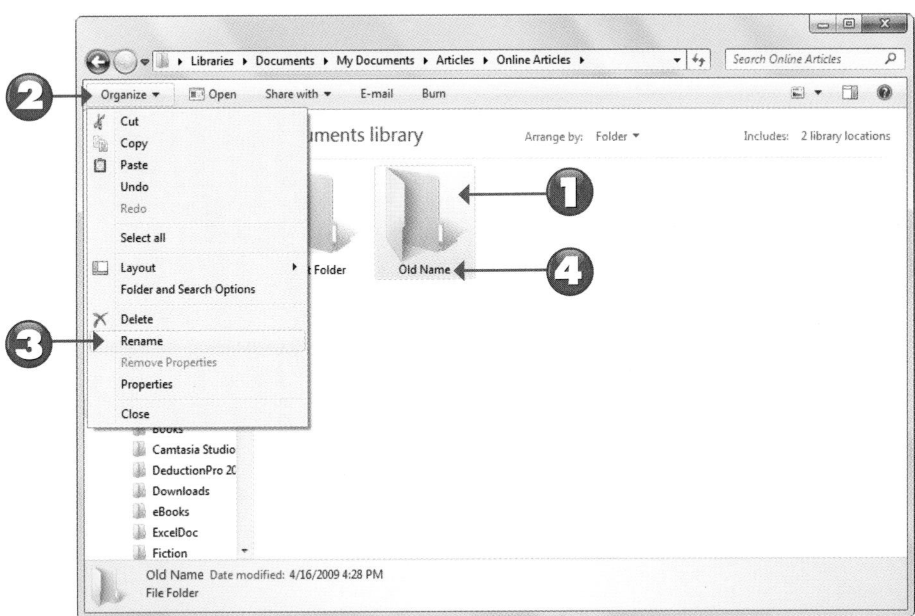

1. Click the file or folder you want to rename.
2. Click the **Organize** button.
3. Click **Rename**; this highlights the filename.
4. Type a new name for your folder (which overwrites the current name), and press **Enter**.

End

CAUTION

Don't Change the Extension The one part of the filename you should never change is the extension—the part that comes after the "dot" if you choose to show file extensions. Try to change the extension, and Windows will warn you that you're doing something wrong. ■

TIP

Keyboard Shortcut You can also rename a file by selecting the file and pressing F2 on your computer keyboard. This highlights the filename and readies it for editing. ■

COPYING A FILE OR FOLDER

There are many ways to copy a file in Windows 7. The easiest method is to use the Copy and Paste commands on the Organize menu.

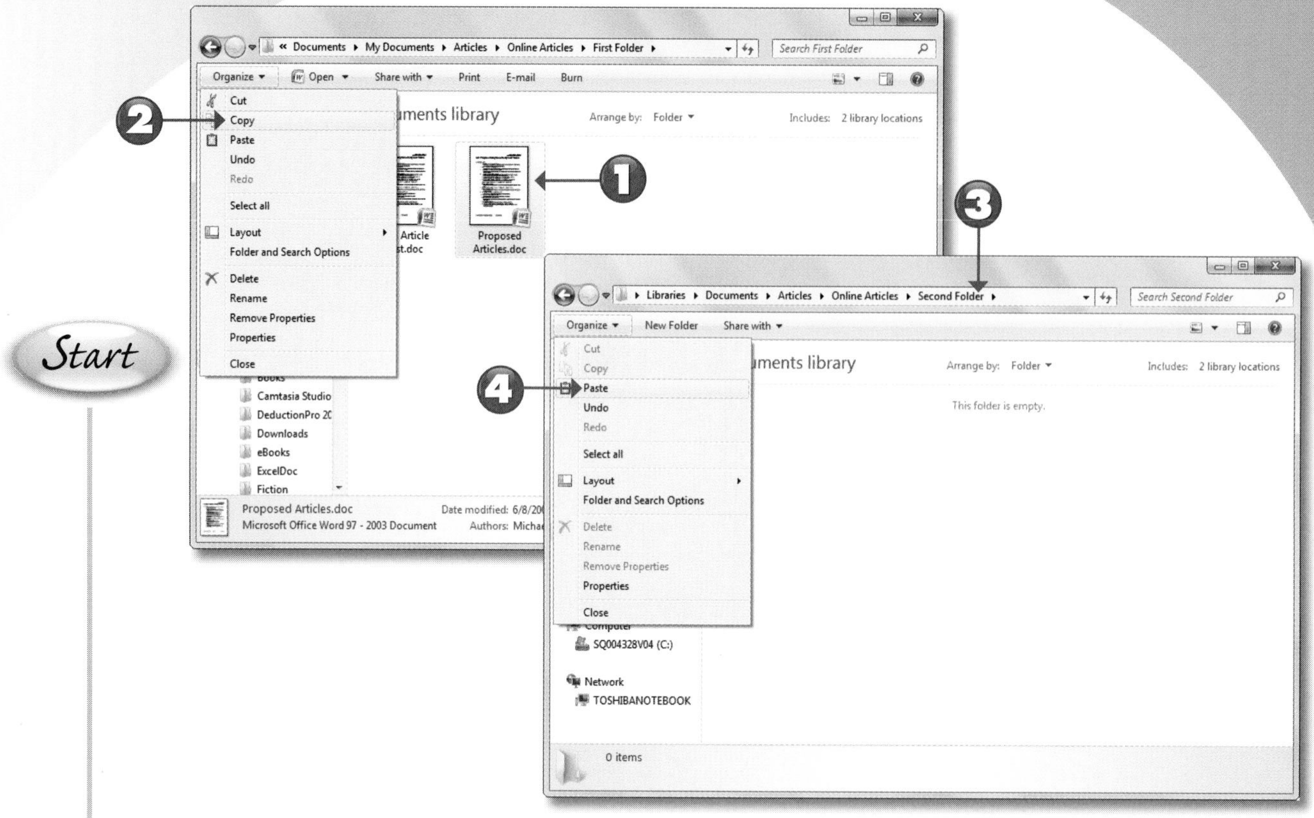

Start

1. Click the item you want to copy.
2. Click the **Organize** button and then click **Copy**.
3. Navigate to and select the new location for the item.
4. Click the **Organize** button and then click **Paste**.

TIP

Copy to a New Folder If you want to copy the item to a new folder, navigate to the new location, pull down the Organize menu, and click New Folder before you click the Paste button. ■

MOVING A FILE OR FOLDER

Moving a file (or folder) is different from copying it. Moving cuts the item from its previous location and pastes it into a new location. Copying leaves the original item where it was *and* creates a copy of the item elsewhere.

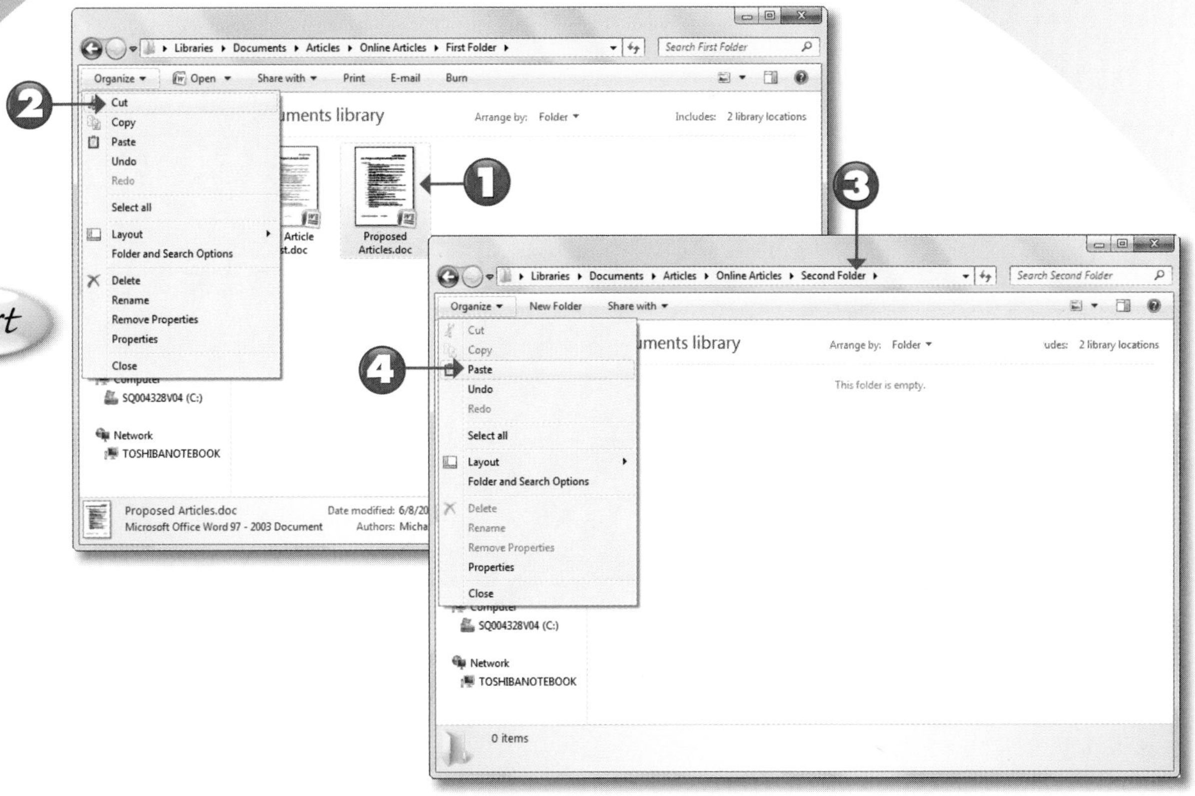

Start

1. Click the item you want to move.
2. Click the **Organize** button and click **Cut**.
3. Navigate to and select the new location for the item.
4. Click the **Organize** button and click **Paste**.

End

TIP

Move to a New Folder If you want to move the item to a new folder, navigate to the new location, pull down the Organize menu, and click New Folder before you click the Paste button. ■

DELETING A FILE OR FOLDER

Keeping too many files eats up too much hard disk space—which is a bad thing. Because you don't want to waste disk space, you should periodically delete those files (and folders) you no longer need. When you delete a file, you send it to the Windows Recycle Bin, which is kind of a trash can for deleted files.

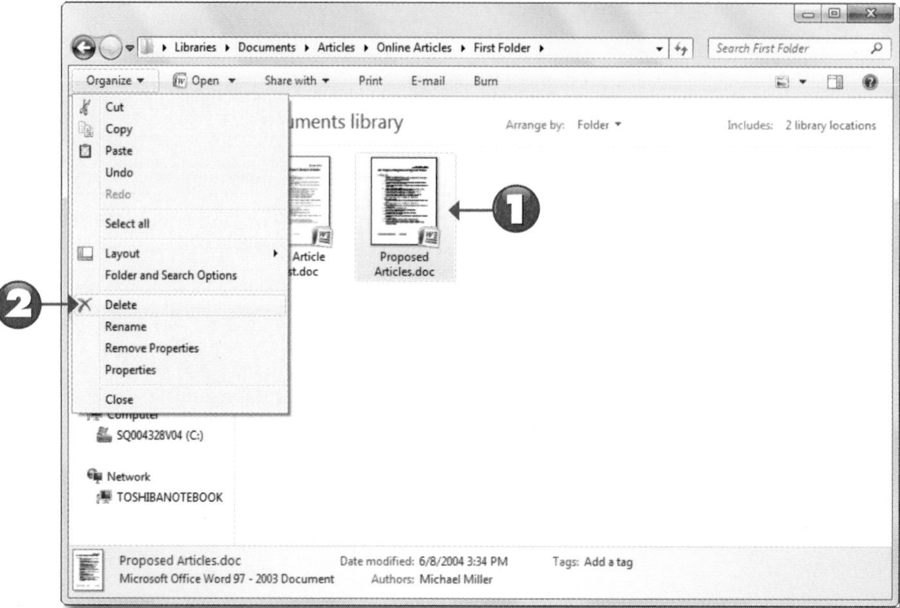

1. Click the file you want to delete.
2. Click the **Organize** button and click **Delete**.

End

TIP

Other Ways to Delete You can also delete a file by dragging it from the folder window onto the Recycle Bin icon on the desktop or by highlighting it and pressing the Delete key on your computer keyboard. ■

RESTORING DELETED FILES

Have you ever accidentally deleted the wrong file? If so, you're in luck. Windows stores the files you delete in the Recycle Bin, which is actually a special folder on your hard disk. For a short period of time, you can "undelete" files from the Recycle Bin back to their original locations.

1. Double-click the **Recycle Bin** icon on your desktop to open the Recycle Bin folder.
2. Click the file you want to restore.
3. Click the **Restore This Item** button.

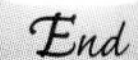

EMPTYING THE RECYCLE BIN

By default, the deleted files in the Recycle Bin can occupy 4GB plus 5% of your hard disk space. When you've deleted enough files to exceed this limit, the oldest files in the Recycle Bin are automatically and permanently deleted from your hard disk. You can also manually empty the Recycle Bin and thus free up some hard disk space.

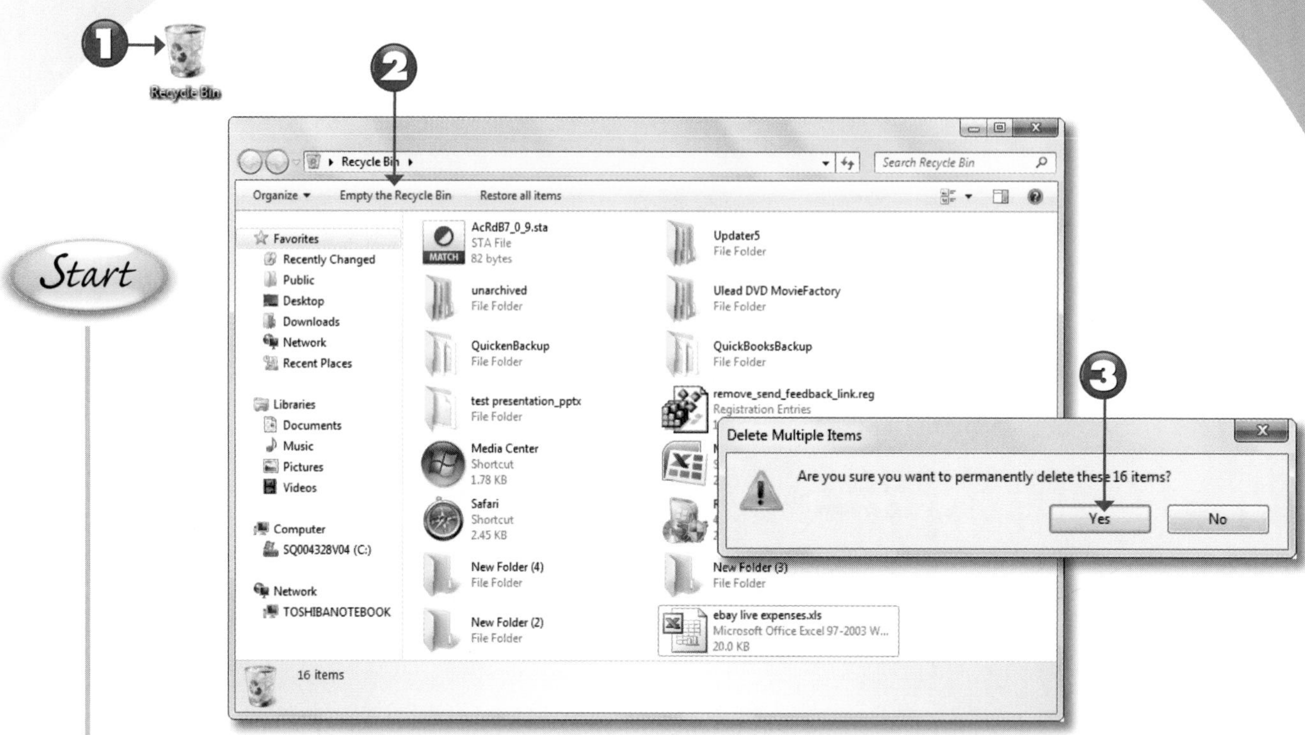

1. Double-click the **Recycle Bin** icon on your desktop to open the Recycle Bin folder.
2. Click the **Empty the Recycle Bin** button.
3. When the Delete Multiple Items dialog box appears, click **Yes** to completely erase the files.

End

TIP

Fast Empty You can also empty the Recycle Bin by right-clicking its icon on the Windows desktop and selecting Empty Recycle Bin from the pop-up menu. ■

WORKING WITH LIBRARIES

Windows 7 includes a new way to manage your files, called *libraries*. A library is kind of a virtual folder; it doesn't physically exist on your hard disk, but instead points to the subfolders and files you place within it.

Start

1. Click the **Windows Explorer** button on the toolbar to open Windows Explorer.
2. Windows's default libraries are displayed in the main Windows Explorer window and in the Navigation pane. Double-click a folder icon (or click the icon in the Navigation pane) to view its contents.
3. Windows Explorer now displays all the included folders and documents, which are located across your computer's hard disk. Double-click an item to open it.

NOTE

Default Libraries Windows 7's default libraries include virtual folders for Documents, Music, Pictures, and Videos. ■

TIP

All Music Windows displays all your digital music files, no matter which folder they're really stored in, in the Music library. All your digital photo files are displayed in the Pictures library. And all your digital video files are displayed in the Videos library. ■

CREATING A NEW LIBRARY

In addition to Windows's default libraries, you can create your own libraries to virtually organize files from any folder on your hard disk.

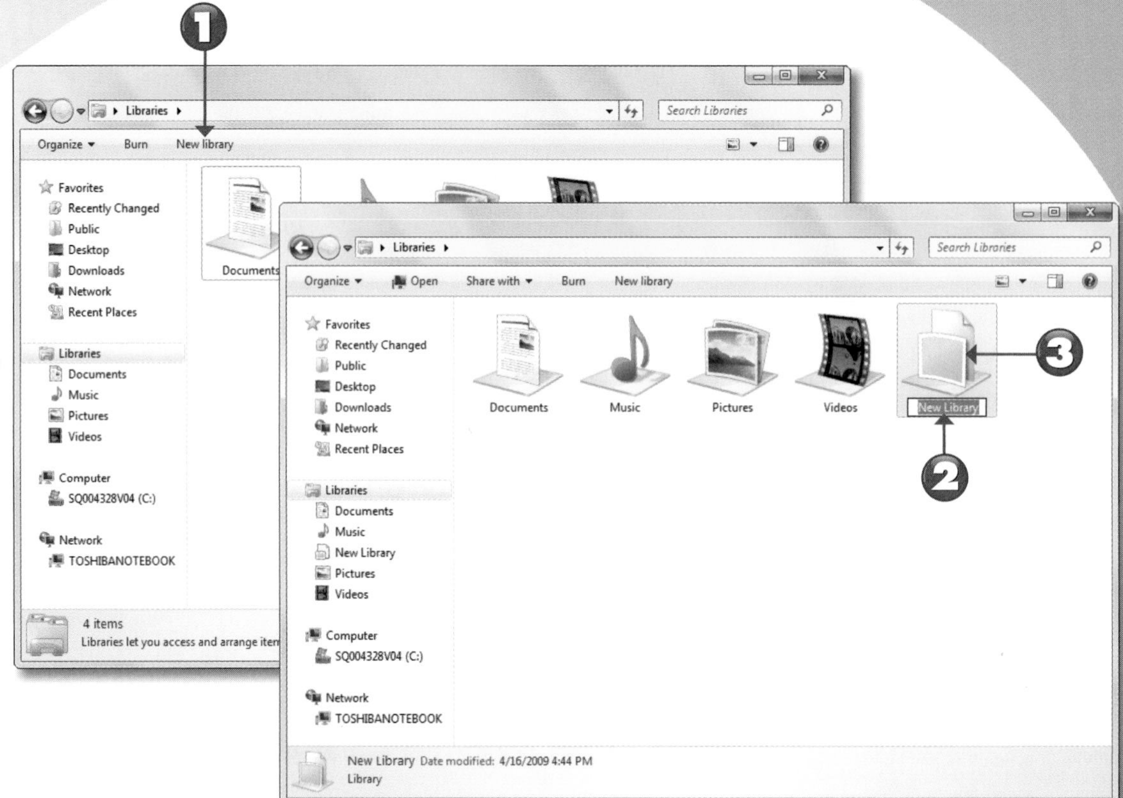

1. Click the **New Library** button on the Windows Explorer toolbar.
2. When the new library icon appears, type a name for the new library.
3. Double-click the icon for the new library.

Continued

TIP

Practical Uses Use libraries to organize files stored in various folders across your hard disk. For example, you might create a library for a project that has Word documents stored in one folder, Excel spreadsheets in another, and photos in still another. ■

4 Click the **Include a Folder** button.

5 Navigate to and click the folder you wish to include in the library.

6 Click the **Include Folder** button.

7 Repeat steps 3–6 to include additional folders in this library.

End

NOTE

Live Libraries When you create or save a new file in a folder assigned to a library, that file automatically appears when you next open the library folder. ■

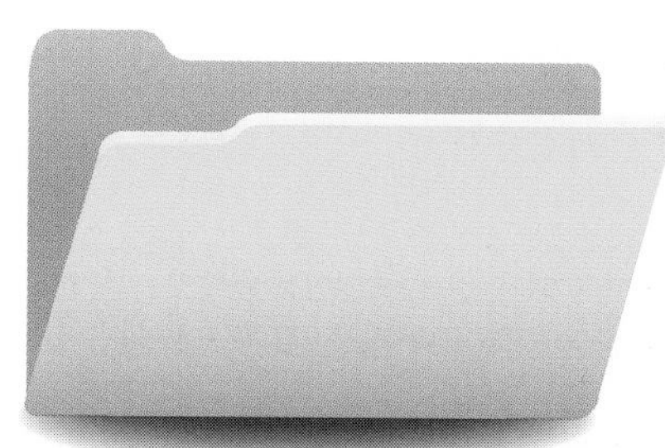

COMPRESSING A FILE

Really big files can be difficult to copy or share. Fortunately, Windows 7 lets you create *compressed* folders, which take big files and compress them in size (called a "zipped" file). After the file has been transferred, you can then uncompress the file back to its original state.

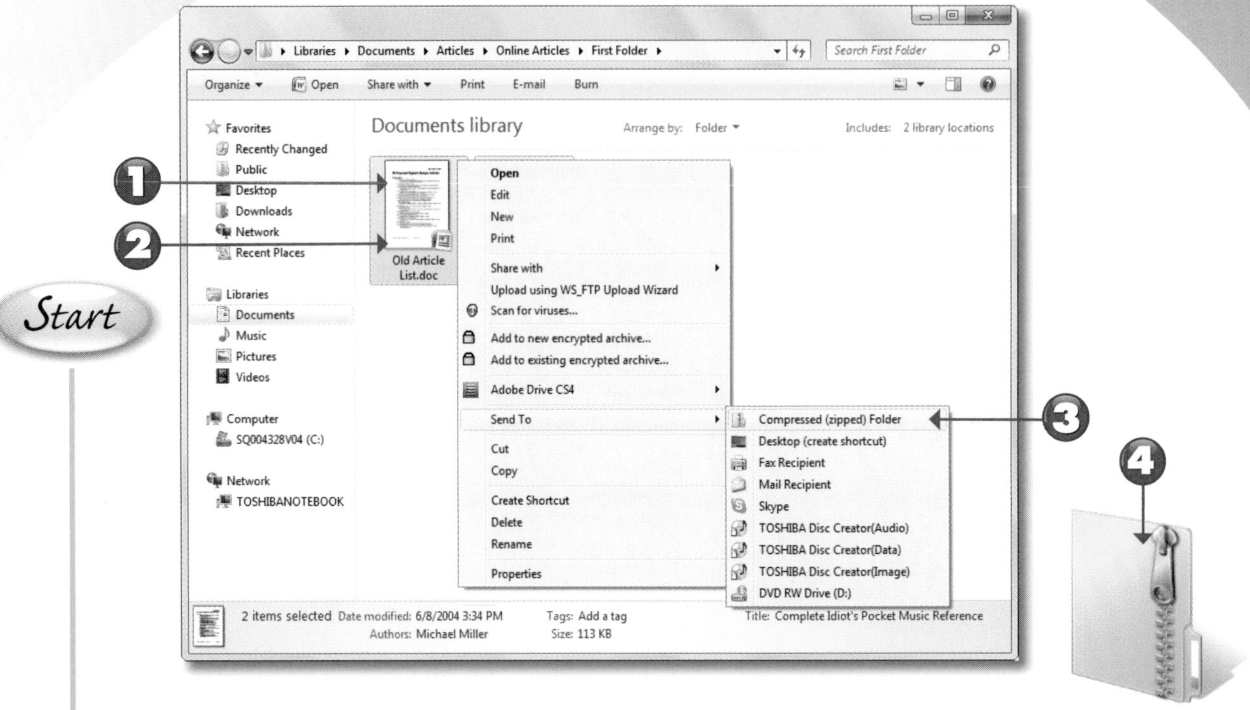

Proposed Articles.zip

1. Click the file(s) you want to compress. (To select more than one file, hold down the **Ctrl** key when clicking.)

2. Right-click the selected file(s) to display the pop-up menu.

3. Select **Send To**, **Compressed (Zipped) Folder**.

4. Windows creates a new zipped folder in this same folder that contains copies of the selected files.

End

NOTE

Zip Files The compressed folder is actually a file with a .zip extension, so it can be used with other compression/decompression programs, such as WinZip. ■

EXTRACTING FILES FROM A COMPRESSED FOLDER

The process of decompressing a file is actually an *extraction* process. That's because you extract the original file(s) from the compressed folder. In Windows 7, this process is eased by the use of the Extraction Wizard.

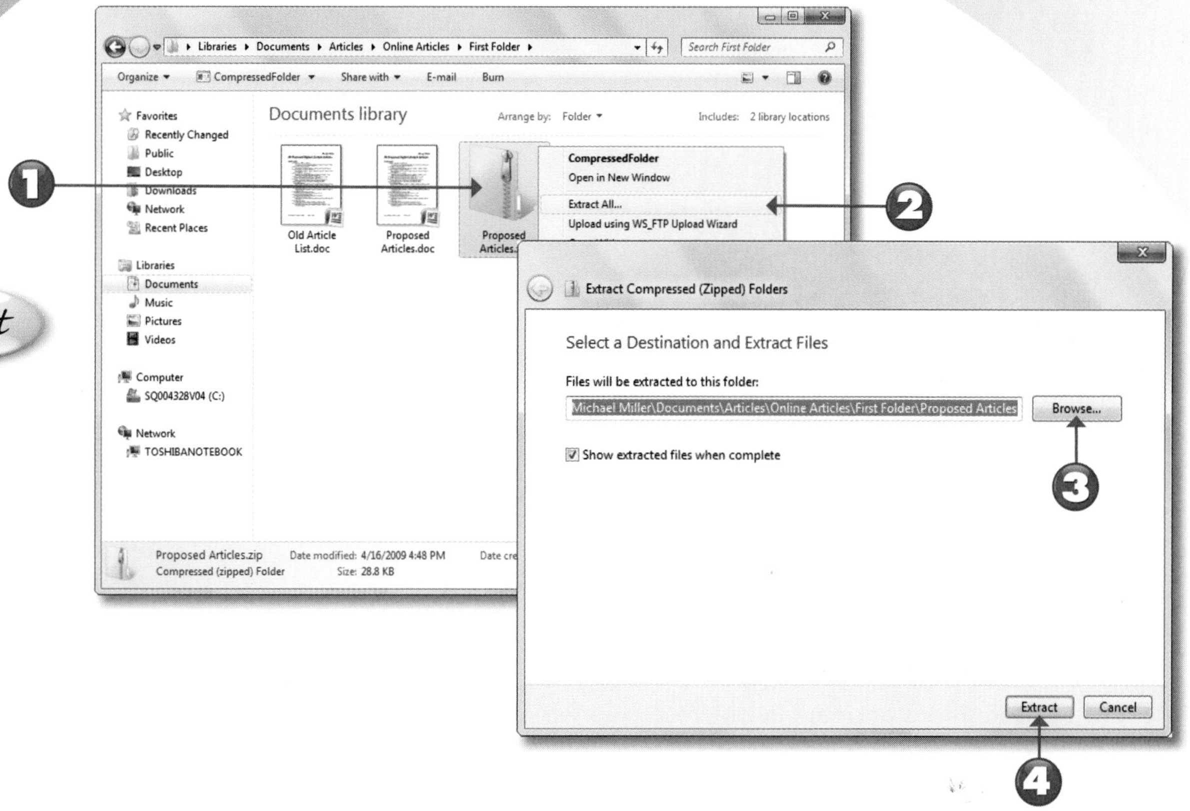

Start

1. Right-click the compressed folder to display the pop-up menu.
2. Click **Extract All**.
3. Click **Browse** to select the folder to which you want to extract the files.
4. Click the **Extract** button. Windows now extracts the files to the location you selected.

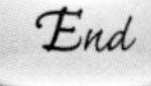

TIP

Extracted Folder By default, compressed files are extracted to a new folder with the same name. You can change this, however, to extract to any folder you like. ■

TIP

Zipper Icon Compressed folders are distinguished by the little zipper on the folder icon. ■

USING MICROSOFT WORD

When you want to write a letter, fire off a quick memo, create a fancy report, or publish a newsletter, you use a type of software program called a *word processor*. For most computer users, Microsoft Word is the word processing program of choice. Word is a full-featured word processor, and it's included on many new PCs and as part of the Microsoft Office suite and some versions of Microsoft Works. You can use Word for all your writing needs—from basic letters to fancy newsletters and everything in between.

You start Word from the Windows Start menu, by selecting Start, All Programs, Microsoft Office, Microsoft Office Word 2007. When Word launches, a blank document appears in the Word workspace. Word can display your document in one of five views: Print Layout, Full Screen Reading, Web Layout, Outline, and Draft. You select a view by using the View buttons at the bottom left of the Word window or by making a selection from the View ribbon.

THE WORD 2007 WORKSPACE

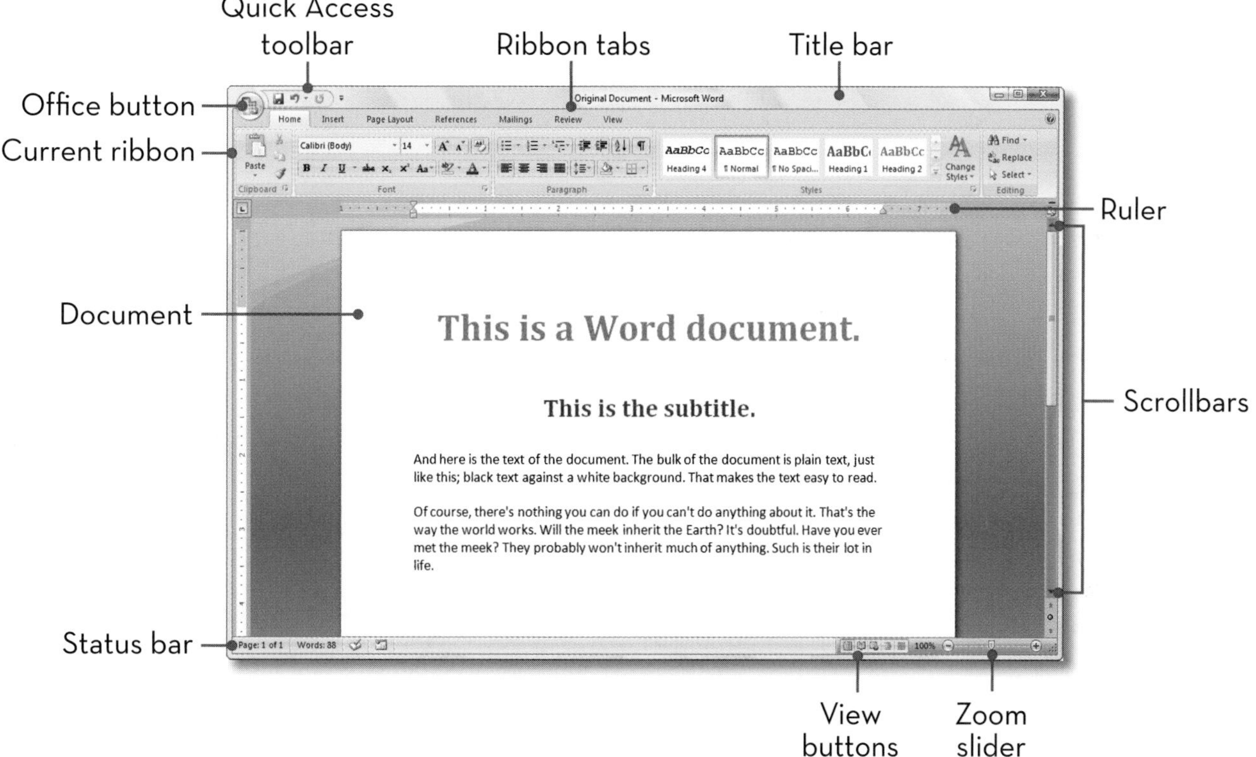

NAVIGATING WORD 2007

Microsoft Word 2007 introduced a new interface that uses toolbar-like ribbons in place of the traditional menu bar and toolbar. Each ribbon contains buttons and controls for specific operations; for example, the Page Layout ribbon contains controls for Margins, Columns, Indent, Spacing, and the like.

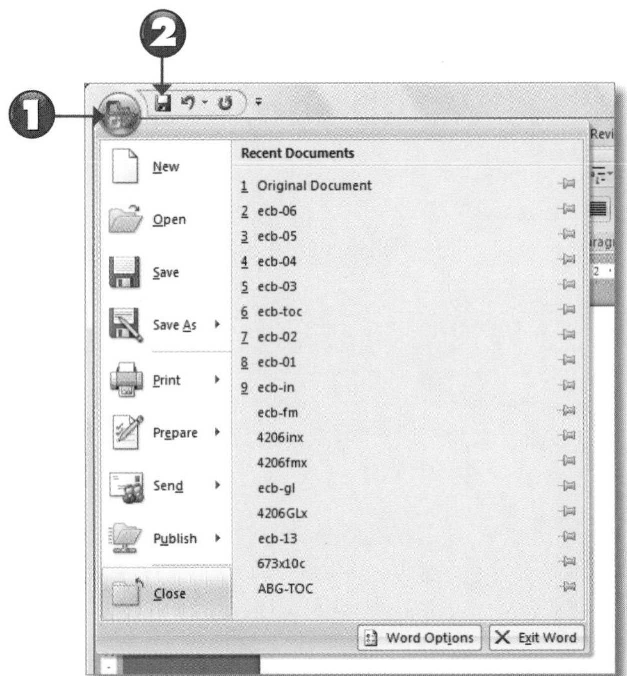

1. Click the **Office** button to access a pull-down menu with common operations and recently used files.

2. Click any icon on the Quick Access toolbar to perform common operations such as Save and Undo.

Continued

NOTE

Microsoft Word 2007 This section covers Microsoft Word 2007, included in Microsoft Office 2007. If you have a different version of Word, consult the program's Help file for information on how to perform common operations. ■

NOTE

Upgrading from Previous Versions If you're accustomed to previous versions of Word, Word 2007 takes a little getting used to. But once you've figured out what's where, the ribbon-based interface is a lot easier to use. ■

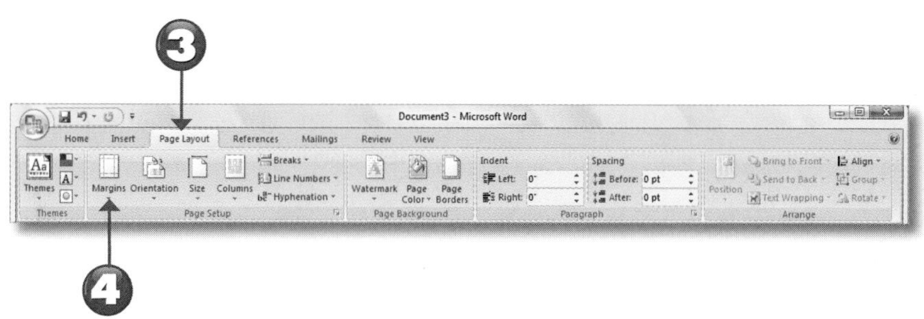

3. Click any tab to display the related ribbon.

4. Click a button or control on the ribbon to perform the given operation.

End

TIP

Context-Sensitive Ribbons Some ribbons appear automatically when you perform a specific task. For example, if you insert a picture and then select that picture, a new Format ribbon tab (not otherwise visible) will appear, with controls for formatting the selected picture. ■

TIP

Customize the Quick Access Toolbar You can add icons to the Quick Access toolbar by clicking the down arrow to the right of the toolbar and checking the items you want to add. ■

CREATING A NEW DOCUMENT

Any new Word document you create is based on what Word calls a *template*. A template combines selected styles and document settings—and, in some cases, prewritten text or calculated fields—to create the building blocks for a specific type of document. You use templates to give yourself a head start on specific types of documents.

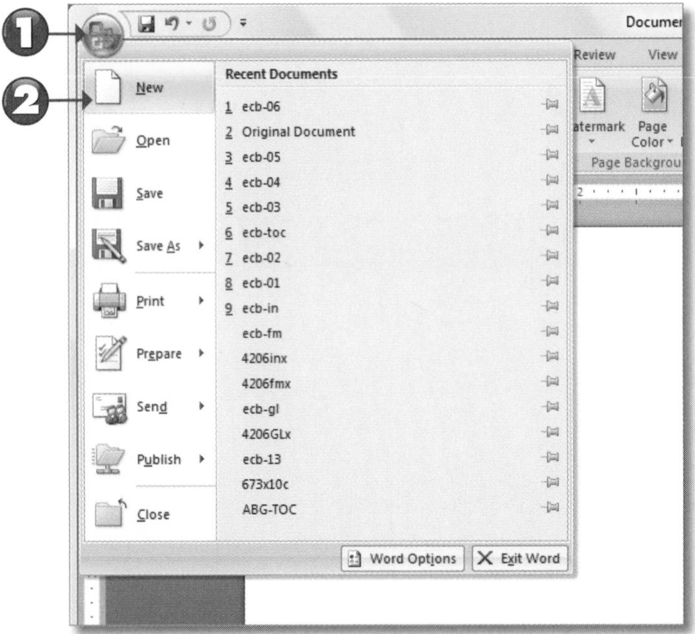

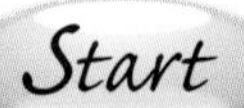

1. Click the **Office** button.
2. Select **New** from the pull-down menu.

Continued

NOTE

Working with Documents Anything you create with Word—a letter, memo, newsletter, and so on—is called a document. A document is nothing more than a computer file that can be copied, moved, deleted, or edited from within Word. ■

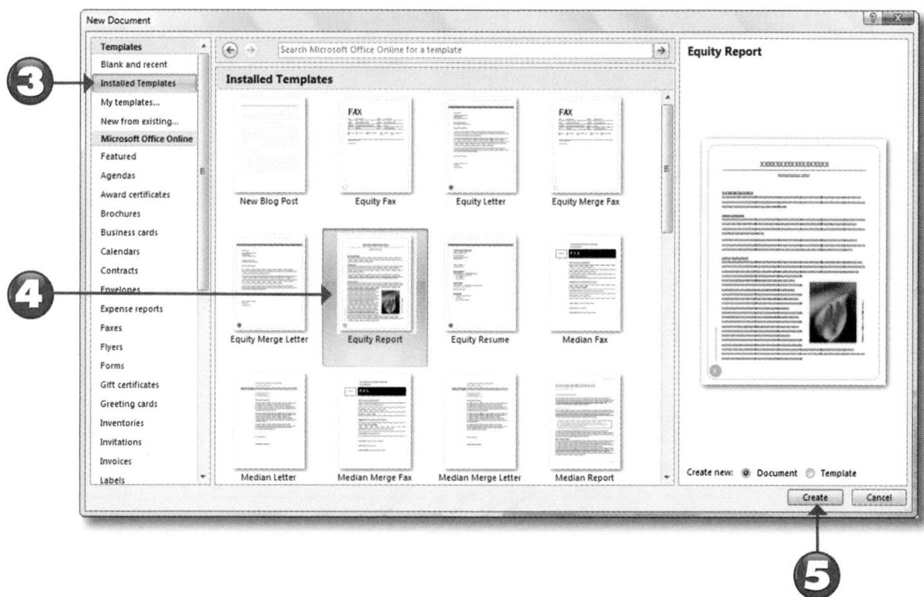

3. Click the type of template you want to create from the list on the left.

4. Click the icon for the template you want.

5. Click the **Create** button to create a new document based on this template.

End

NOTE

Downloading Templates If you choose to download a template from Microsoft Office Online, you'll need to be connected to the Internet. These templates are free to download for your personal use. ■

SAVING A DOCUMENT

Every document you create that you want to keep must be saved to a new file. The first time you save a file, you have to specify a filename and location.

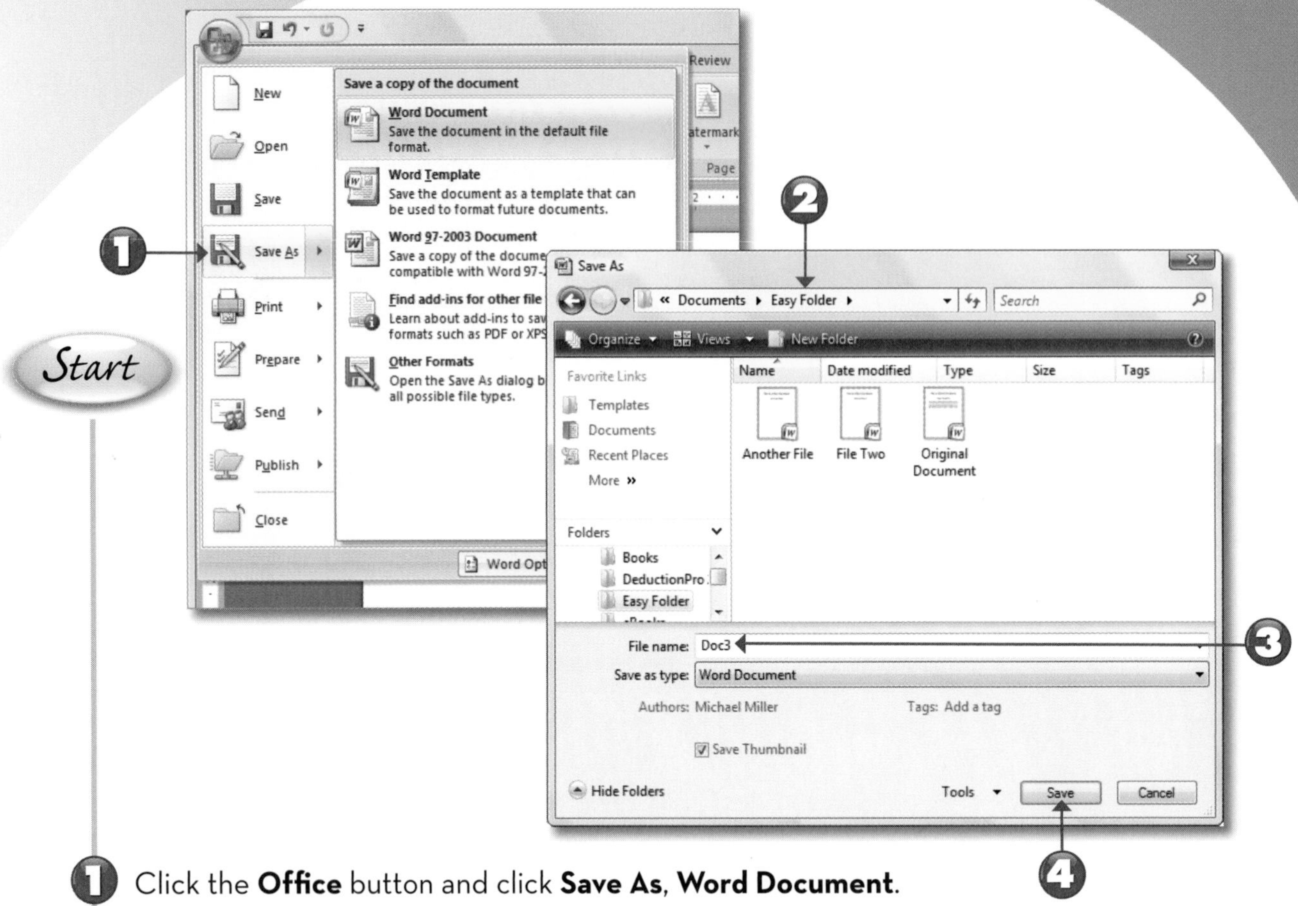

Start

1. Click the **Office** button and click **Save As**, **Word Document**.
2. Navigate to the folder where you want to save the file.
3. Enter a name for the new file.
4. Click the **Save** button.

End

TIP

Saving Again After you've saved a file once, you don't need to go through the whole Save As routine again. To "fast save" an existing file, click the Save button on Word's Quick Access toolbar—or pull down the Office menu and select Save. ■

TIP

Compatibility Saving your new document as a Word document saves the file in the new .docx file format used exclusively by Word 2007. If you want your document to be compatible with older versions of Word, save it as a Word 97-2003 document (.doc file format), instead. ■

OPENING AN EXISTING DOCUMENT

After you've created a document, you can reopen it at any time for additional editing.

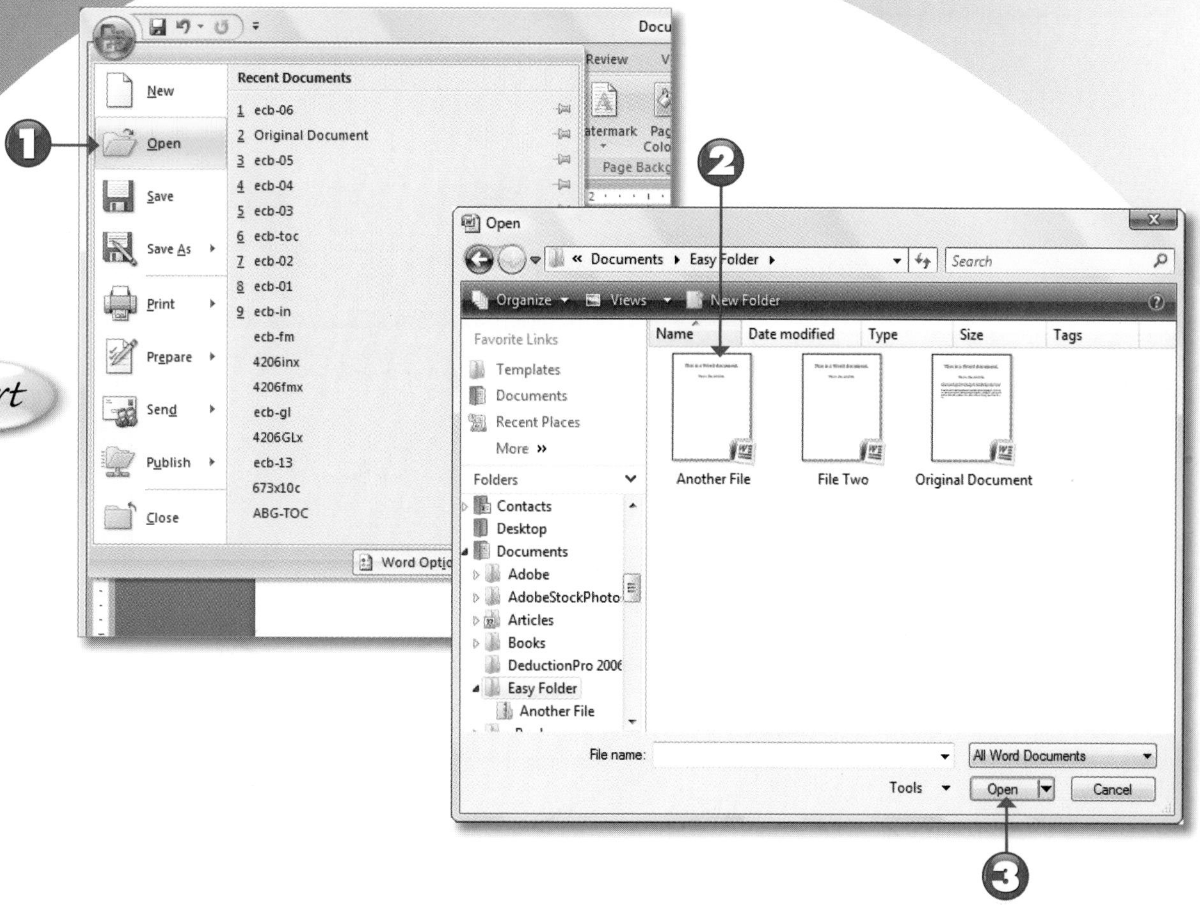

Start

1. Click the **Office** button and then click **Open**.
2. Navigate to and select the file you want to open.
3. Click **Open**.

End

TIP

Easy Opening You can also open a document by double-clicking the file icon from within the Open dialog box.

ENTERING TEXT

You enter text in a Word document at the *insertion point*, which appears onscreen as a blinking cursor. When you start typing on your keyboard, the new text is added at the insertion point.

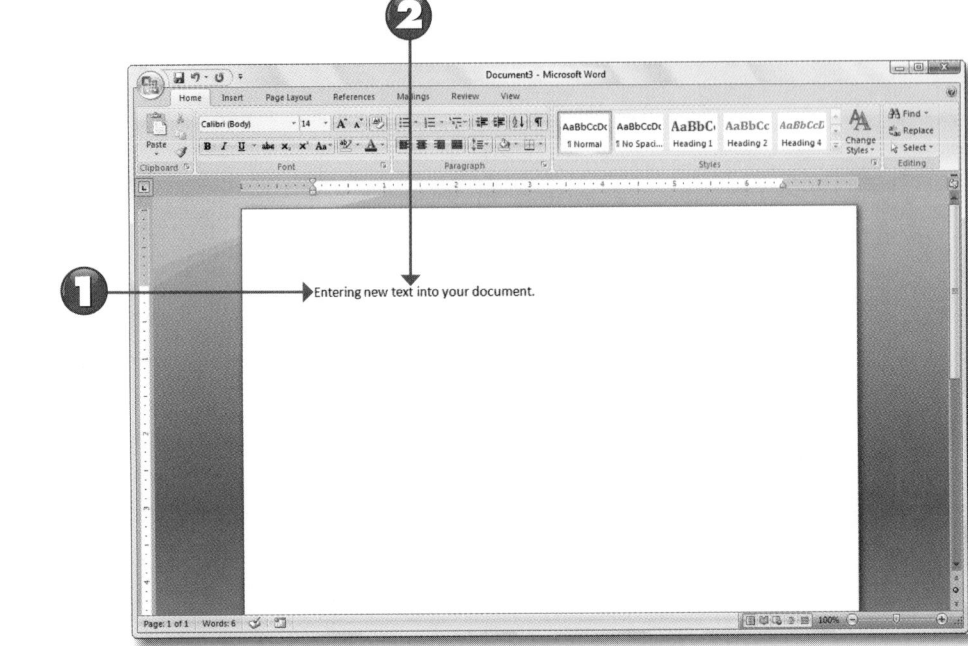

1. Within your document, click where you want to enter the new text.

2. Type the text.

End

TIP

Move the Insertion Point You move the insertion point with your mouse by clicking a new position in your text. You move the insertion point with your keyboard by using your keyboard's arrow keys. ■

CUTTING/COPYING AND PASTING TEXT

Word lets you cut, copy, and paste text—or graphics—to and from anywhere in your document or between documents. Use your mouse to select the text you want to edit, and then select the appropriate command from the Home ribbon.

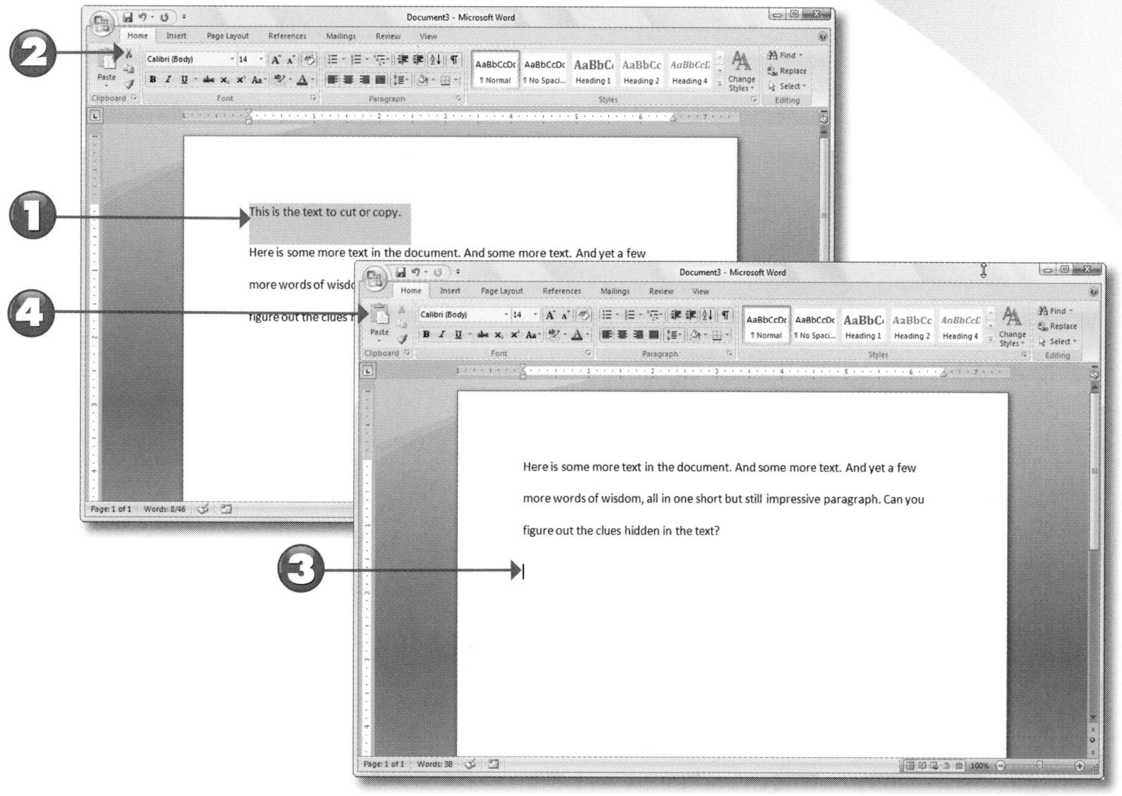

Start

1. Click and drag the cursor to select the text you want to copy or cut.
2. From the Home ribbon, click **Copy** to copy the text or **Cut** to cut the text.
3. Within the document, click where you want to paste the cut or copied text.
4. From the Home ribbon, click **Paste**.

End

TIP

Keyboard Shortcuts You also can select text using your keyboard; use the Shift key—in combination with other keys—to highlight blocks of text. For example, Shift + left arrow selects one character to the left. ■

NOTE

Cut Versus Copy Cutting text removes the text from the original location and then pastes it into a new location. Copying text leaves the text in the original location and pastes a copy of it into a new location—essentially duplicating the text. ■

FORMATTING TEXT

After your text is entered and edited, you can use Word's numerous formatting options to add some pizzazz to your document.

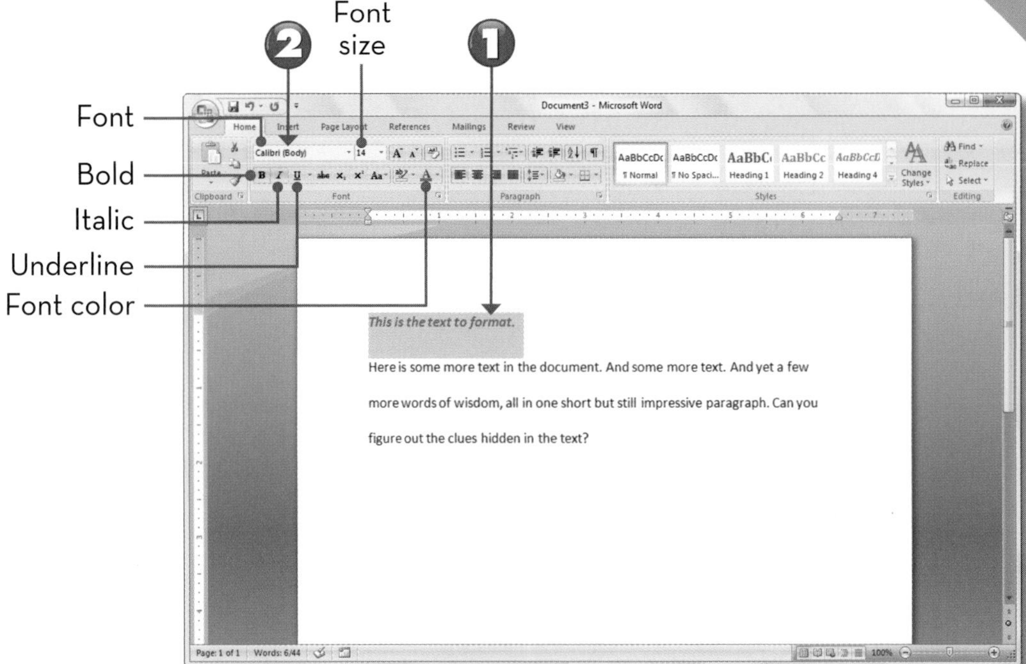

1. Click and drag the cursor over the text you want to edit.

2. Click the desired button in the Font section of the Home ribbon—**Font**, **Font Size**, **Bold**, **Italic**, **Underline**, or **Font Color**.

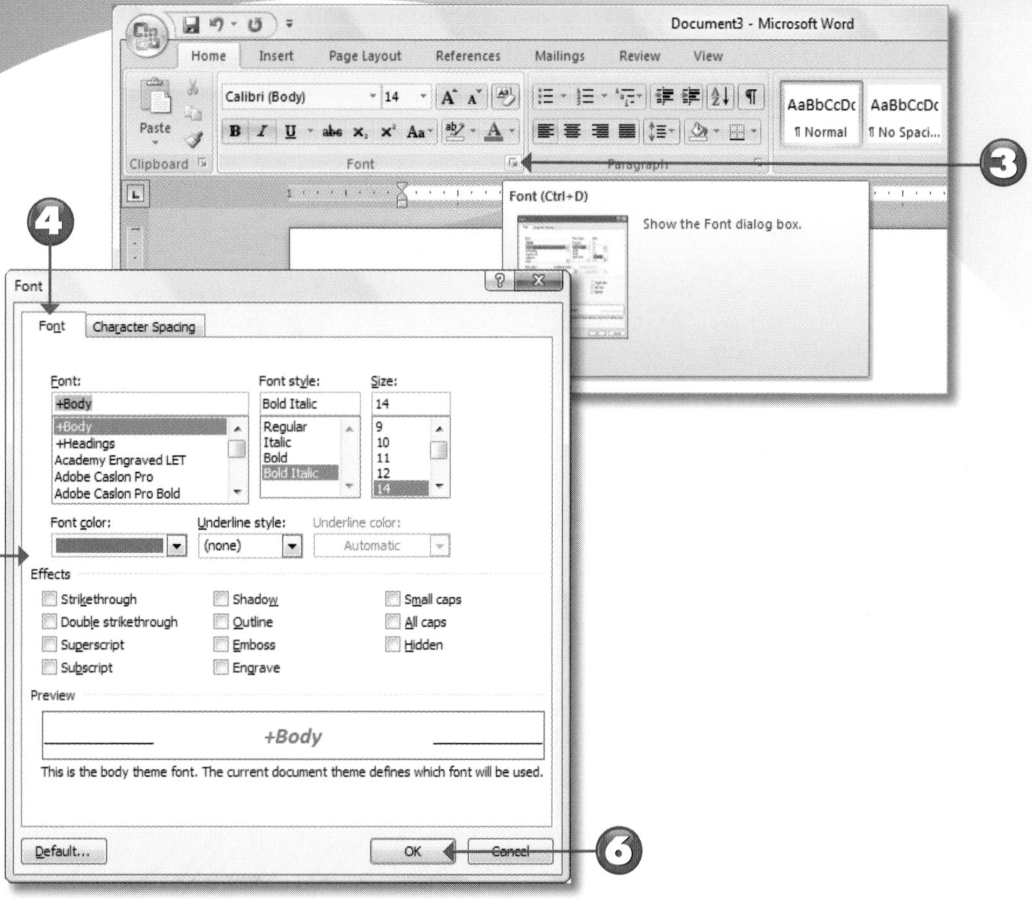

Start

3 For additional formatting options, click the right arrow on the bottom right of the Font section of the Home ribbon; this displays the Font dialog box.

4 Click the **Font** tab.

5 Select the type of formatting you want.

6 Click **OK** when done.

End

TIP

See Your Formatting It's easiest to format text when you're working in Print Layout view because this displays your document as it will look when printed. To switch to this view, select the View ribbon and then click Print Layout.

FORMATTING PARAGRAPHS

When you're creating a complex document, you need to format more than just a few words here and there. To format complete paragraphs, use Word's Paragraph formatting options on the Home ribbon.

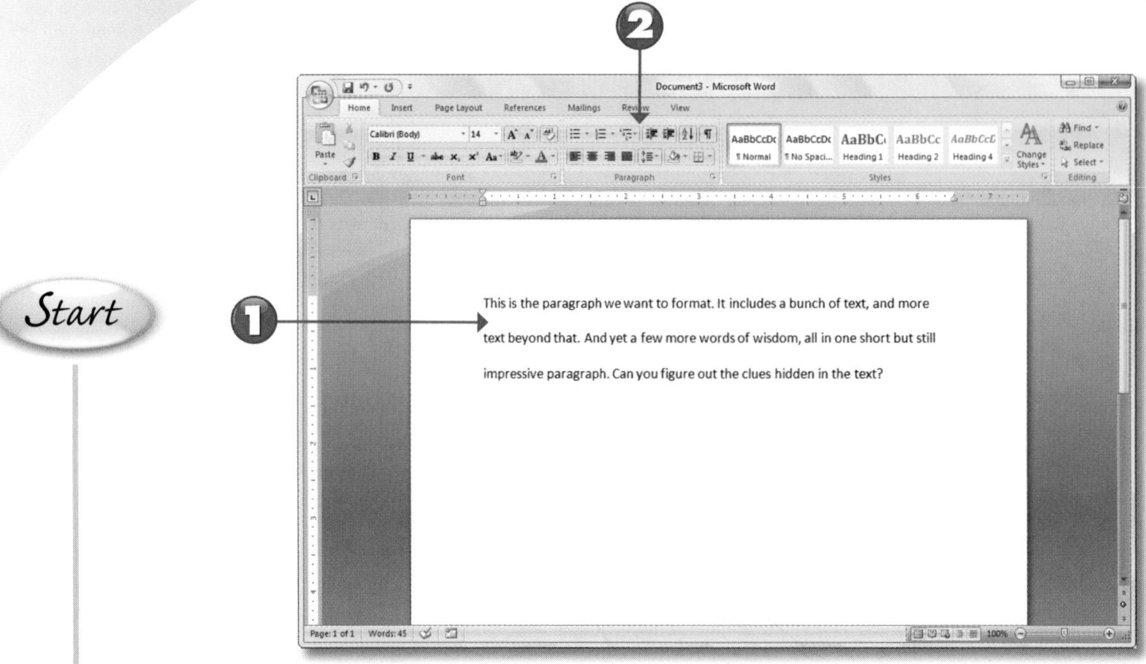

1. Click anywhere within the paragraph you want to format.
2. Click the desired button in the Paragraph section of the Home ribbon—including **Bullets**, **Numbering**, **Decrease Indent**, **Increase Indent, Line Spacing**, or any of the four **Align Text** options.

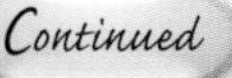

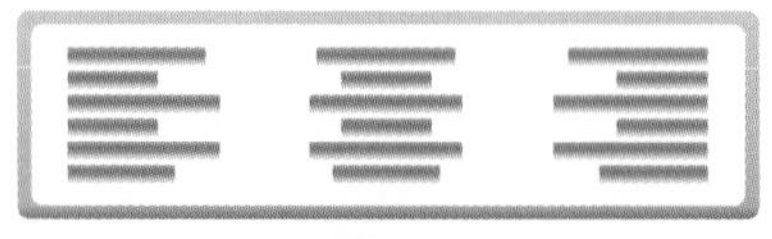

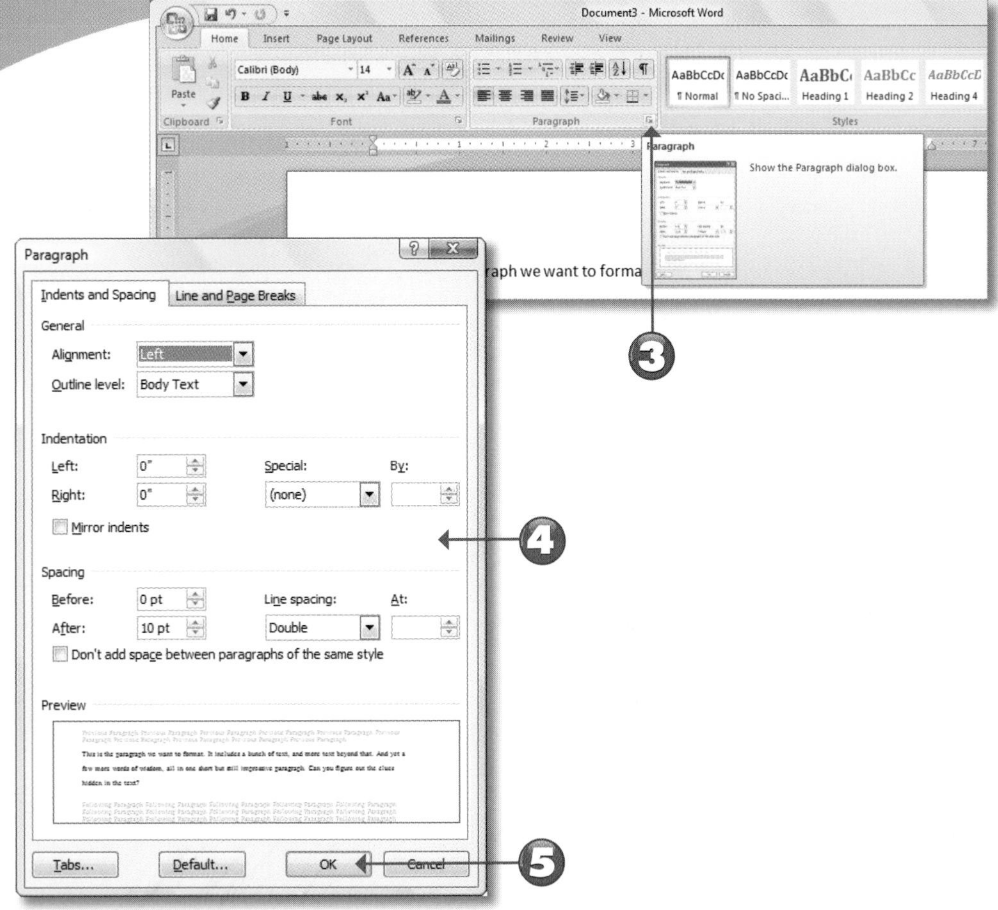

3. For additional paragraph formatting options, click the right arrow at the bottom right of the Paragraph section of the Home ribbon; this displays the Paragraph dialog box.

4. Select the necessary options to adjust how the entire paragraph appears, including indentation, line spacing, and alignment.

5. Click **OK** when done.

End

TIP

Line and Page Breaks Click the Line and Page Breaks tab in the Paragraph dialog box to add a page break before the current paragraph, keep lines together, and configure widow/orphan control.

APPLYING STYLES

If you have a preferred paragraph formatting you use repeatedly, you don't have to format each paragraph individually. Instead, you can assign all your formatting to a paragraph *style* and then assign that style to specific paragraphs throughout your document.

Start

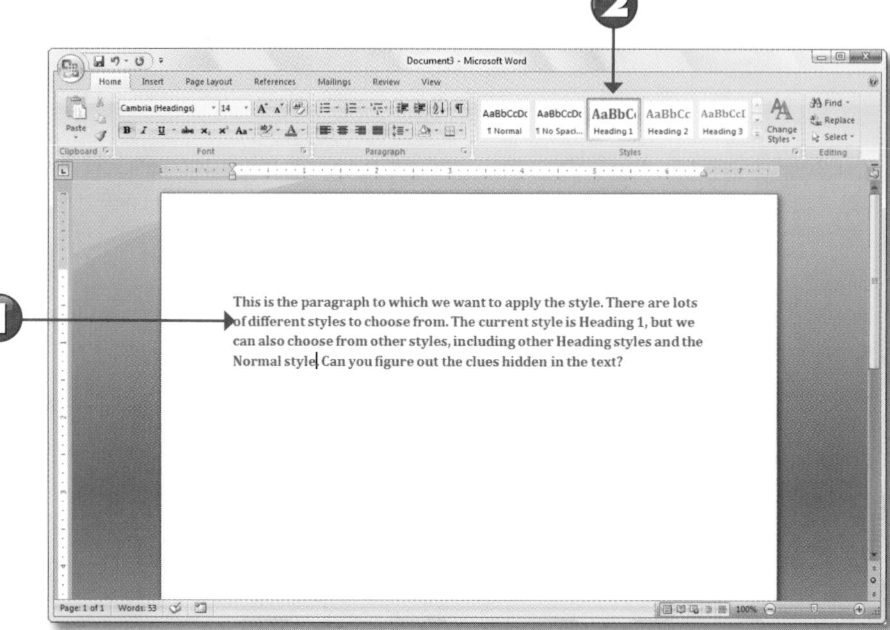

1. Click anywhere within the paragraph to which you want to apply the style.

2. Select a paragraph style from the Styles section of the Home ribbon.

NOTE

Style Elements Styles include formatting for fonts, paragraphs, tabs, borders, numbering, and more. ■

3. To change the entire look of your document, switch style sets by clicking the **Change Styles** button on the Home ribbon.

4. Click **Style Set**.

5. Select a new style set from the list.

End

NOTE

Changing Style Sets Word 2007 includes several style sets, each of which has its own distinct look. ■

91

CHECKING YOUR SPELLING

If you're not a great speller, you'll appreciate Word's automatic spell checking. You can see it right onscreen; just deliberately misspell a word, and you'll see a squiggly red line under the misspelling. That's Word telling you you've made a spelling error!

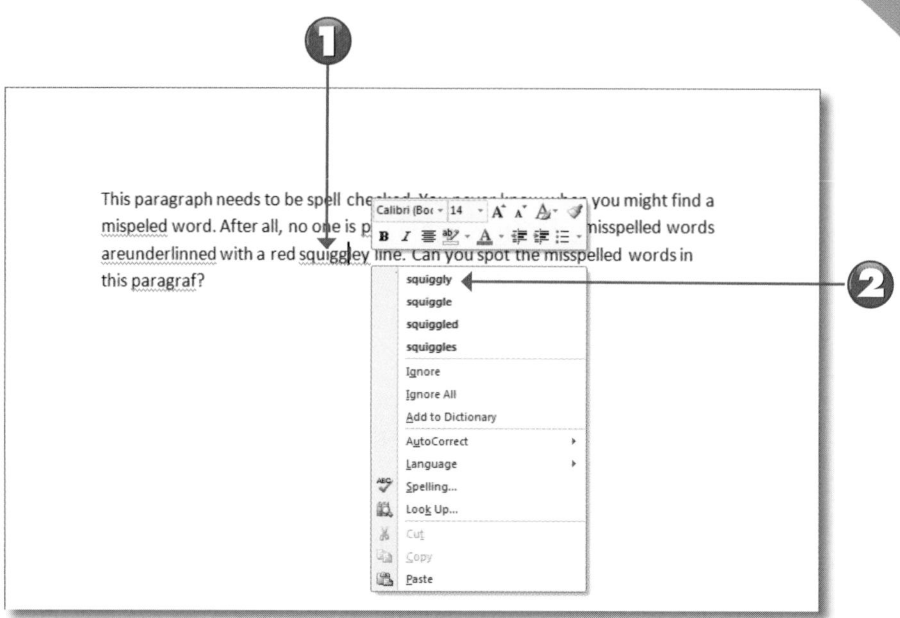

Start

1. Position your cursor over a misspelled word and right-click with your mouse.
2. Choose a replacement word from the list.

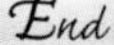

TIP

Add New Words If Word doesn't recognize a legitimate word and marks it as misspelled, you can add it to the spelling dictionary by selecting Add to Dictionary from the pop-up menu. ■

PRINTING A DOCUMENT

When you've finished editing your document, you can instruct Word to send a copy to your printer. When you want to print multiple copies, print only selected pages, or print to a different (nondefault) printer, use Word's Print dialog box.

Start

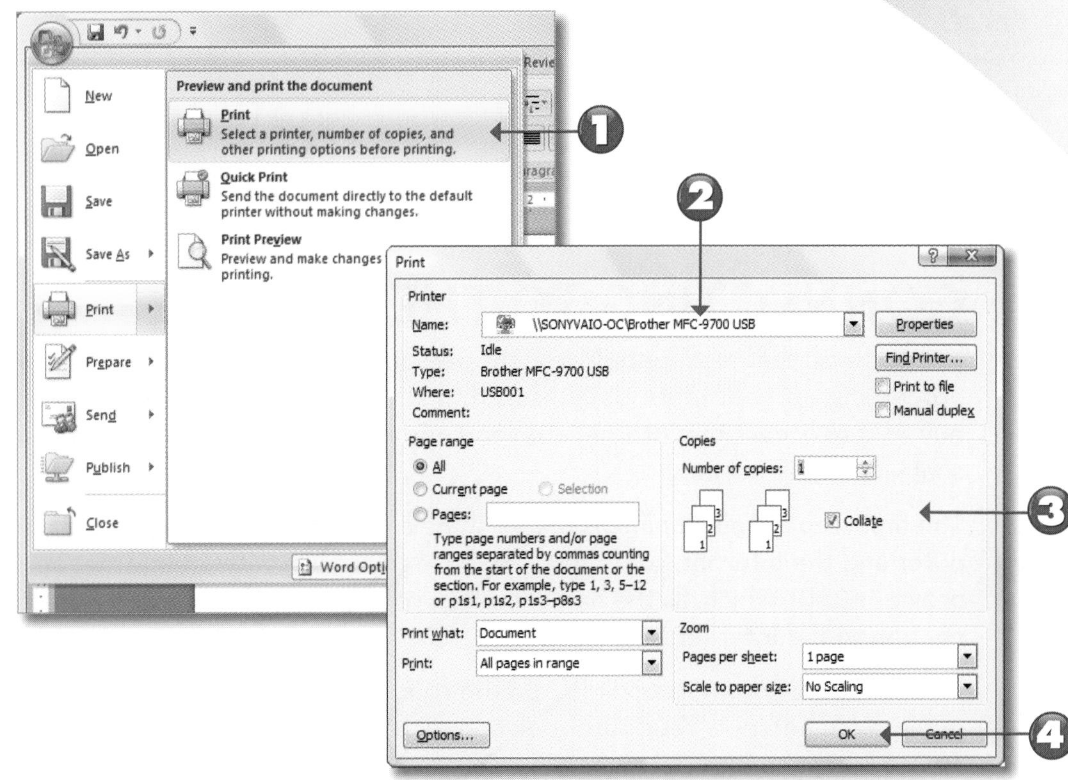

1. Click the **Office** button and then click **Print**, **Print**.
2. Pull down the Name list and select your printer.
3. Select which part(s) of your document to print and how many copies you want.
4. Click the **OK** button to print the document.

TIP

Quick Print The fastest way to print a document is with Word's quick print option. You activate a quick print by opening the Office menu and selecting Print, Quick Print. This bypasses the Print dialog box and all other configuration options. ■

CONNECTING TO THE INTERNET

It used to be that most people bought personal computers to do work—word processing, spreadsheets, databases, that sort of thing. But today, many people buy PCs to access the Internet—to send and receive email, surf the Web, and chat with other users.

The first step in going online is establishing a connection between your computer and the Internet. To do this, you have to sign up with an Internet service provider (ISP), which, as the name implies, provides your computer with a connection to the Internet.

If you're using your notebook PC on the road, all you have to do is look for a public WiFi hotspot. Your notebook connects to the hotspot, which then connects you to the Internet, simple as pie.

HOW THE INTERNET WORKS

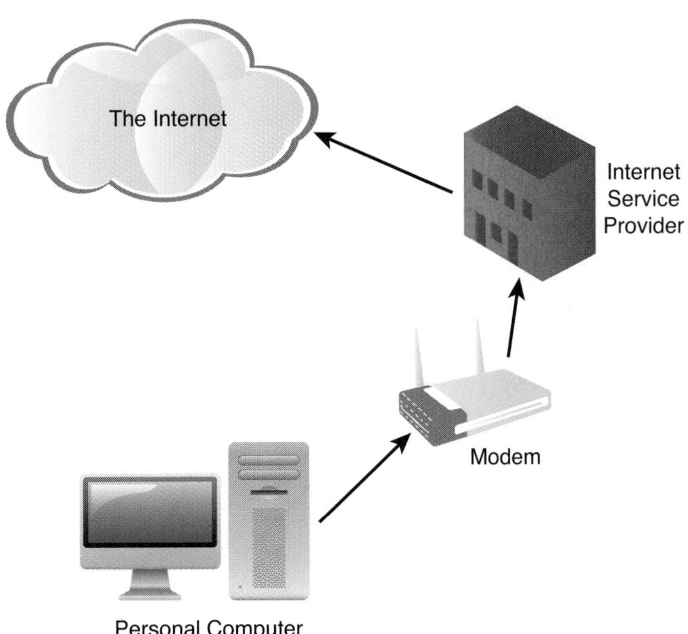

CONNECTING A BROADBAND MODEM

If you have a broadband connection to your Internet service provider (ISP), you connect your PC to the broadband modem. The connection is similar whether you're connecting via cable Internet or DSL; most broadband modems connect via either USB or Ethernet.

Start

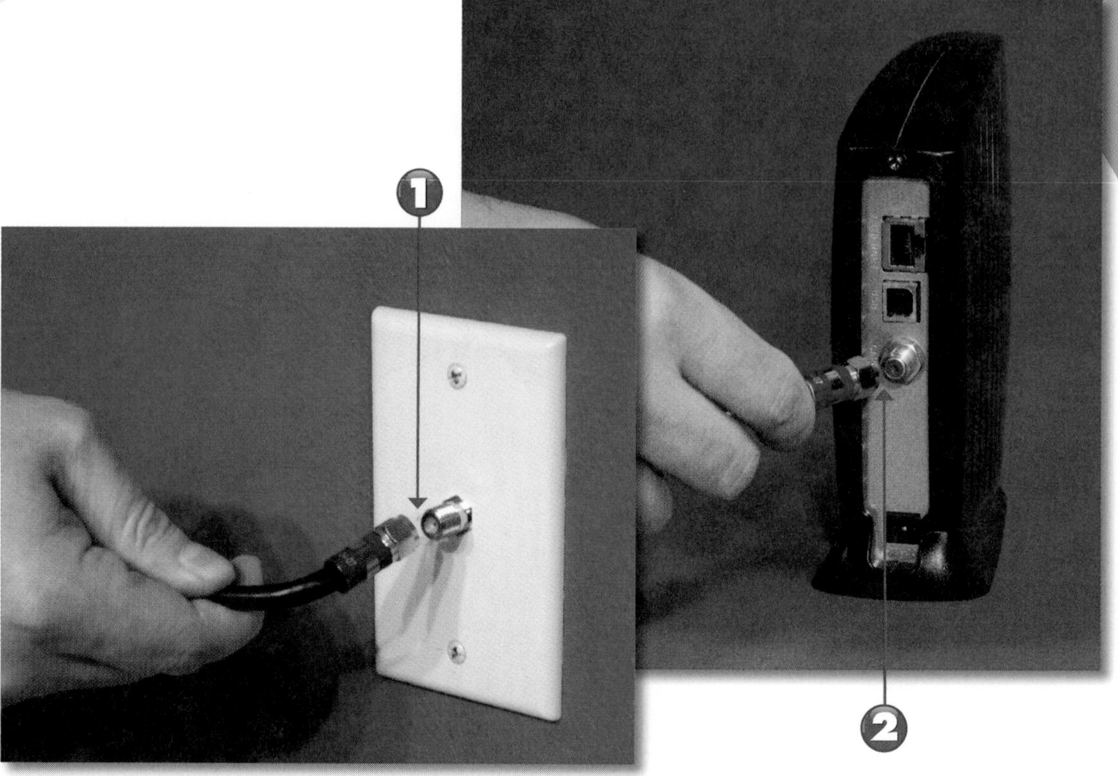

1. Connect one end of the supplied cable to the cable or telephone outlet on a nearby wall.
2. Connect the other end of the supplied cable to the input jack on the back of your broadband modem.

Continued

NOTE

Dial-Up Internet Some ISPs still offer a dial-up Internet connection. This type of connection uses your standard phone line but is extremely slow—just 56.6 kilobits per second (kbps) as opposed to the 3,000kbps or higher connection speeds possible with broadband connections. ■

NOTE

Cable or DSL? Your cable company and phone company both offer broadband Internet access. Both cable Internet and your phone company's digital subscriber line (DSL) offerings provide the same always-on, super-fast Internet connection. ■

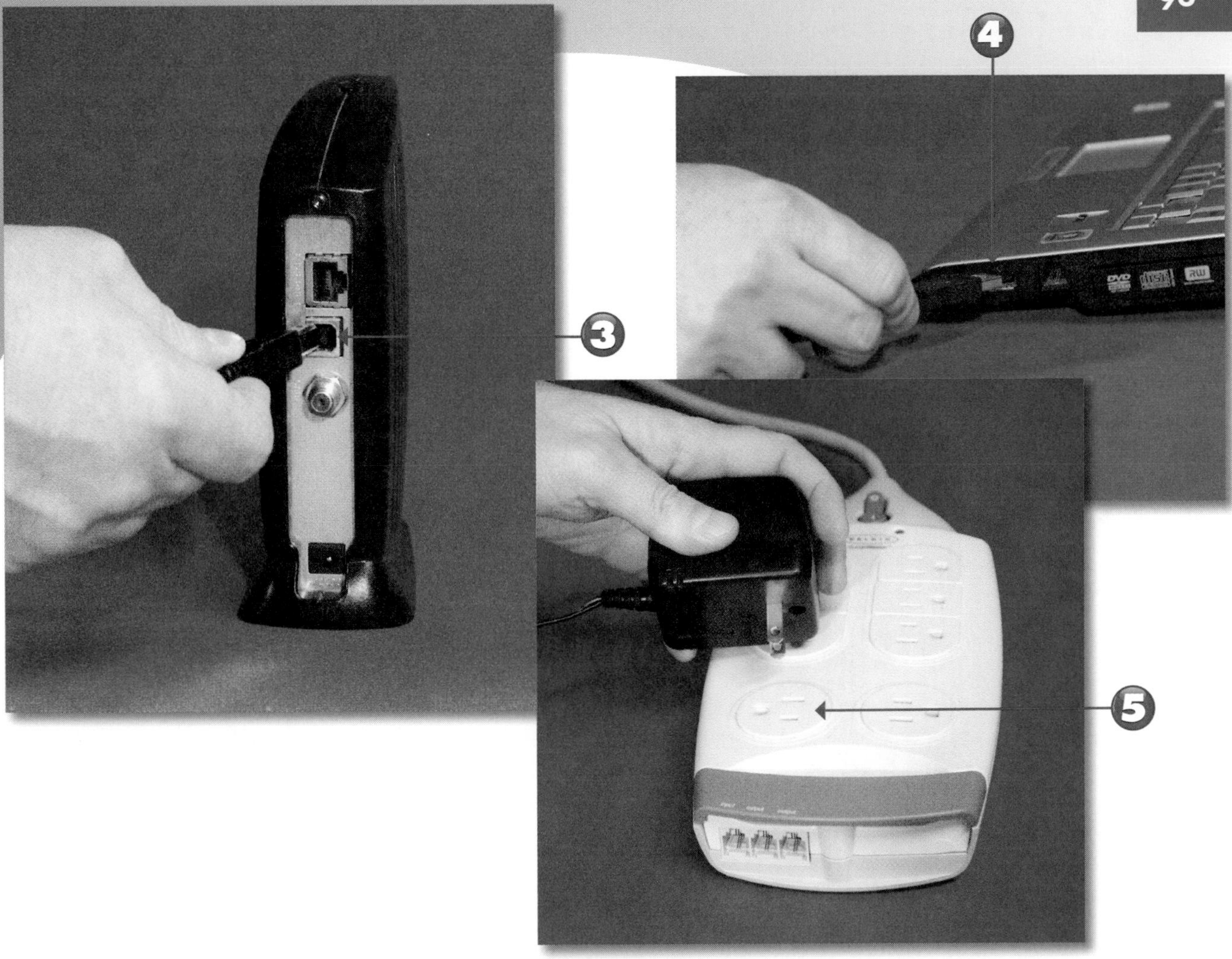

3 Connect one end of a USB cable to the USB "out" port on the back of the broadband modem.

4 Connect the other end of the USB cable to an open USB port on your notebook PC.

5 Connect the power cable on your broadband modem to a power source. The modem should now turn on.

End

NOTE

Connecting via Wireless If you prefer not to anchor yourself to a wired Internet connection, you can connect your broadband modem to a wireless network router and then connect your notebook PC wirelessly. Learn more in Chapter 9, "Setting Up a Wireless Home Network." ■

SETTING UP A NEW HOME INTERNET CONNECTION

After you sign up for your home Internet service, you need to configure your computer to work with your ISP. Windows 7 makes this simple; just connect your broadband modem (cable or DSL) to your computer and then perform a few simple steps.

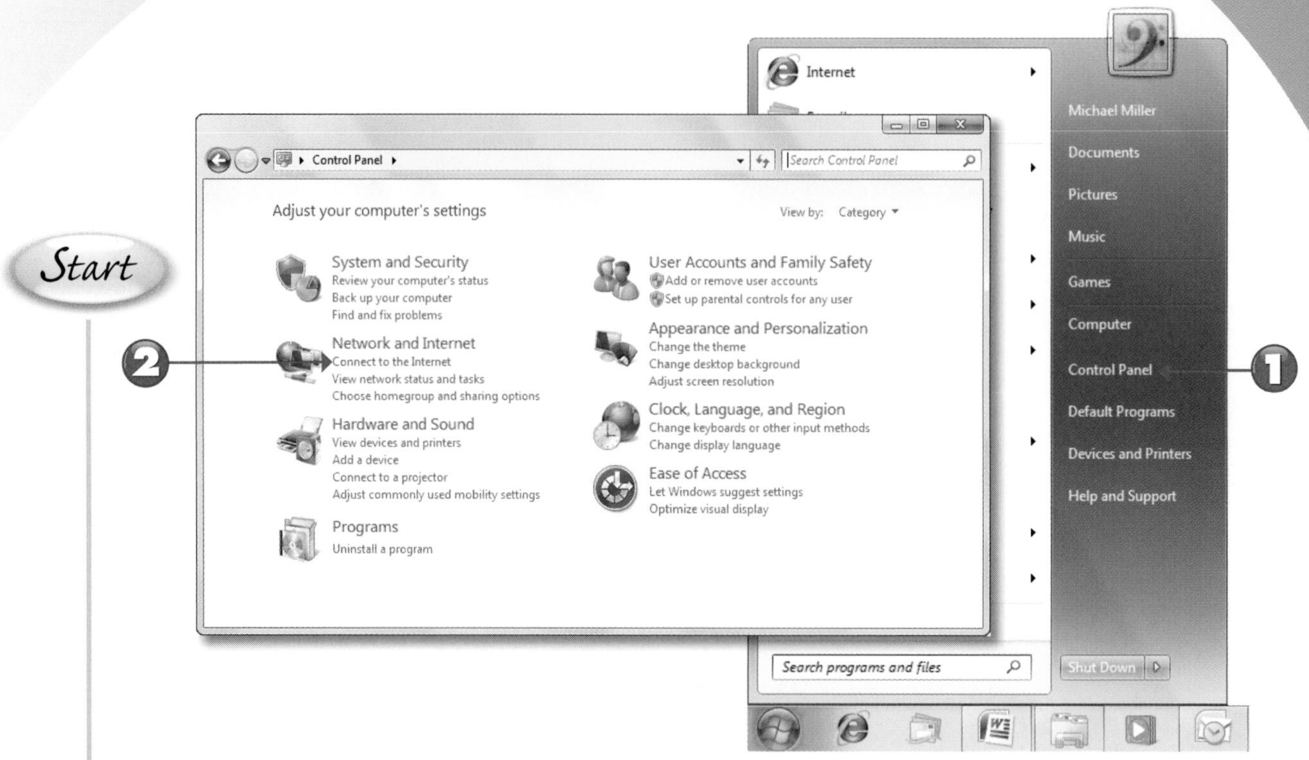

Start

1. Click the **Start** button and then click **Control Panel**.

2. Click **Connect to the Internet** (in the Network and Internet section).

Continued

NOTE

Plug and Surf In many instances, you don't even have to perform these steps. Try launching your Web browser after you connect your broadband modem. If you can connect to a website, your computer was configured automatically and no manual setup is required. ■

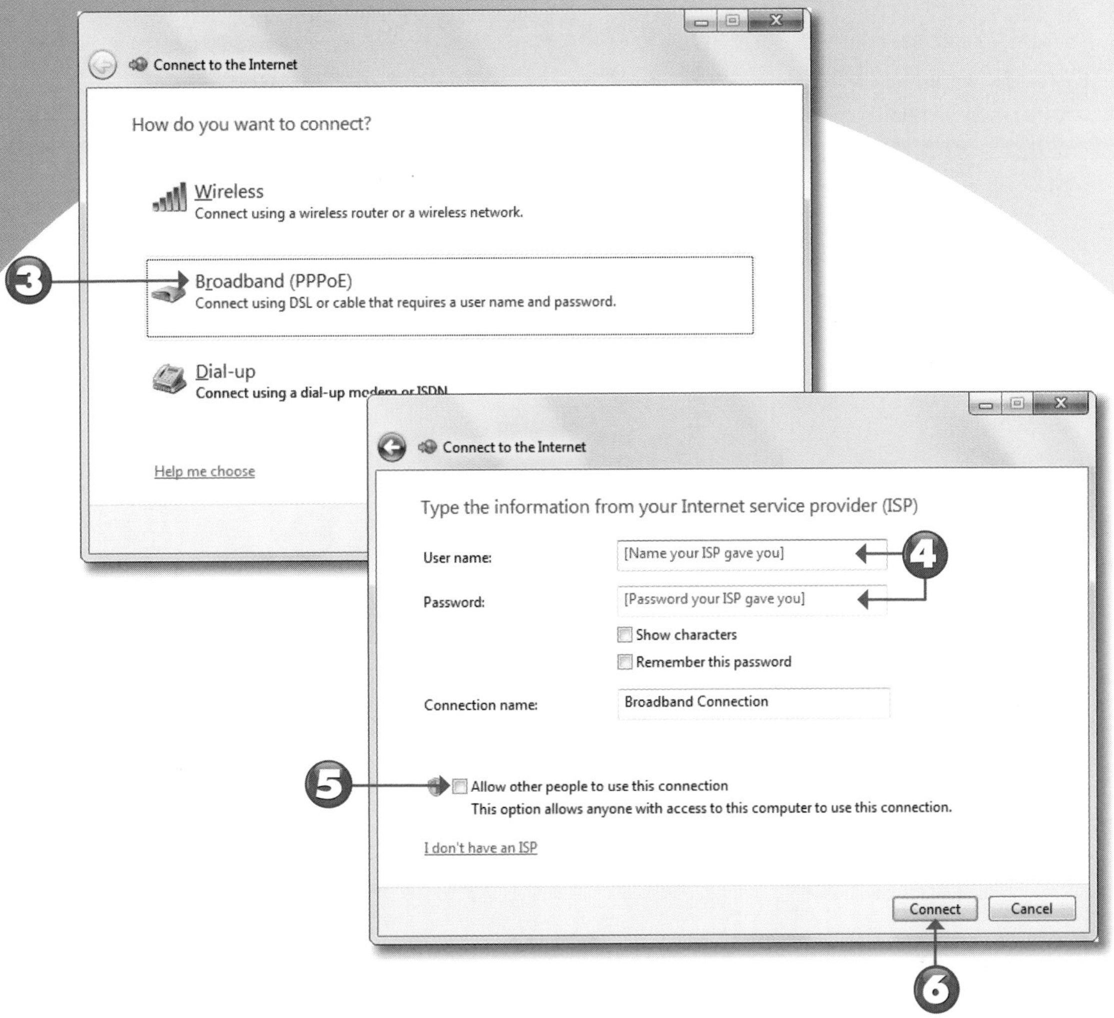

Connect to the Internet

How do you want to connect?

Wireless
Connect using a wireless router or a wireless network.

3 Broadband (PPPoE)
Connect using DSL or cable that requires a user name and password.

Dial-up
Connect using a dial-up modem or ISDN.

Help me choose

Connect to the Internet

Type the information from your Internet service provider (ISP)

User name: [Name your ISP gave you] 4

Password: [Password your ISP gave you]

Show characters

Remember this password

Connection name: Broadband Connection

5 Allow other people to use this connection
This option allows anyone with access to this computer to use this connection.

I don't have an ISP

Connect Cancel

6

3. Click **Broadband**.
4. If your ISP provided a username and password, enter that information now. (Most broadband connections do not require this information.)
5. If you want other users of your computer to use this Internet connection, check **Allow Other People to Use This Connection**.
6. Click **Connect**.

NOTE

Dial-Up Connections These instructions cover connecting to a broadband (cable or DSL) Internet connection. If you're connecting via a slower dial-up connection, consult your ISP for setup instructions. ■

CONNECTING TO AN INTERNET WIFI HOTSPOT

If you have a notebook PC, you have the option to connect to the Internet when you're out and about. Many coffeehouses, restaurants, libraries, and hotels offer wireless WiFi Internet service, either free or for an hourly or daily fee. Assuming that your notebook has a built-in WiFi adapter (and it probably does), connecting to a public WiFi hotspot is a snap.

1. Click the **Network** icon in the notification area of the Windows taskbar.
2. The pop-up window should now list all available WiFi networks. Click the network you wish to connect to.
3. Click **Connect**.

Continued

NOTE

Finding the WiFi Signal When you're near a WiFi hotspot, your PC should automatically pick up the WiFi signal. Just make sure that your WiFi adapter is turned on (some notebooks have a switch for this, either on the front or on the side of the unit), and then look for a wireless connection icon in Windows' system tray or notification area. ■

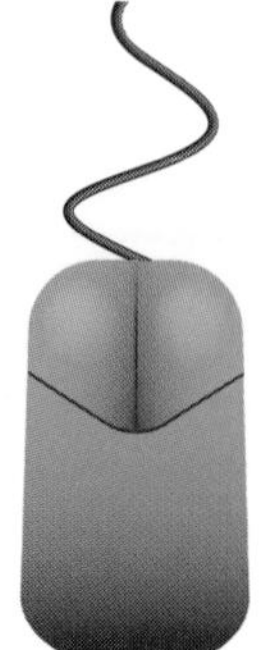

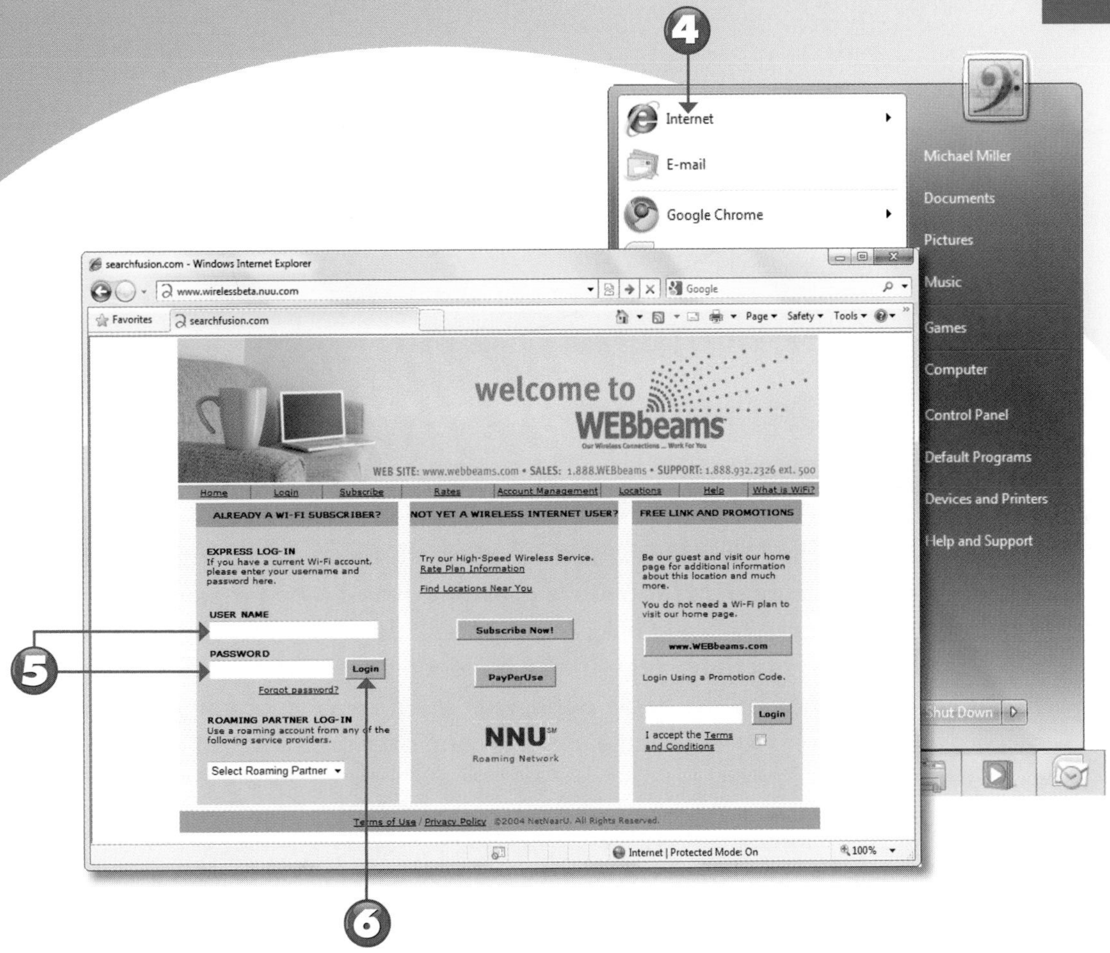

4. Click the Start menu and click **Internet** to launch the Internet Explorer Web browser.

5. Some hotspots will ask for your username and password or require a credit card for payment. Enter the necessary information.

6. Click the **Login** or **Enter** button to access the hotspot.

End

NOTE

Logging In to the Hotspot After Windows connects to the selected hotspot, you can log on to the wireless network, which you do by opening Internet Explorer. If the hotspot has free public access, you'll be able to surf normally. If the hotspot requires a password, payment, or other logon procedure, it will intercept the request for your normal home page and instead display its own login page. ■

BROWSING THE WEB

The World Wide Web is probably the most interesting and popular part of the Internet. Information on the Web is presented in *web pages*, each of which contains text, graphics, and links to other web pages. A web page resides at a *website*, which is nothing more than a collection of web pages. The main page of a website is called the *home page*, which serves as an opening screen that provides a brief overview and a sort of menu of everything you can find at that site.

You view web pages with a software program called a *web browser*. Internet Explorer is the web browser included with Microsoft Windows 7, and it's extremely easy to use—just a matter of entering an address or clicking a link.

INTERNET EXPLORER

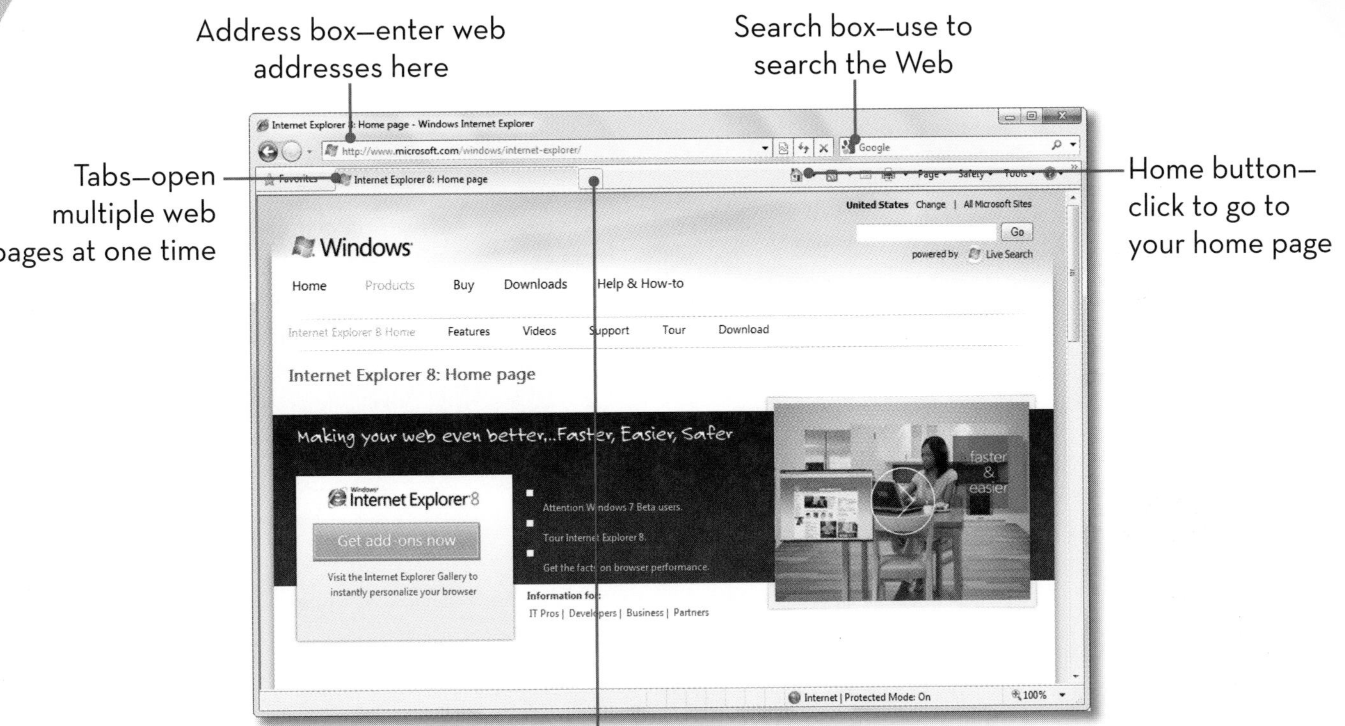

SURFING THE WEB WITH INTERNET EXPLORER

Internet Explorer (IE) is a web browser that lets you quickly and easily browse the World Wide Web. When you enter a new web address in the Address box and press Enter (or click the Go button), IE loads the new page. You can also click any link on a web page to go to the new page. Let's demonstrate with a quick tour of the Web.

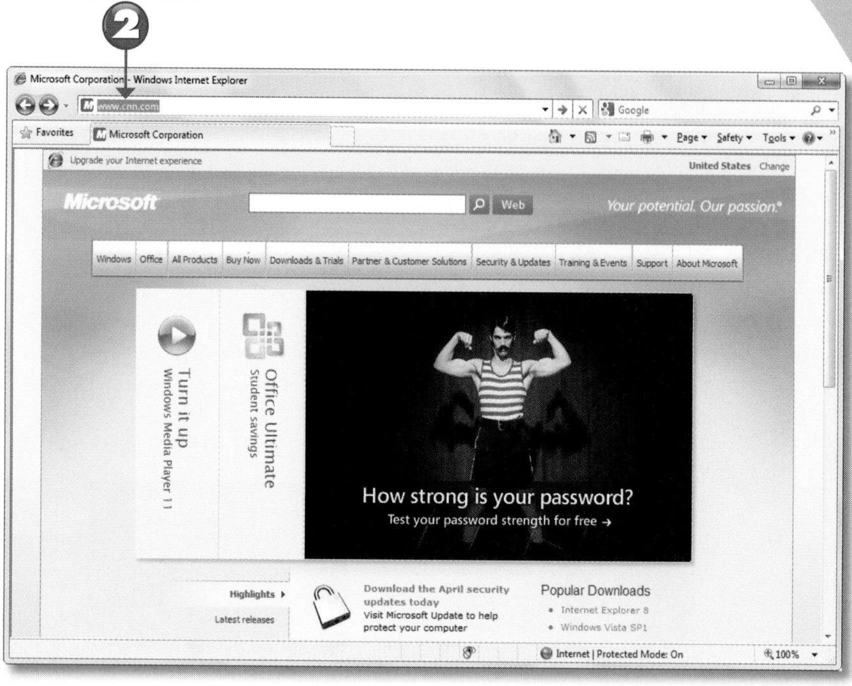

Start

1. Launch Internet Explorer by clicking the **Internet Explorer** button on the Windows taskbar.
2. Let's find out what's happening out in the real world by heading over to one of the most popular news sites. Enter **www.cnn.com** in the Address box, and then press **Enter**.

Continued

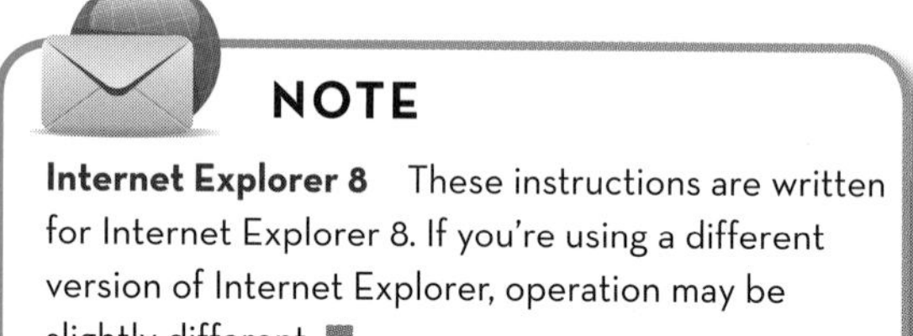

NOTE

Internet Explorer 8 These instructions are written for Internet Explorer 8. If you're using a different version of Internet Explorer, operation may be slightly different.

3. Click any headline or link to read the complete story.

4. Click the down scroll button to read more of the story.

Continued

TIP

Change IE's Home Page When you launch Internet Explorer, it loads your predefined home page. To change Internet Explorer's home page, go to the new page, click the down arrow next to the Home button on the toolbar, select Add or Change Home Page, select Use This Webpage as Your Only Home Page, and click Yes. ■

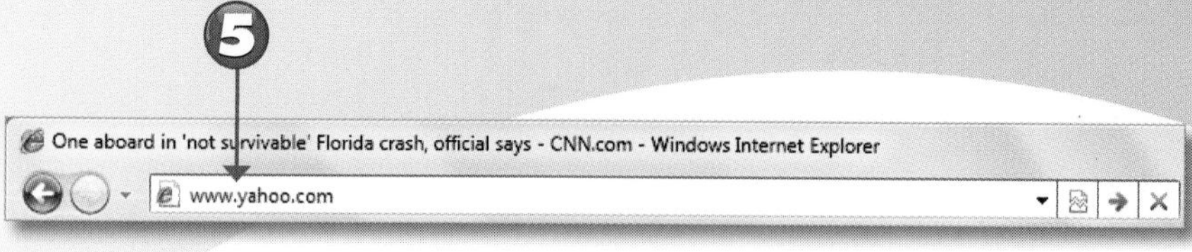

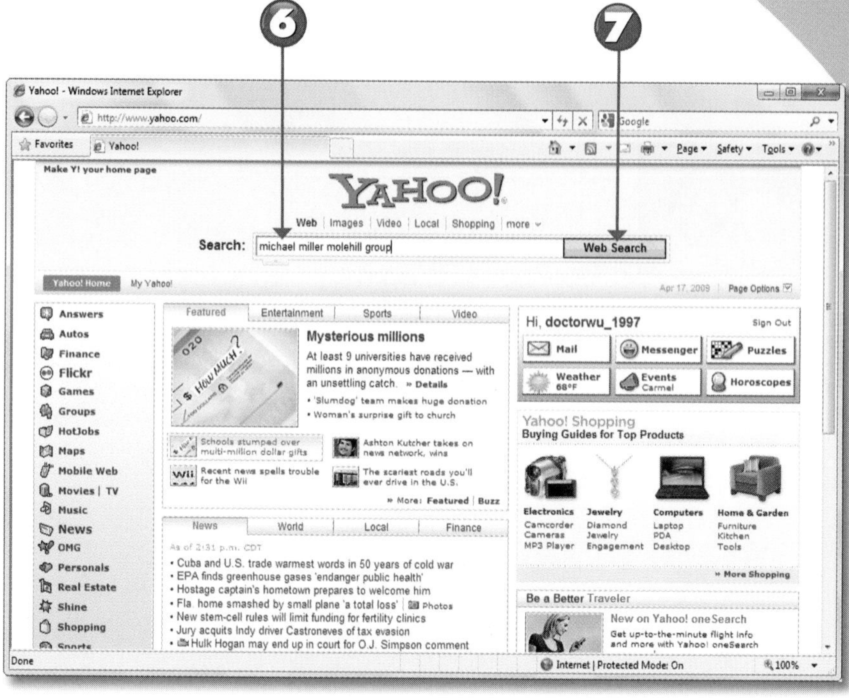

1. Now, let's do a little searching at Yahoo!. Enter **www.yahoo.com** in the Address box and press **Enter**.

2. Ready to search? Enter **michael miller molehill group** in the Search box at the top of the page.

3. Click the **Web Search** button to begin the search.

Continued

TIP

Searching the Web To find a particular page on the Web, you use a search site. These sites, such as Google and Yahoo!, let you enter a query and search for web pages that contain those keywords. ■

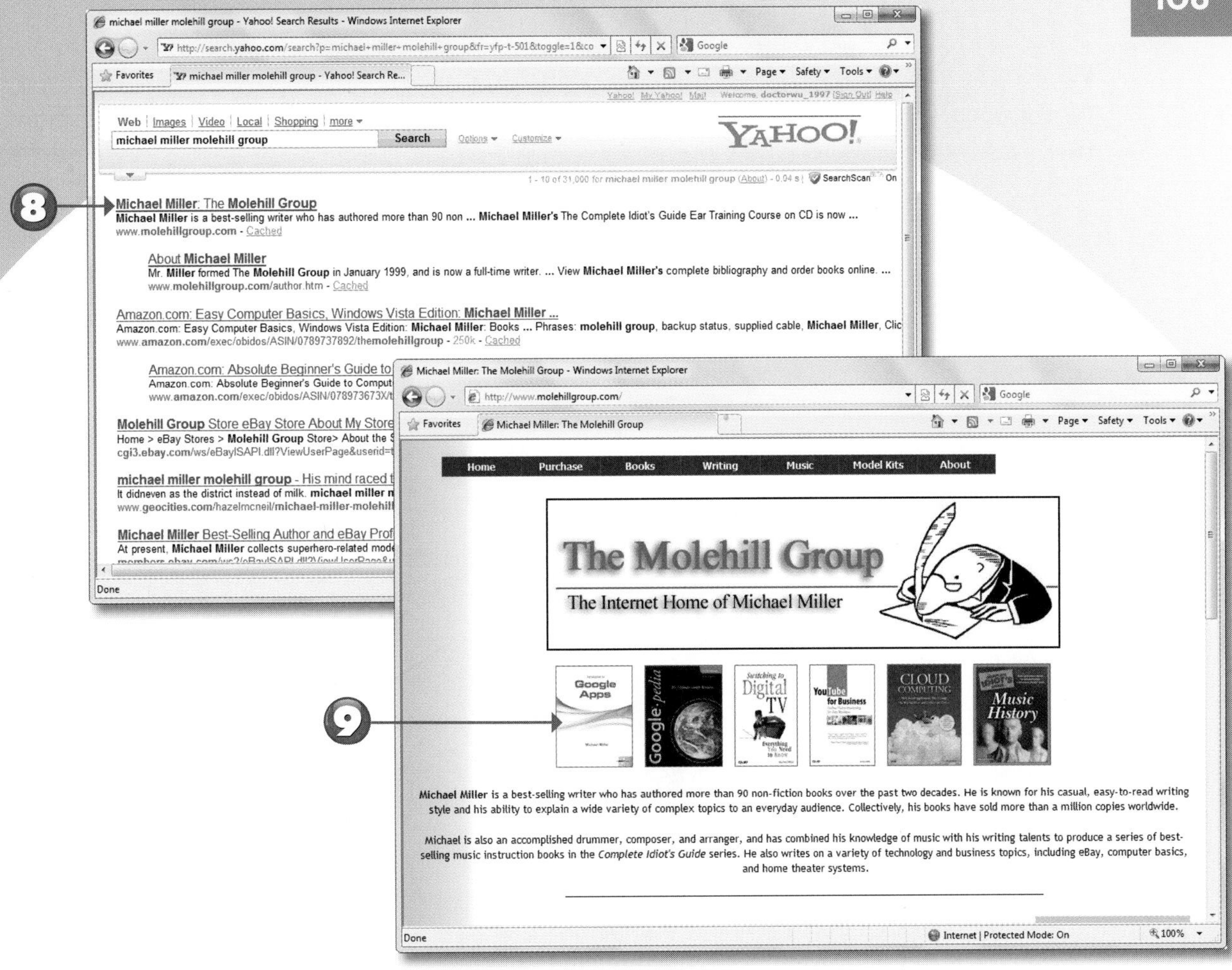

8. When the search results page appears, find the listing for The Molehill Group (it should be near the top) and click the link.

9. You're now taken to *my* website, The Molehill Group. Click one of the book pictures at the top of the page to read more about that book.

End

TIP

Going Back To return to the last-viewed web page, click the Back button next to the Address box, or press the Backspace key on your keyboard. If you've backed up several pages and want to return to the page you were on last, click the Forward button.

SAVING YOUR FAVORITE PAGES

When you find a web page you like, you can add it to a list of Favorites within Internet Explorer. This way, you can easily access any of your favorite sites just by selecting them from the list.

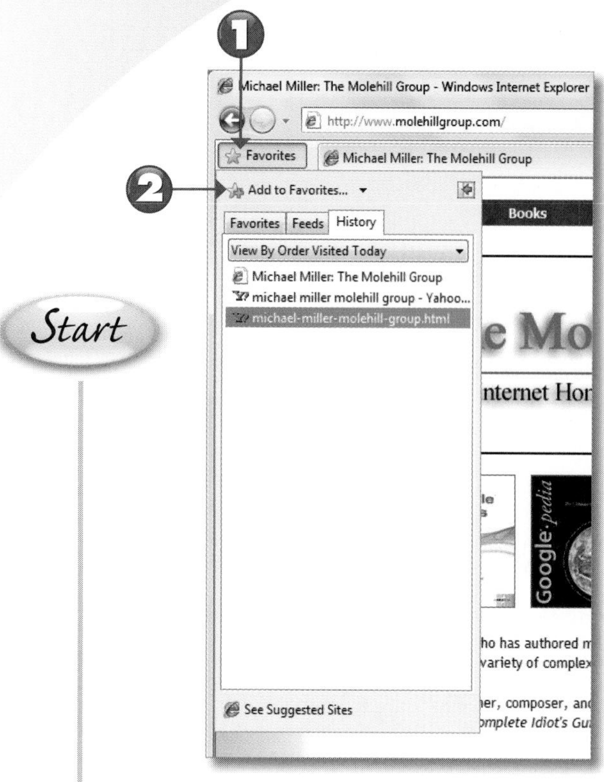

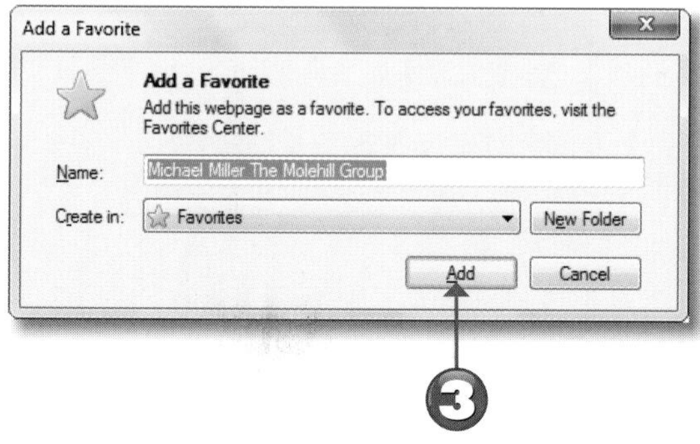

Start

1. Go to the web page you want to add to your Favorites list, and then click the **Favorites** button.
2. Click **Add to Favorites**.
3. Confirm the page's name and then click the **Add** button.

TIP

Organizing Favorites You can store your favorite websites in the main Favorites folder, or you can create additional subfolders for different types of Favorites. ■

RETURNING TO A FAVORITE PAGE

After a web page is saved to your Favorites list, you can return to that page at any time by selecting it from the list—no need to reenter that page's web address.

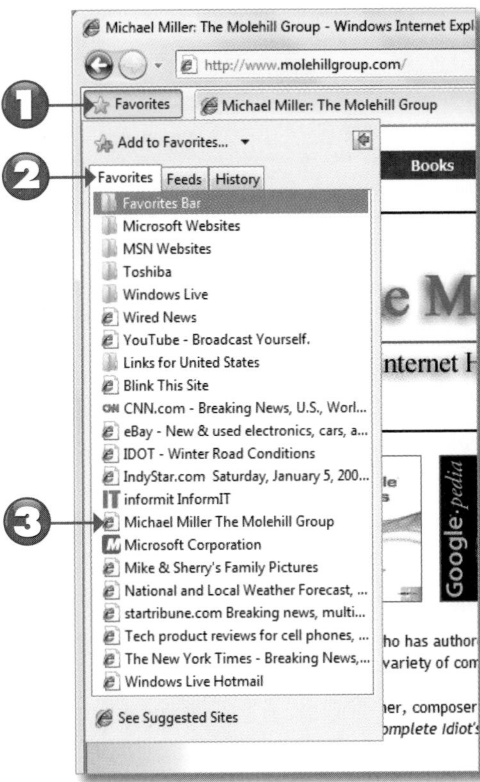

1. Click the **Favorites** button on the toolbar.
2. Click the **Favorites** tab to display the Favorites list.
3. Click a favorite page, and IE goes to that page.

TIP

Hide the Favorites Pane Click the Favorites button again to hide the Favorites pane. ■

REVISITING HISTORY

Internet Explorer keeps track of web pages you've recently visited so you can easily revisit them without having to reenter the web page address.

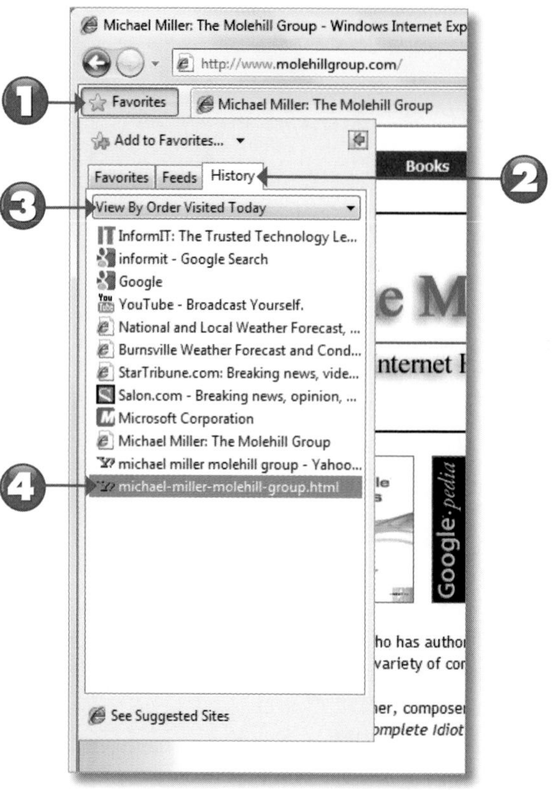

1. Click the **Favorites** button on the toolbar.
2. Click the **History** tab to display the History list.
3. Click the **View By** list and select how you want to view—by date, site, most visited, or order visited today.
4. Click a specific page to display that page in the right pane.

End

TIP

Recent History To revisit one of the last half-dozen or so pages viewed in your current session, click the down arrow on the Back button. This drops down a menu containing the last nine pages you've visited. Click a page to return to it. ■

SEARCHING THE WEB WITH GOOGLE

A web search engine lets you search for virtually anything online. The most popular search engine today is Google (www.google.com), which indexes billions of individual web pages. Google is very easy to use and returns extremely accurate results.

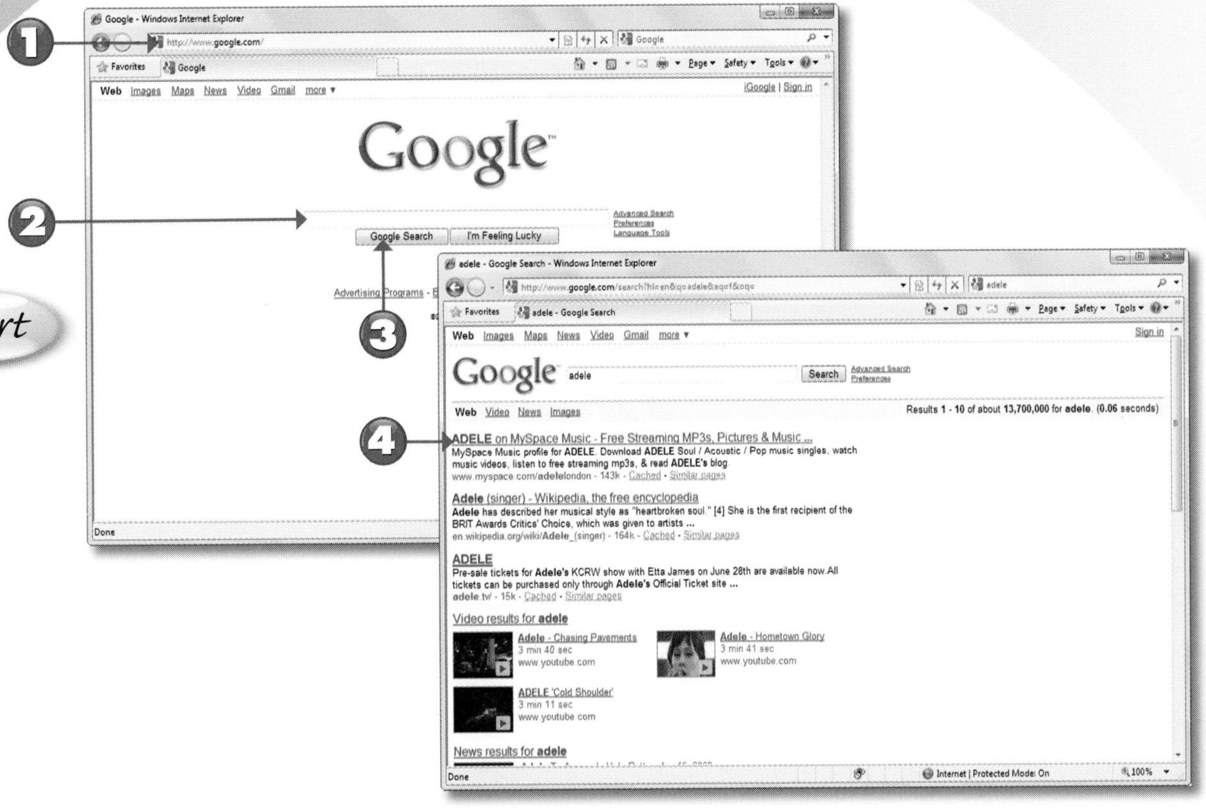

Start

1. Go to **www.google.com**.
2. Enter one or more keywords into the search box.
3. Click the **Google Search** button.
4. When the results are displayed, click any page link to view that page.

End

TIP

Advanced Searching Google also offers a variety of advanced search options to help you fine-tune your search. Just click the Advanced Search link and choose the appropriate options. ■

TIP

Internet Explorer Search Box You can also search the web from Internet Explorer's search box, located next to the address box. To choose a search provider, click the down arrow next to the search box, select Find More Providers, and when the Add Search Providers page appears, click Google. ■

FINDING NEWS AND OTHER INFORMATION ONLINE

The Web is a terrific source for all sorts of news and information. Let's take a quick look at some of the most popular news, weather, and sports sites—the best way to stay informed online!

Start

1. For the top headlines from a variety of sources, go to Google News (**news.google.com**).
2. For in-depth international news, go to BBC News (**news.bbc.co.uk**).

Continued

TIP

More News Other full-service news sites include ABC News (abcnews.go.com), CBSNews.com (www.cbsnews.com), CNN.com (www.cnn.com), and MSNBC (www.msnbc.msn.com). ■

3 For comprehensive sports coverage, go to ESPN.com (**espn.go.com**).

4 For additional sports coverage, go to SportingNews.com (**www.sportingnews.com**).

Continued

NOTE

Sports on the Web The best sports sites on the Web resemble the best news sites—they're actually portals to all sorts of content and services, including up-to-the-minute scores, post-game recaps, in-depth reporting, and much more. ■

TIP

Local Sports If you follow a particular sports team, check out that team's local newspaper on the Web. Chances are you'll find a lot of in-depth coverage there that you won't find at other sites. ■

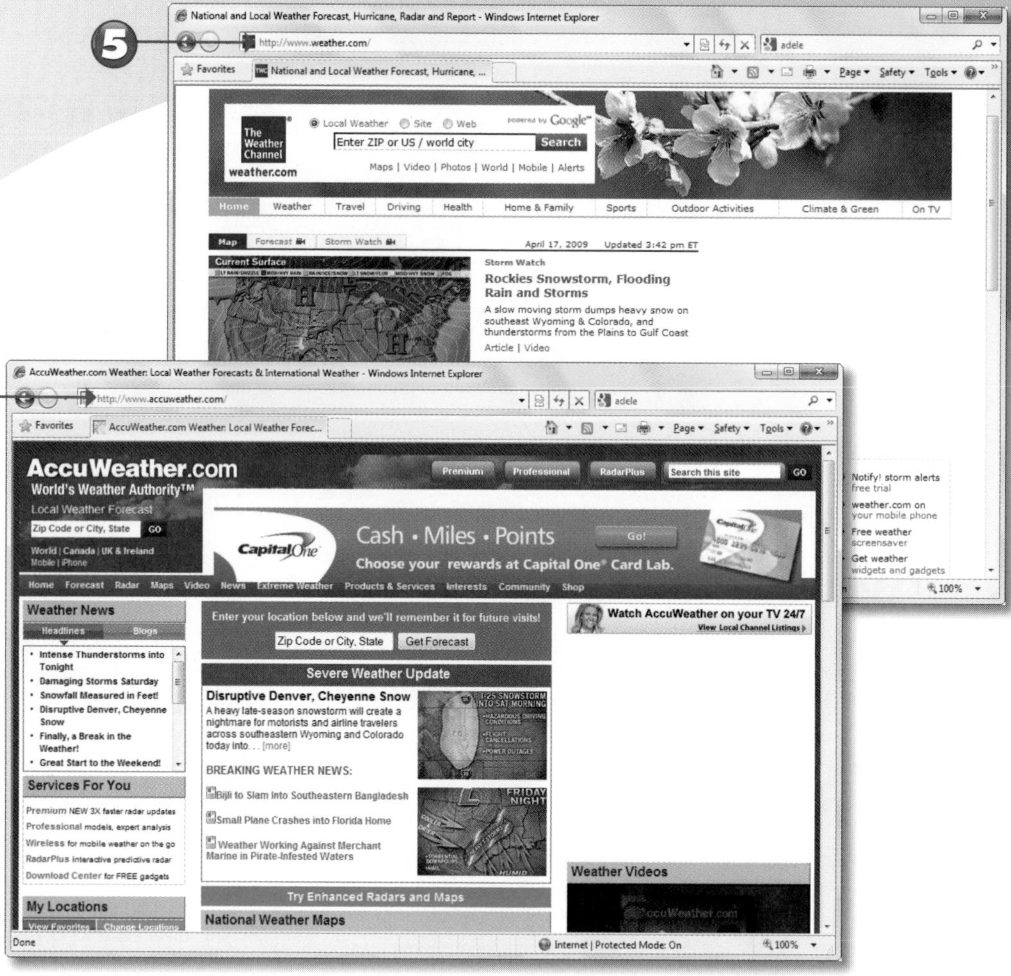

Start

5. The online site for The Weather Channel is found at **www.weather.com**.

6. For additional weather forecasts and information, go to AccuWeather.com (**www.accuweather.com**).

Continued

TIP

Weather on the Web Weather reports and forecasts are readily available on the Web; most of the major news portals and local websites offer some variety of weather-related services. There are also a number of dedicated weather sites on the Web, all of which offer local and national forecasts, weather radar, satellite maps, and more.

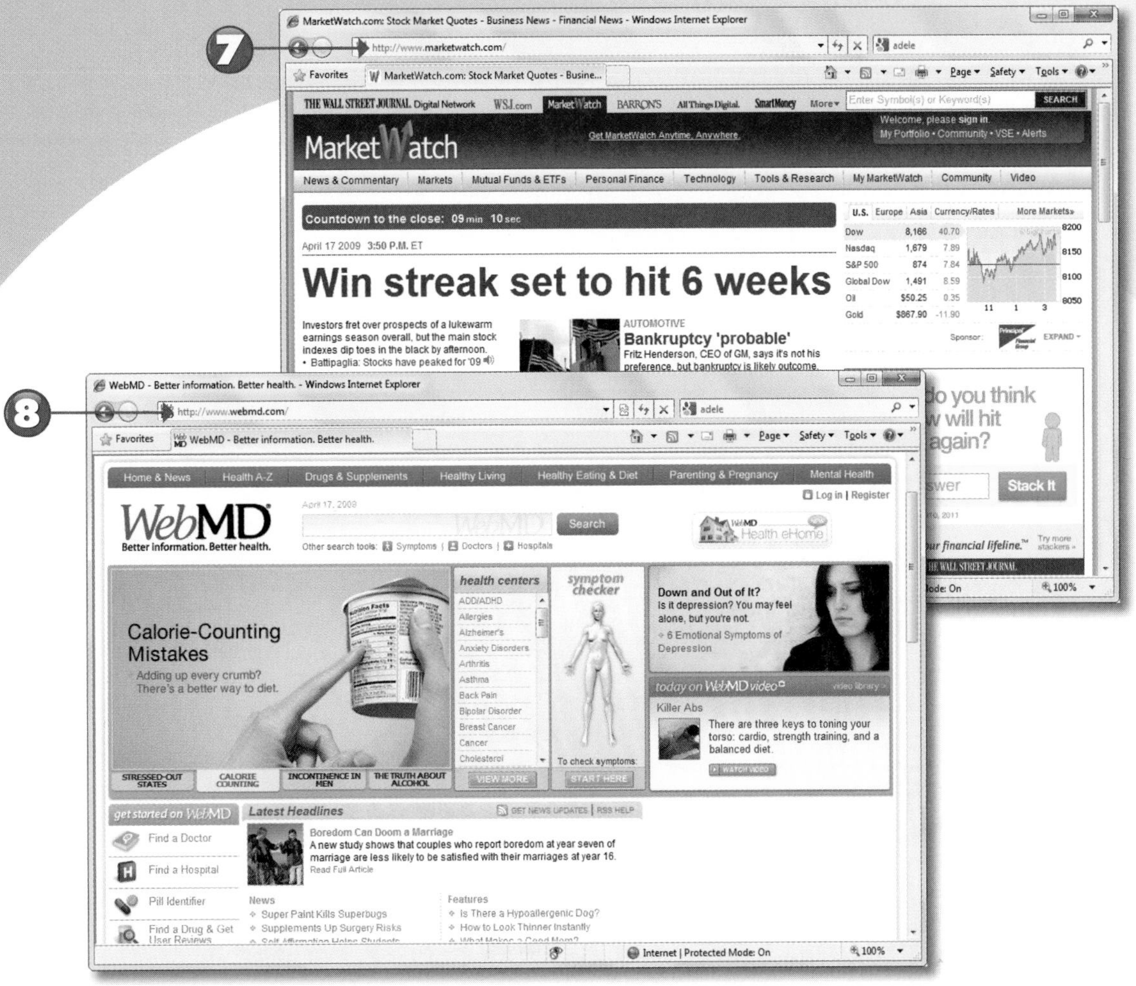

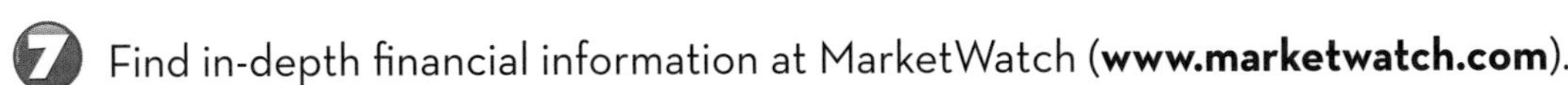

7 Find in-depth financial information at MarketWatch (**www.marketwatch.com**).

8 For health and medical information, go to WebMD (**www.webmd.com**).

End

TIP

More Financial Sites Other popular financial sites include Motley Fool (www.fool.com), MSN Money (moneycentral.msn.com), and TheStreet.com (www.thestreet.com).

CAUTION

Health Information Online As useful as online health sites are, they should not and cannot serve as substitutes for a trained medical opinion.

SHOPPING FOR BARGAINS AT SHOPPING.COM

When you're shopping for bargains online, numerous sites let you perform automatic price comparisons. Search for the product you want, and then search for the lowest price—it's that easy. One of the most popular of these shopping comparison sites is Shopping.com (www.shopping.com).

Start

1. Go to **www.shopping.com**.
2. Click a category in the left column.
3. Fine-tune your search by price range, condition, brand, and other parameters.
4. When you find the product you want, click the **Compare Prices** button.

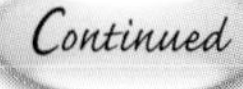

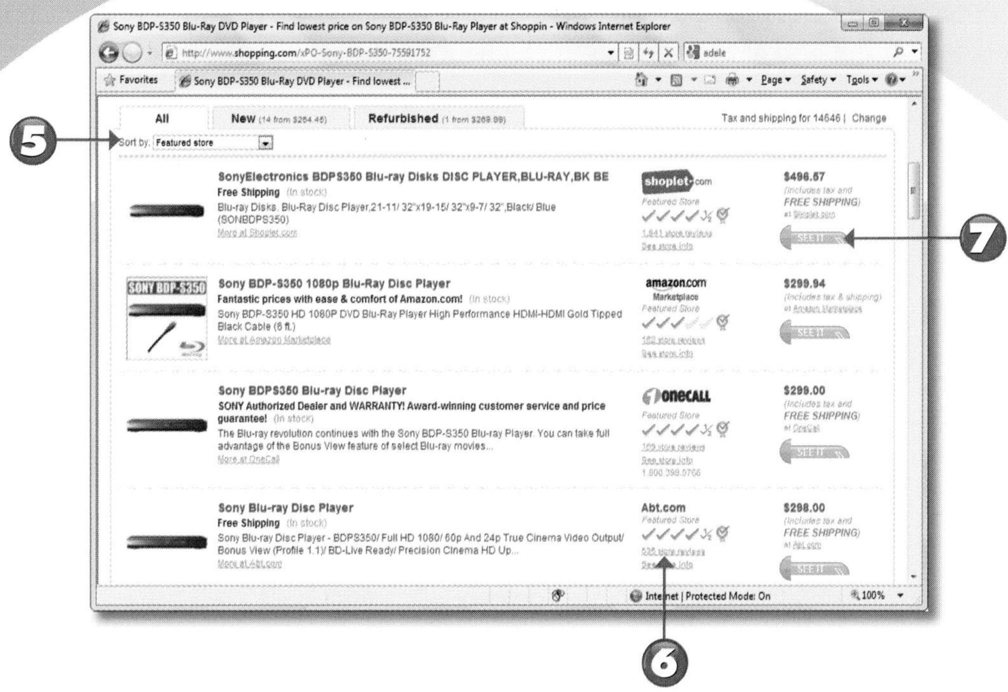

5 Click the **Sort by** list to sort by price, store name, or store rating.

6 Click a **Store Reviews** link to find out what other customers think of a particular retailer.

7 Click the **See It** or **Buy It** button to go to a store and make a purchase.

End

TIP

Shipping Costs Often the merchant with the lowest price also has the highest shipping costs. Enter your ZIP Code to calculate the total price for the item, including shipping costs. Base your decision on the total price you'll have to pay. ■

CAUTION

Merchant Reputation Some online retailers might be bait-and-switch artists, offer poor service, or take forever to ship items. Check the retailer ratings, and take the time to read the customer reviews. Skip those merchants that rate poorly. ■

BIDDING FOR ITEMS ON EBAY

Some of the best bargains on the Web come from other consumers selling items via online auction at eBay (www.ebay.com). An eBay auction is a web-based version of a traditional auction. You find an item you'd like to own and then place a bid on it. Other users also place bids, and at the end of the auction the highest bidder wins.

Start

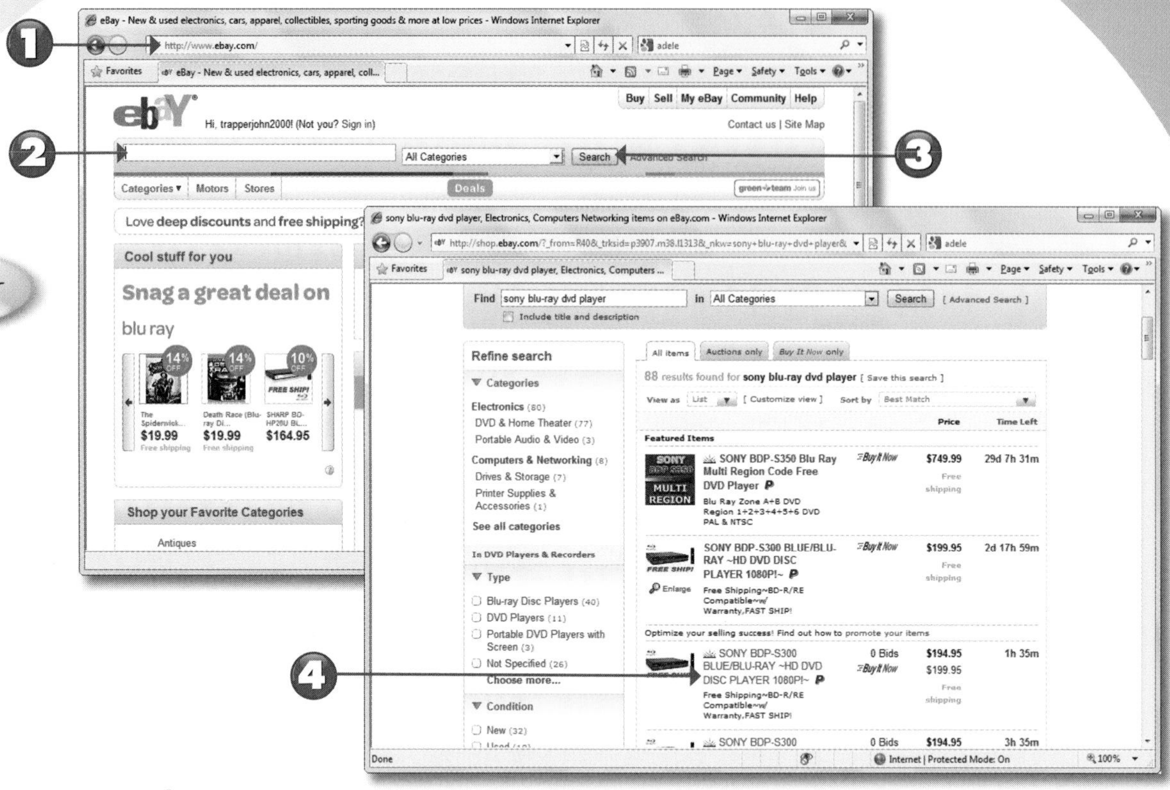

1. Go to **www.ebay.com**.
2. Enter keywords describing the item you're looking for into the search box.
3. Click the **Search** button.
4. When the search results page appears, click the link for the item you're interested in.

Continued

TIP

Learn More About eBay Learn more about eBay in my companion book, *Absolute Beginner's Guide to eBay*, Fifth Edition (Que, 2008). ■

TIP

Place Your Best Bid Always bid the highest amount you're willing to pay. eBay's proxy software enters only the minimum bid necessary, without revealing your maximum bid amount. Your bid will be automatically raised when other users bid until the bid amount reaches your maximum. ■

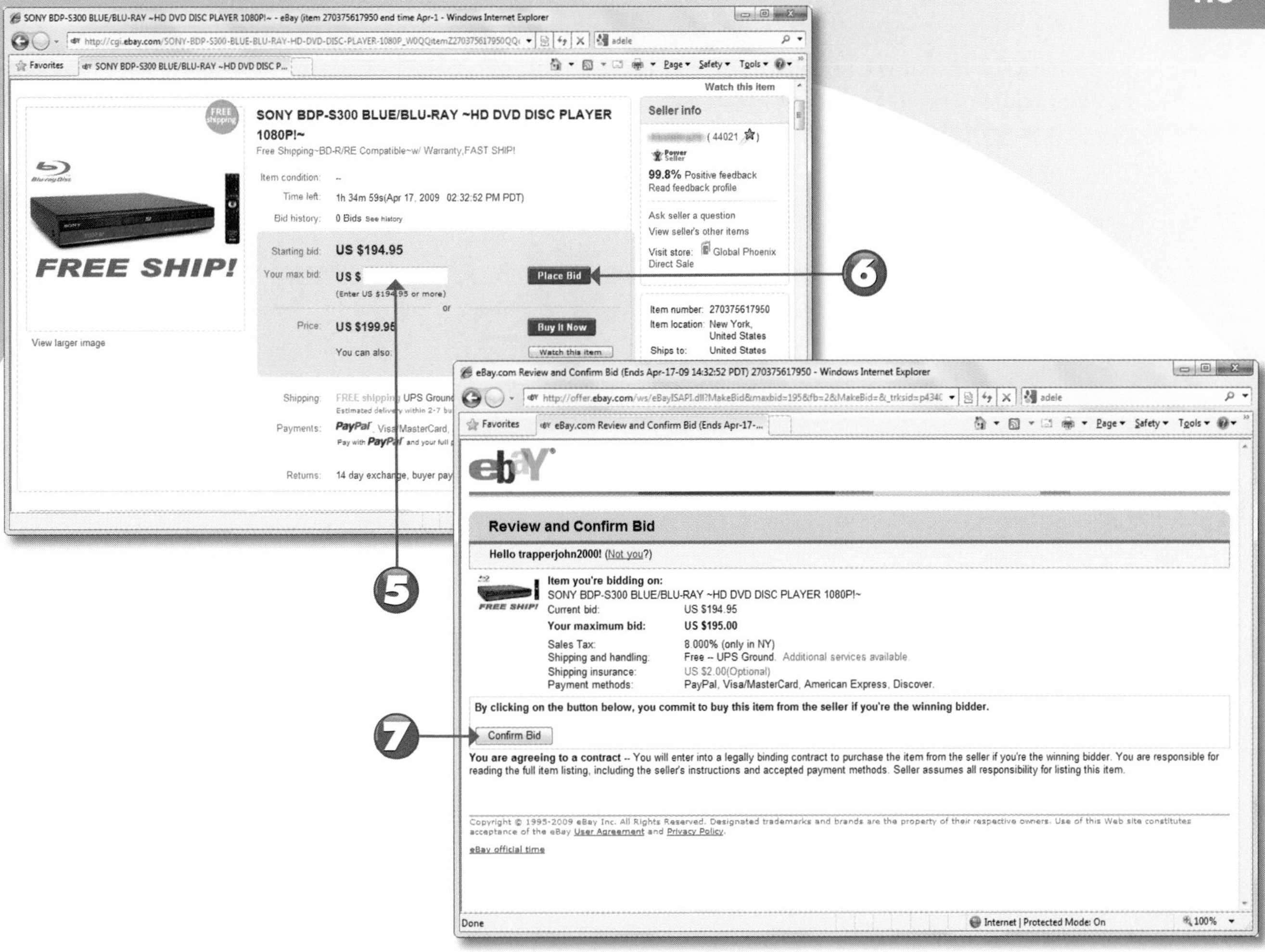

5 Enter the maximum amount you're willing to pay into the Your Max Bid **max bid** box.

6 Click the **Place Bid** button.

7 When the Review and Confirm Bid page appears, click the **Confirm Bid** button.

End

TIP

You Win! If you're the high bidder at the end of the auction period, you win! When you receive the end-of-auction notification email from eBay, click the Pay For It button and follow the onscreen instructions from there. ■

TIP

Buy It Now Some sellers offer the option of buying the item without bidding, for a fixed price. Look for the Buy It Now option to buy an item immediately! ■

BUYING ITEMS ON CRAIGSLIST

When you're looking to buy something locally, you can often find great bargains on craigslist (www.craigslist.org), an online classified advertising site. Browse the ads until you find what you want, and then arrange with the seller to make the purchase.

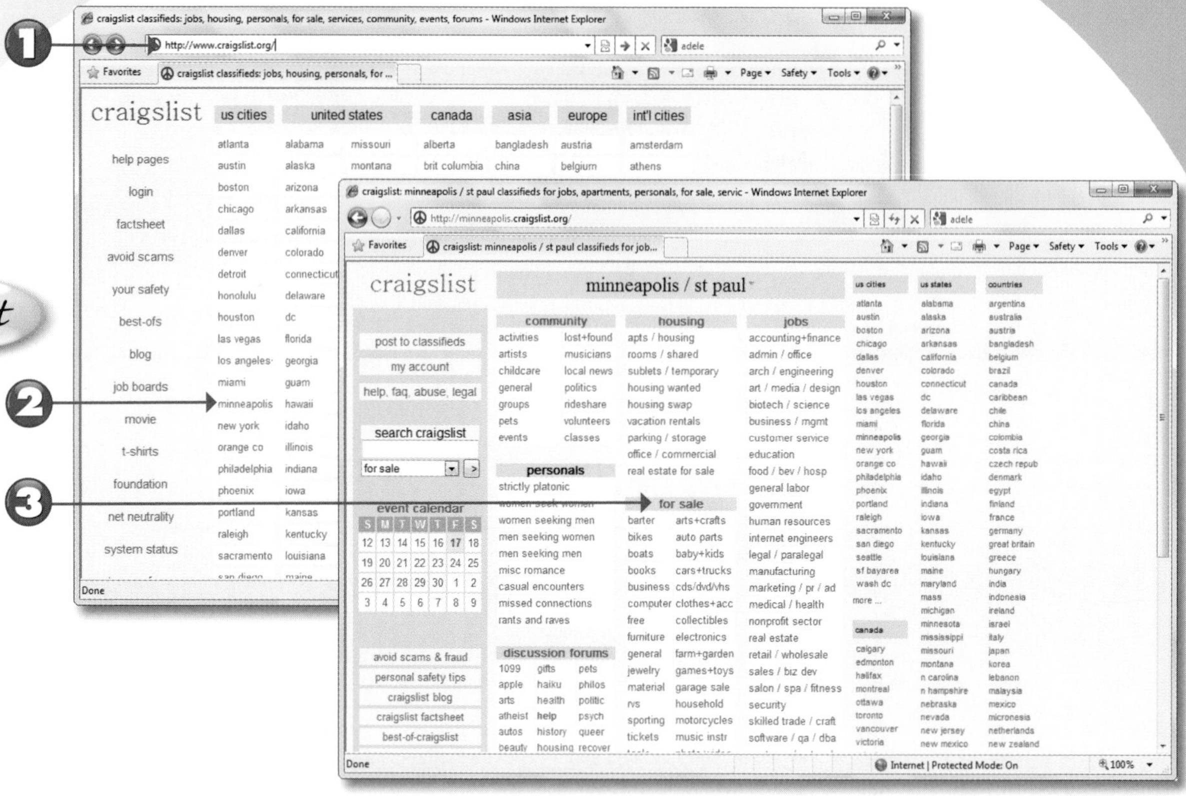

Start

1. Go to **www.craigslist.org**.
2. Click the name of your city or state.
3. Go to the **For Sale** section and click the category you're looking for.

Continued

NOTE

Classified Ads Listings on craigslist are just like traditional newspaper classified ads. All transactions are between you and the seller; craigslist is just the "middleman." ■

TIP

Contacting the Seller When you contact the seller via email, let him know you're interested in the item and would like to see it in person. The seller should reply with a suggested time and place to view and possibly purchase the item. ■

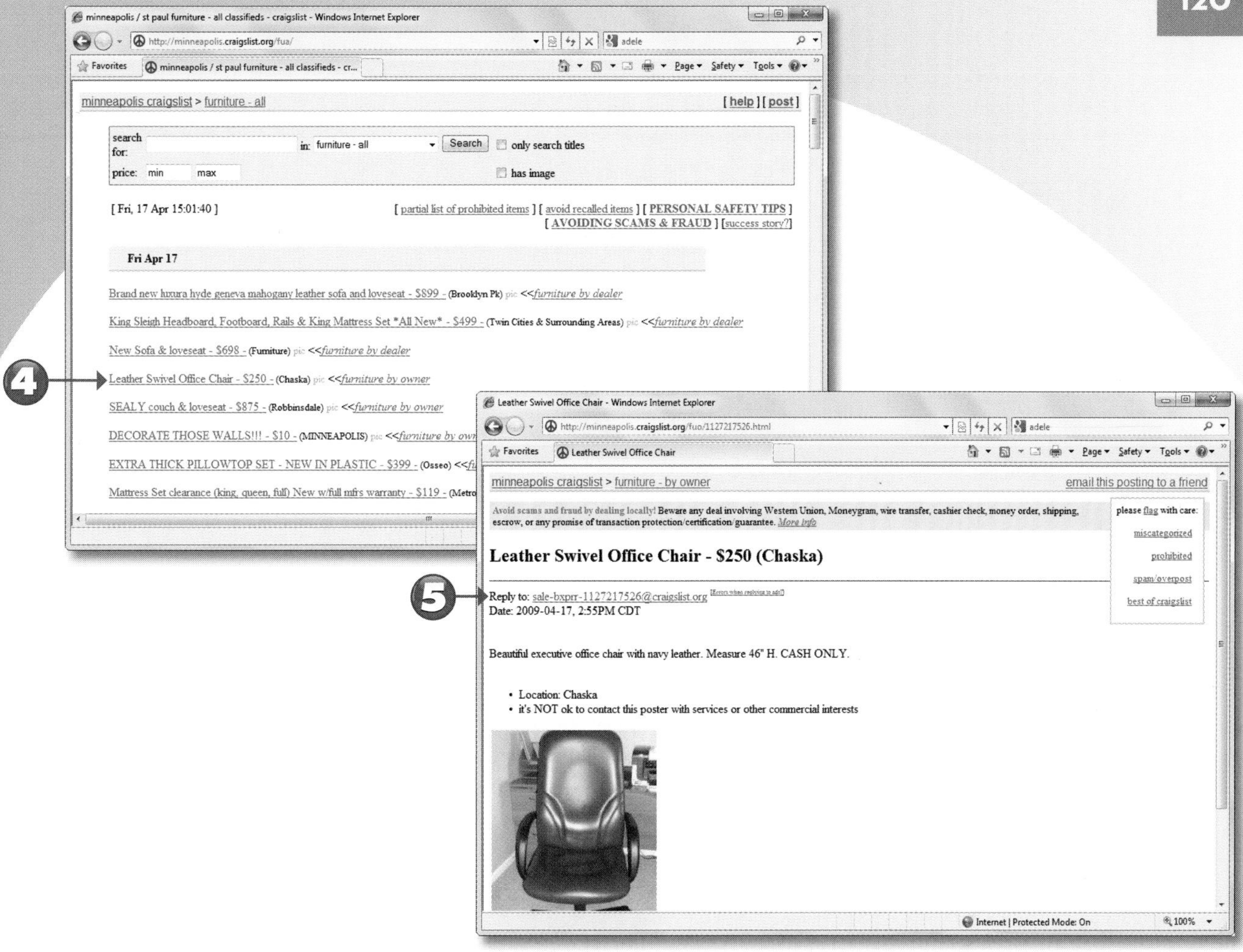

4 Click the link for the item you're interested in.

5 Click the **Reply To** link to email the seller and express your interest.

End

TIP

Pay in Cash When you purchase an item from a craigslist seller, expect to pick up the item in person and pay in cash.

CAUTION

Buyer Beware Just as with traditional classified ads, craigslist offers no buyer protections. Make sure you inspect the item before purchasing!

SELLING ITEMS ON CRAIGSLIST

The craigslist site is also a great place to sell items you want to get rid of. Just place an ad and wait for potential buyers to contact you!

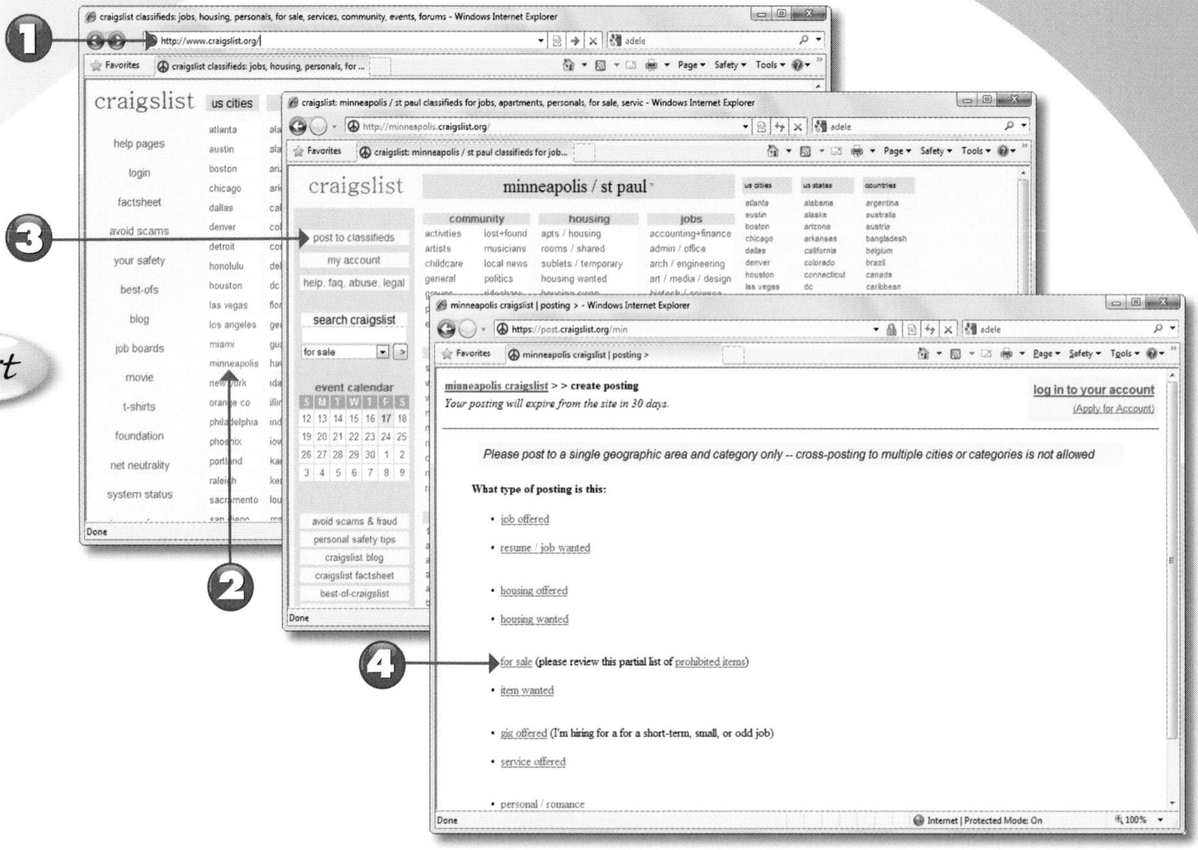

Start

1. Go to **www.craigslist.org**.
2. Click the name of your city or state.
3. Click the **Post to classifieds** link.
4. Click the category that best fits what you're selling. (If necessary, click through to an appropriate subcategory.)

Continued

TIP

Selling Locally Selling on craigslist is better than eBay when you have a big or bulky item that might be difficult to ship long distances. Local buyers will pick up the items they purchase.

NOTE

Contact Email For your protection, craigslist displays an anonymized email address in your item listing. Buyers email this anonymous address, and the emails are forwarded to your real email address.

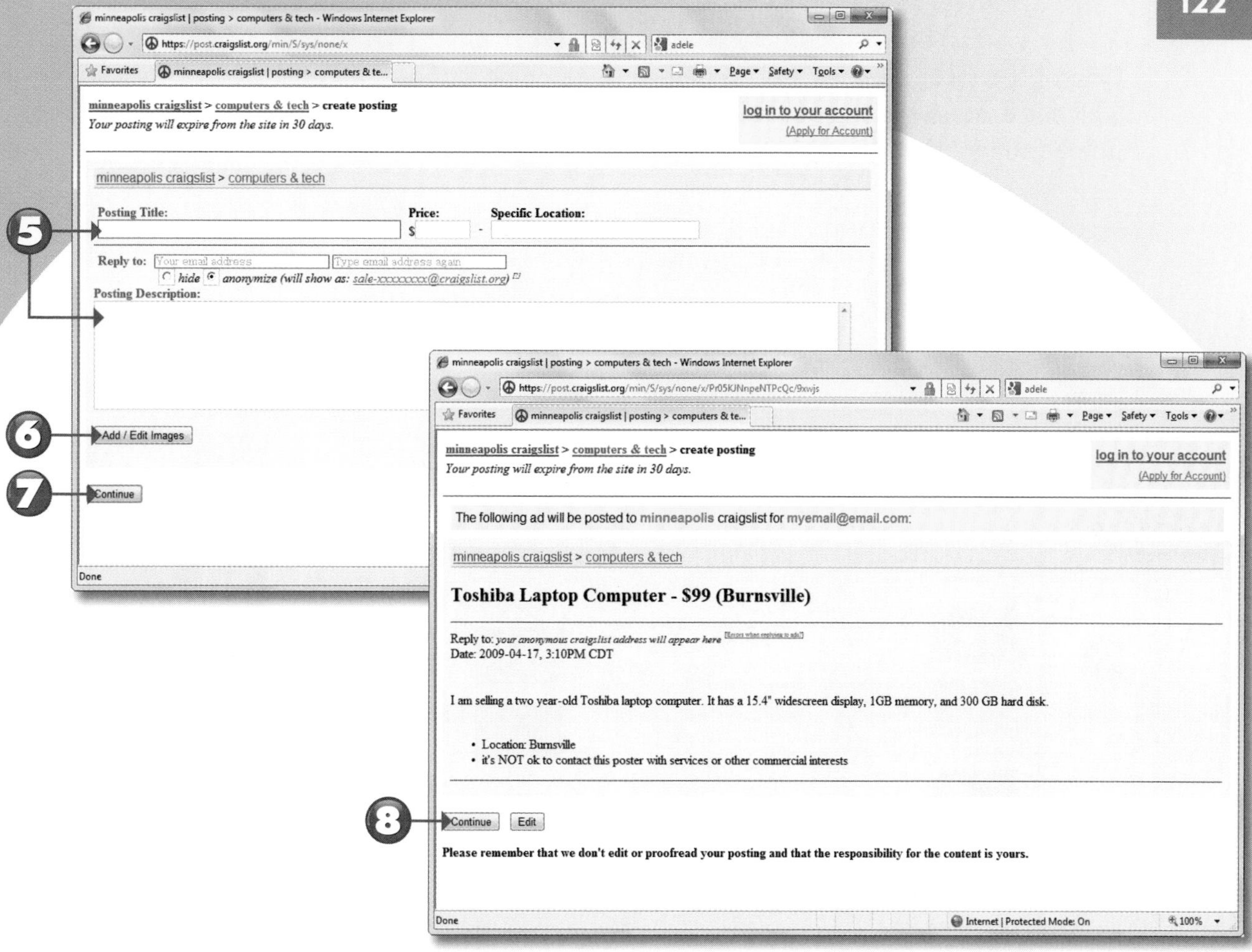

5. Enter a title, asking price, and location for your listing, as well as your email address and a posting description.

6. Click the **Add/Edit Images** button to include digital photos of your item.

7. Click the **Continue** button.

8. Confirm the listing details, and then click the **Continue** button to finalize the listing.

End

CAUTION

Safety First Make sure someone else is with you before you invite potential buyers into your home to look at the item you have for sale—or arrange to meet buyers at a safe, neutral location. ■

TIP

Other Services The craiglist site isn't just for buying and selling merchandise. You can also use craigslist for look for or offer services, jobs, and housing. ■

WATCHING WEB VIDEOS ON YOUTUBE

One of the most popular Web activities is watching videos. The best site for this is YouTube, which is a video-sharing community; users can upload their own videos and watch videos uploaded by other members.

Start

1. Go to **www.youtube.com**.
2. Enter the type of video you're looking for into the search box.
3. Click the **Search** button.
4. When the list of matching videos appears, click the video you want to watch.

Continued

TIP

Sharing Videos Find a video you think a friend would like? Click the Share link under the video player. Scroll down to the Sent This Video from You-Tube section, enter your friend's email address into the To box, and then click the Send button. ■

TIP

Favorites To add a video to your list of favorite videos, click the Favorite link under the video player. View your favorites by clicking the down arrow next to your name (at the top of the page), and then click Favorites. ■

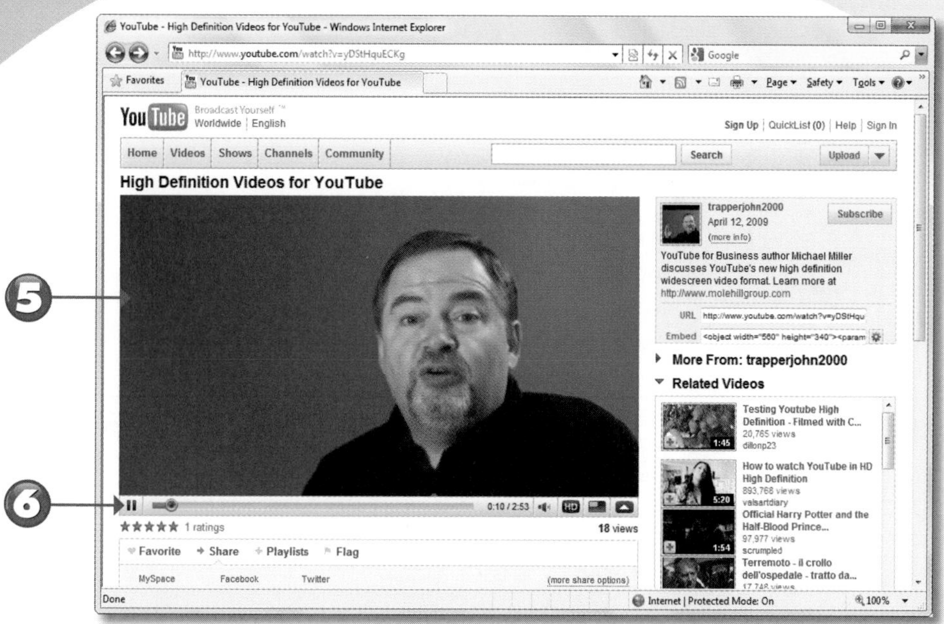

5 When the video page appears, the video begins playing automatically.

6 Click the **Pause** button to pause playback; click the button again to resume playback.

End

TIP

Watching Full Screen To watch a video on your entire computer screen, click the full-screen button at the lower right of the video player. ■

TIP

High Definition Some YouTube videos are now being offered in high definition mode. To view a video in high definition, click the HD button under the video player. (If there's no HD button, the video isn't available in high definition.) ■

UPLOADING YOUR OWN YOUTUBE VIDEOS

Anyone can upload movies and videos to the YouTube site. Once uploaded, all users can view the video—and if you're lucky, the video will go viral!

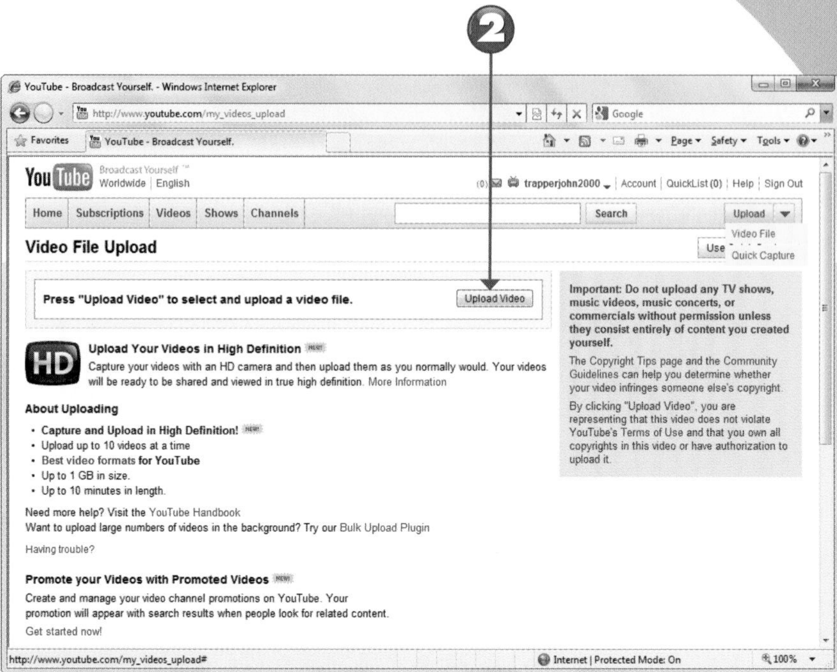

Start

1. Click the **Upload** button at the top of any YouTube page and select **Upload Video File**.

2. Click the **Upload Video** button.

Continued

TIP

Video Specs The videos you upload to YouTube should be less than 10 minutes in length, less than 1GB in size, and recorded at either 640x480 (standard definition) or 1280x720 (high definition) resolution. ■

TIP

File Formats YouTube lets you upload video files in any of the following file formats: .AVI, .MOV, .MPG, and .WMV. ■

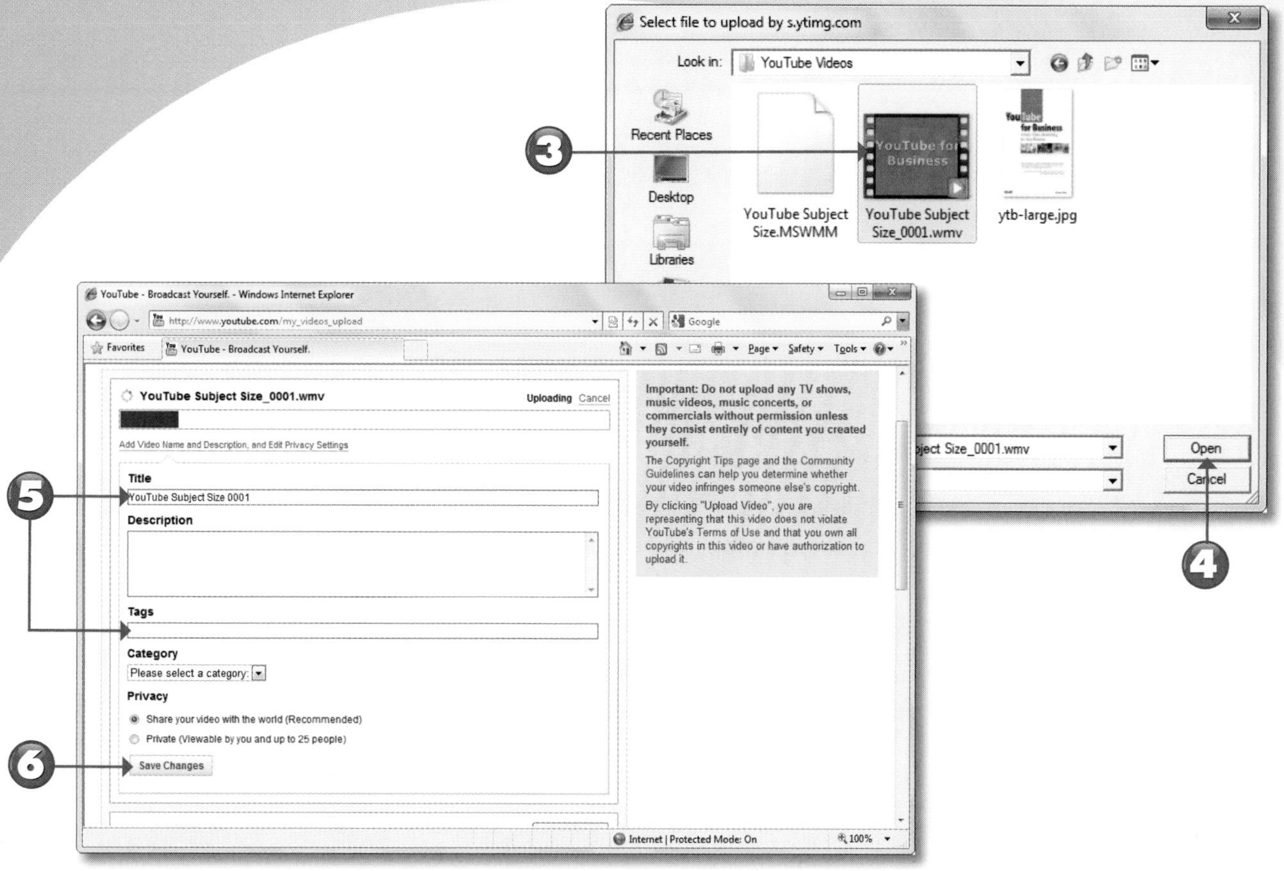

3. Navigate to and select the video you want to upload.

4. Click **Open**.

5. While the video uploads, enter the requested information (title, description, tags, category, and privacy level).

6. Click **Save Changes**.

End

TIP

Manage Your Videos To manage the videos you've uploaded, click the down arrow next to your name at the top of the YouTube home page and click My Videos. You can then edit, annotate, or even delete individual videos. ■

TIP

Video Insight To learn more about who is watching your videos, go to your My Videos page and click the Insight button for a specific video. ■

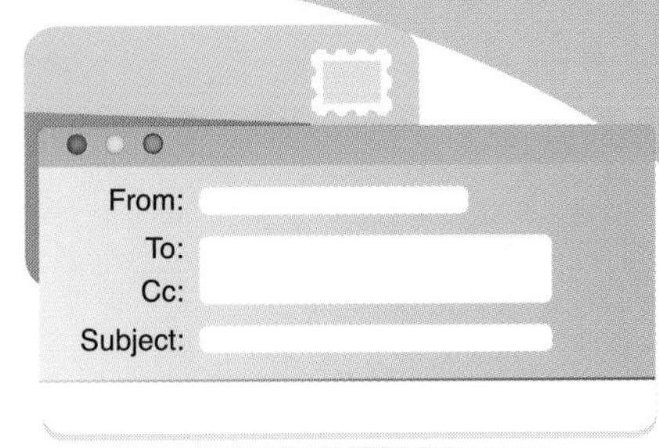

COMMUNICATING ONLINE

An email message is like a regular letter, except that it's composed electronically and delivered almost immediately via the Internet. You can use email to send both text messages and computer files (such as digital photos) to friends, family, and colleagues.

There are two types of email on the Internet: POP email, which requires an account with your Internet service provider (ISP) and a separate email program, and web mail, which can be accessed using any web browser. Web mail is probably the easiest to use, with free services available from Google (Gmail), Microsoft (Windows Live Hotmail), and Yahoo! (Yahoo! Mail).

GMAIL

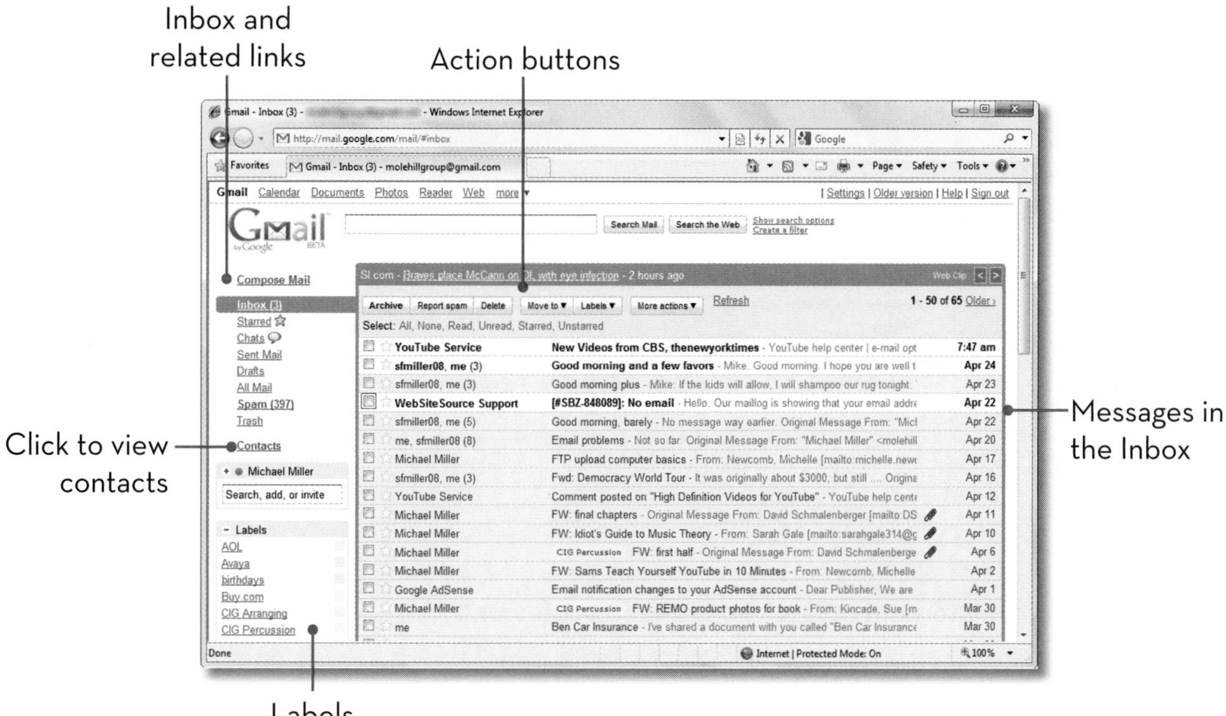
Inbox and related links
Action buttons
Messages in the Inbox
Click to view contacts
Labels

SETTING UP A GMAIL ACCOUNT

Google's Gmail is one of the most popular free web mail services. Anyone can sign up for a free Gmail account and then access email from any computer with an Internet connection, using any web browser.

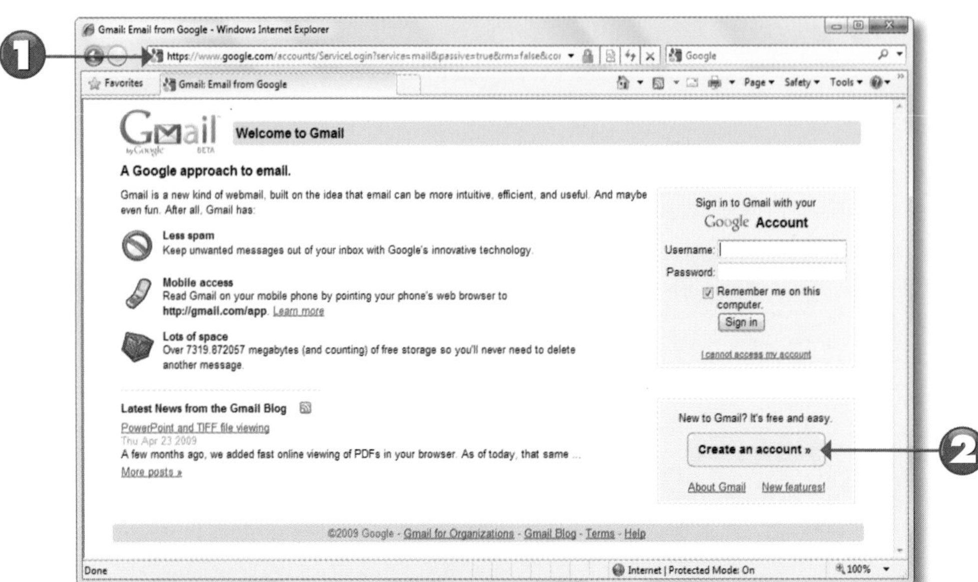

1. From within Internet Explorer, go to **mail.google.com**.

2. Click the **Create an Account** button.

Continued

NOTE

Other Web Mail Services Other popular web mail services include Microsoft's Windows Live Hotmail (www.hotmail.com) and Yahoo! Mail (mail.yahoo.com). ■

NOTE

POP Email POP (Post Office Protocol) email is available from most ISPs. It requires the use of a dedicated email program and the configuration of that program with information about the ISP's incoming and outgoing email servers. ■

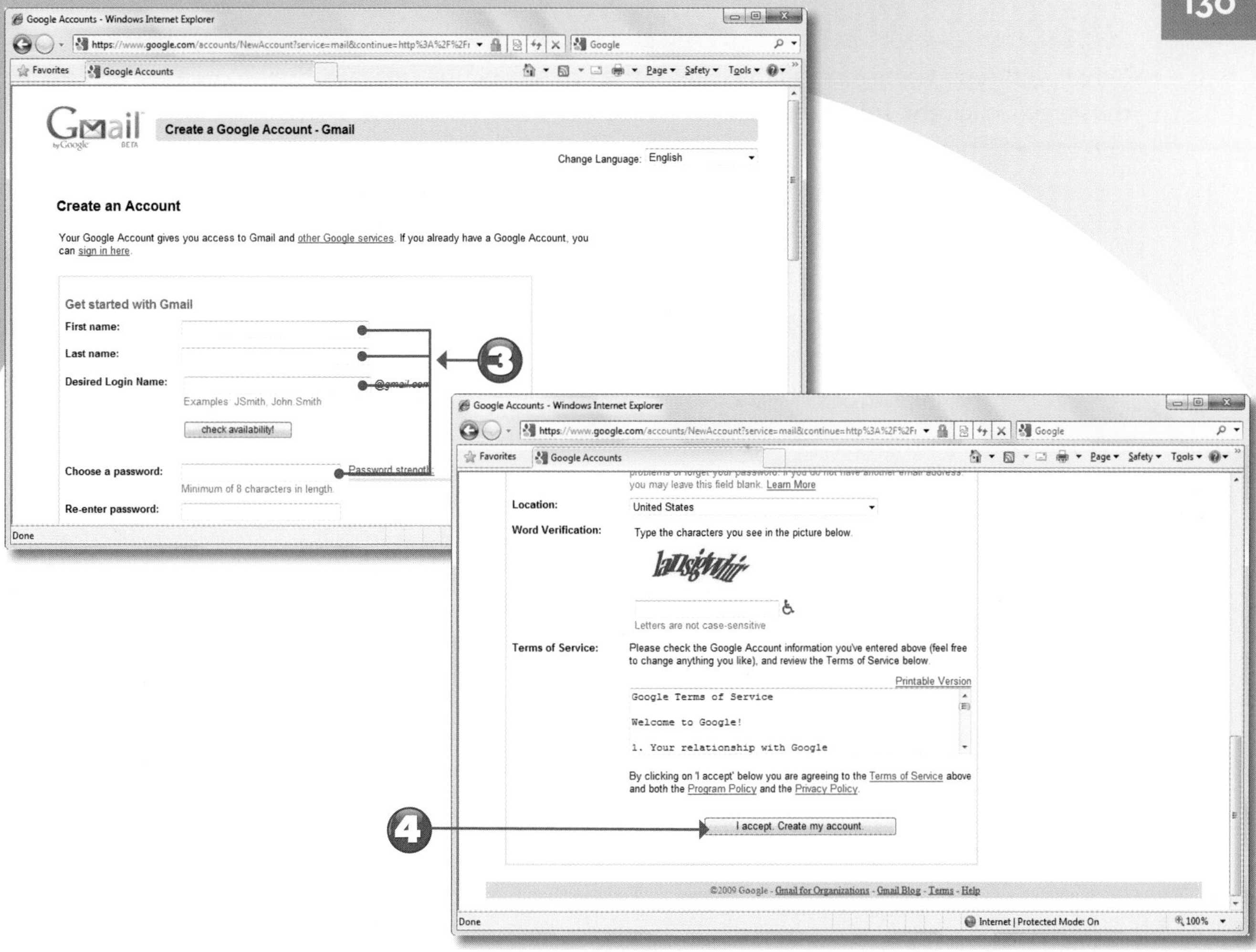

3. Enter the necessary information, including your name, desired email address (login name), and desired password.
4. Click **I Accept. Create My Account.**

End

NOTE

POP Versus Web Mail POP email, like web mail, is typically free. However, you can only access POP email from the email program installed on a single computer; you can't send or receive email from other computers, as you can with web mail. ■

NOTE

POP Email Programs Popular POP email programs include Windows Live Mail (downloadable free with Windows 7), Microsoft Outlook, Outlook Express, and Mozilla Thunderbird. ■

READING AN EMAIL MESSAGE

When you receive new email messages, they're stored in Gmail's Inbox. To display all new messages, click the **Inbox** link.

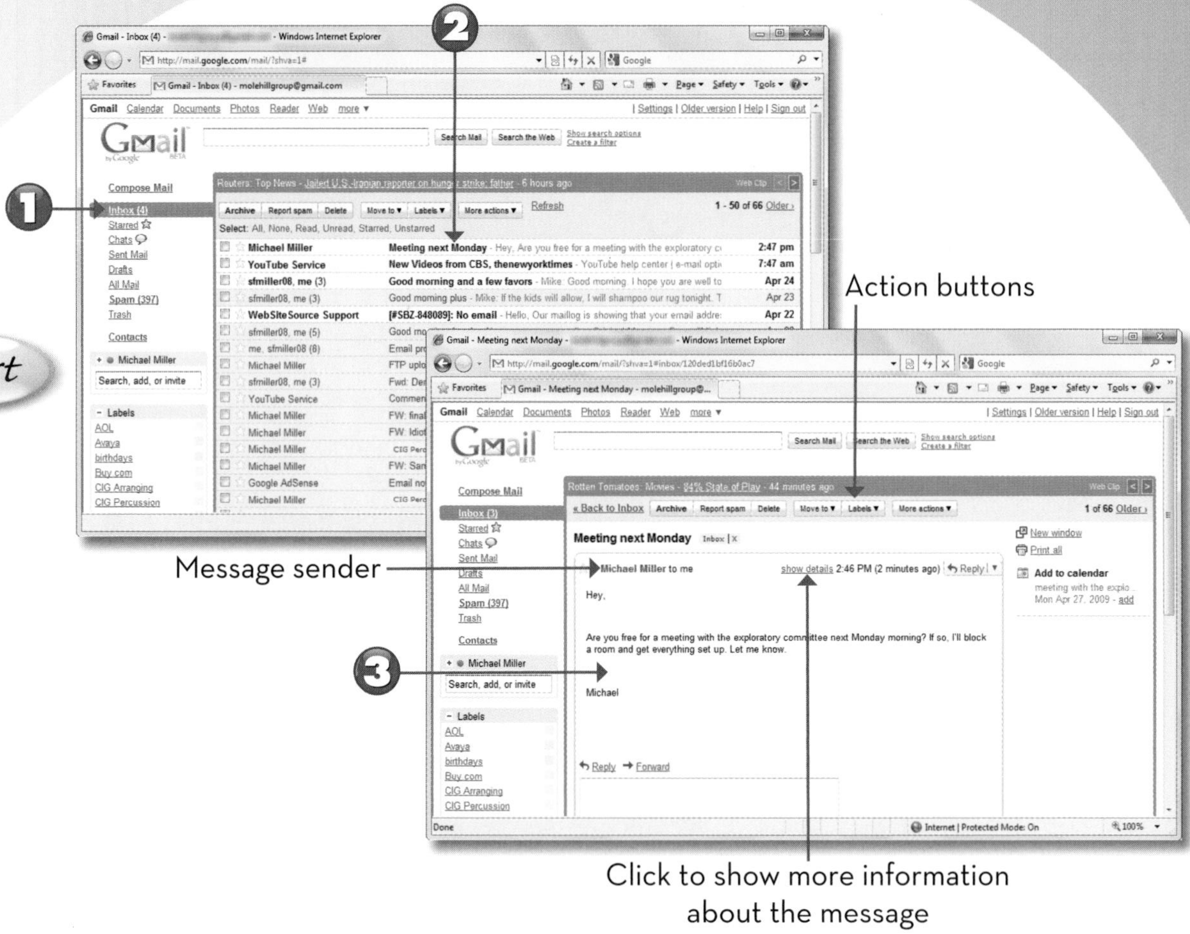

Action buttons

Message sender

Click to show more information about the message

Start

1. On Gmail's main page, click the **Inbox** link.

2. Click the header for the message you wish to view.

3. The selected message now appears; scroll down to read the entire text, if necessary.

End

NOTE

Gmail Home Gmail's home page is located at **mail.google.com**. Before you can view your Inbox , you may be asked to sign in with your username (email address) and password. ■

NOTE

Sender's Address The name of the person who sent you the email is displayed at the top of the message. Click **Show Details** to view the sender's full email address and more information about the message. ■

REPLYING TO AN EMAIL MESSAGE

It's easy to reply to any message you receive. Just click **Reply**, and then enter your new message!

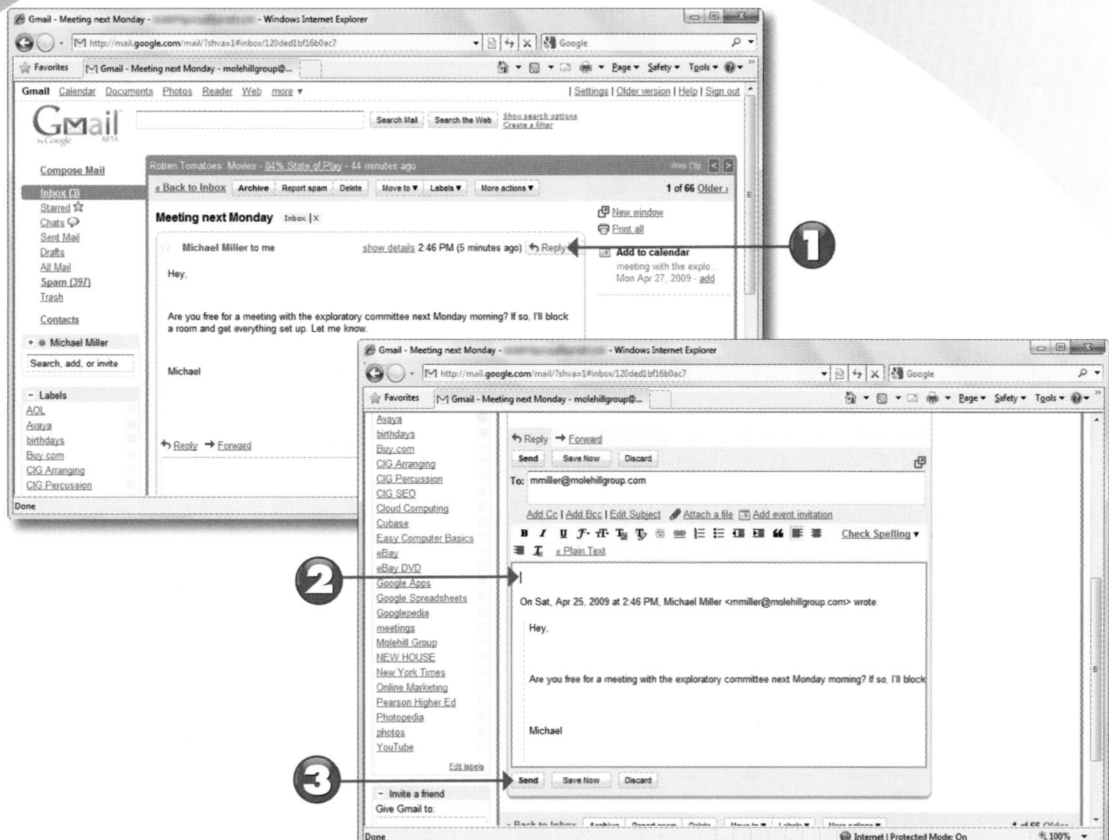

Start

1. From the open message, click **Reply**.
2. Enter your reply text in the message window.
3. Click the **Send** button to send your reply to the original sender.

End

NOTE

Quoted Text The text of the original message is automatically "quoted" at the bottom of the reply message. ■

COMPOSING A NEW EMAIL MESSAGE

Composing a new message is similar to replying to a message. The big difference is that you have to manually enter the recipient's email address.

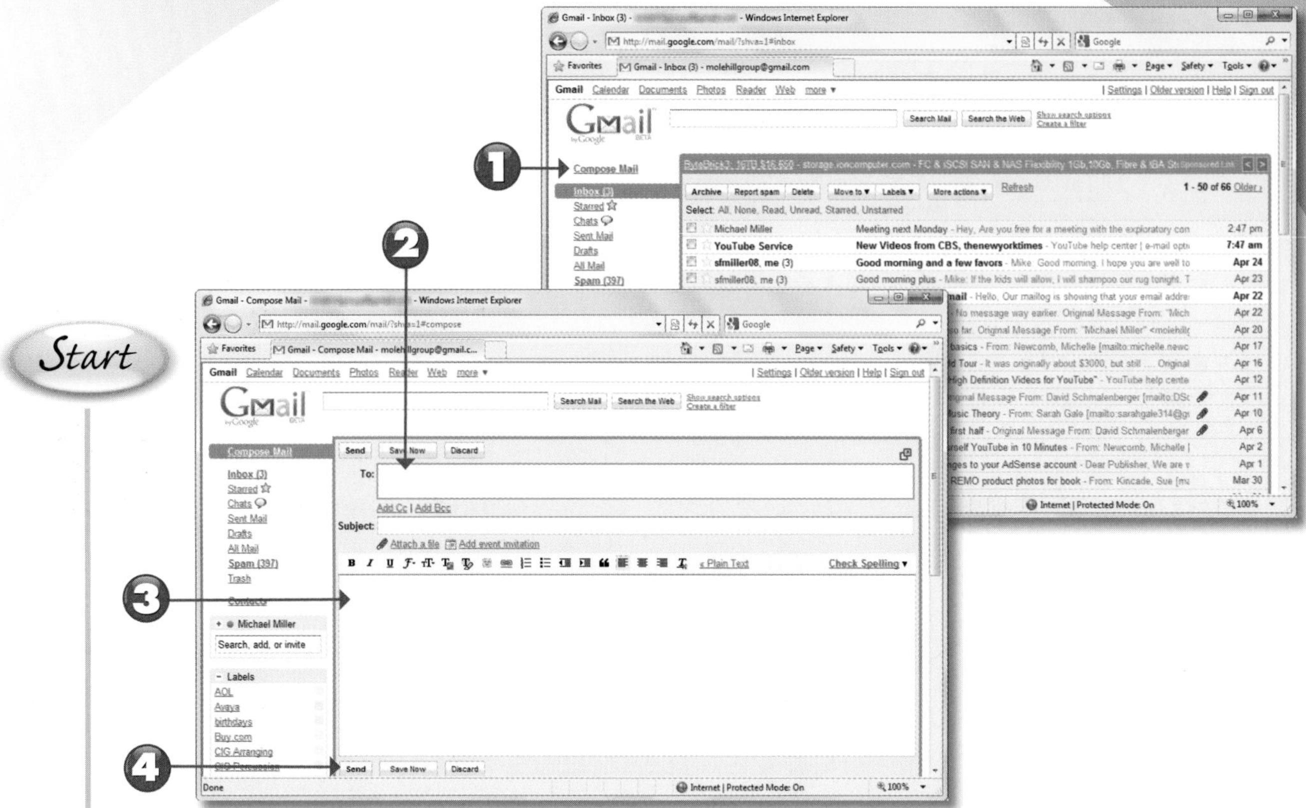

Start

1. Click **Compose Mail** from any Gmail page.
2. Enter the email address of the recipient(s) in the To box; then enter a subject in the Subject box.
3. Move your cursor to the main message area and type your message.
4. When your message is complete, send it to the recipient(s) by clicking the **Send** button.

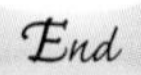

TIP

Send to Multiple Recipients You can enter multiple addresses in the To box, as long as you separate the addresses with a semicolon, like this: books@molehillgroup.com; gjetson@sprockets.com. ■

TIP

Cc and Bcc Gmail also lets you send carbon copies (Cc) and blind carbon copies (Bcc) to additional recipients. (A blind carbon copy is not visible to other recipients.) Just click the **Add Cc** or **Add Bcc** links to add these addresses. ■

SENDING A FILE VIA EMAIL

The easiest way to share a file with another user is via email, as an *attachment*. To send a file via email, you attach that file to a standard email message. When the message is sent, the file travels along with it; when the message is received, the file is right there, waiting to be opened.

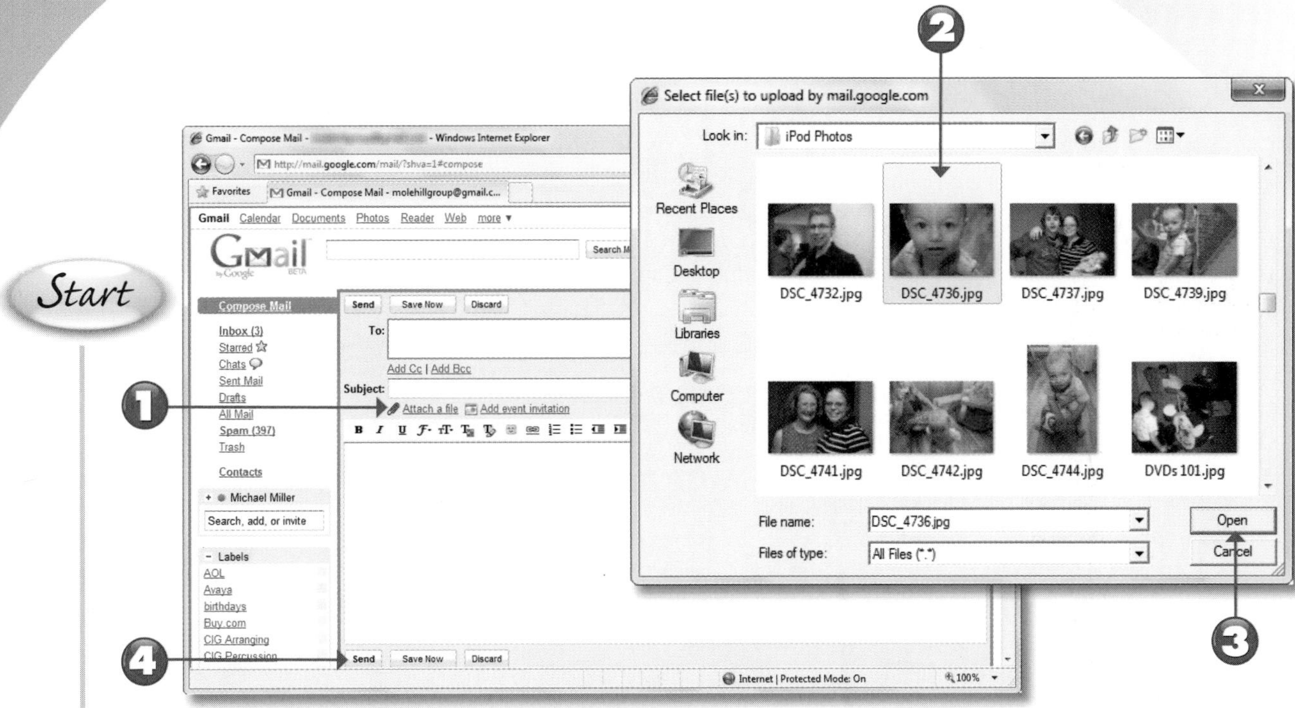

Start

1. Start with a new message and then click **Attach a File**.
2. Navigate to and select the file you want to send.
3. Click **Open**.
4. Complete and send the message as normal by clicking the **Send** button.

End

CAUTION

Large Files Be wary of sending extra-large files over the Internet. They can take a long time to upload—and just as long for the recipient to download when received. ■

CAUTION

Attached Viruses Beware of receiving unexpected email messages with file attachments. Opening the attachment may infect your computer with a virus or spyware! You should never open email attachments that you weren't expecting—or from senders you don't know. ■

MANAGING GMAIL MESSAGES

Gmail groups original messages and their replies (and *their* replies) into connected *conversations*. You can also organize your messages by applying labels and then search for messages with a given label.

Start

1. To view a previous message in a conversation, click that message's header.

2. To apply a label to an email message, click the **Label** button and either select an existing label or enter a new one.

3. To view all messages with a given label, click that label in the **Labels** box.

End

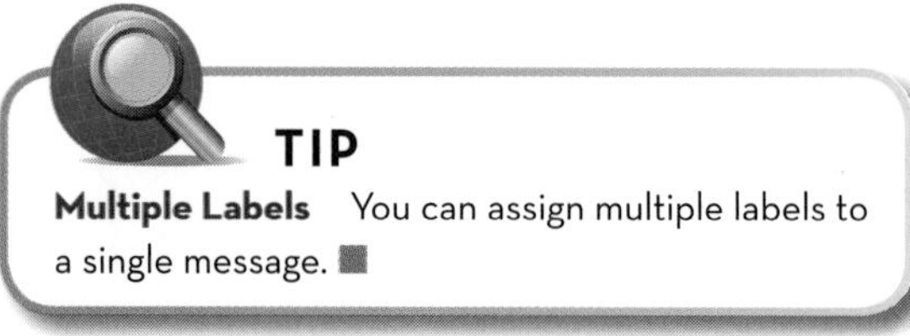

TIP

Multiple Labels You can assign multiple labels to a single message. ■

NOTE

Folders Other email services and programs use folders for organization, but labels are Gmail's way of organizing email messages by topic or content. ■

ADDING GMAIL CONTACTS

You can store frequently emailed addresses in Gmail's Contacts list. Once you've added them, it's easy to send messages to your contacts.

Start

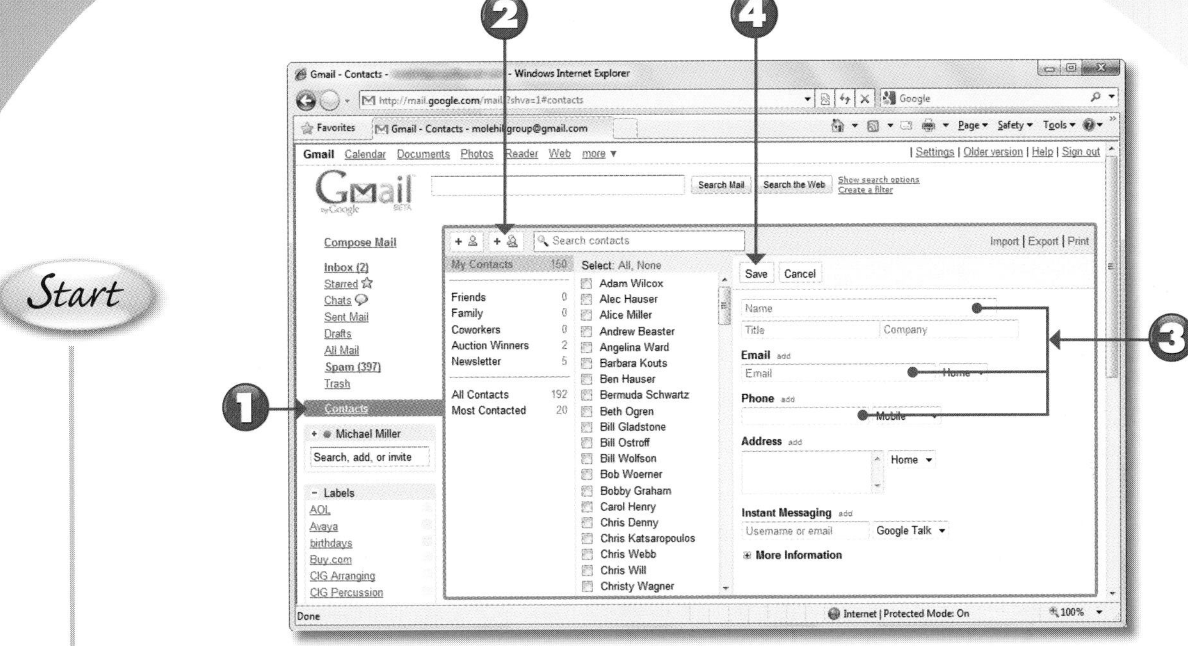

1. Click **Contacts** from any Gmail page.
2. Click the **New Contact** button.
3. Enter the name, email address, and other information for this contact.
4. Click **Save**.

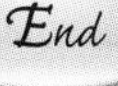

TIP

Emailing Contacts Once a contact has been added, you can email that contact by opening a new message and typing the person's name in the To box. All matching contacts will appear; choose the one you want to email. ■

DOWNLOADING AOL INSTANT MESSENGER

Instant messaging (IM) lets you communicate one on one, in real-time, with your friends, family, and colleagues. One of the most popular IM programs is AOL Instant Messenger, also known as AIM, which is downloadable for free.

1. From within Internet Explorer, go to **www.aim.com**.
2. Click the **Download** button and follow the onscreen instructions.

NOTE

Other IM Services Other popular instant messaging services include Yahoo! Messenger (messenger.yahoo.com), ICQ (www.icq.com), Google Talk (www.google.com/talk/), and Microsoft's Windows Live Messenger (messenger.live.com). ■

NOTE

Screen Name and Password Once you install AOL Instant Messenger on your computer, you'll need to sign up for an AIM screen name. Click the **Get a Screen Name** link at the top of the AIM home page and enter the appropriate information to create your account and create a screen name. ■

INSTANT MESSAGING WITH AOL INSTANT MESSENGER

To send an instant message to another user, both of you have to be online at the same time. If that person is in your Buddies list, he'll show up as being online in AIM; you'll also appear in his online list.

Start

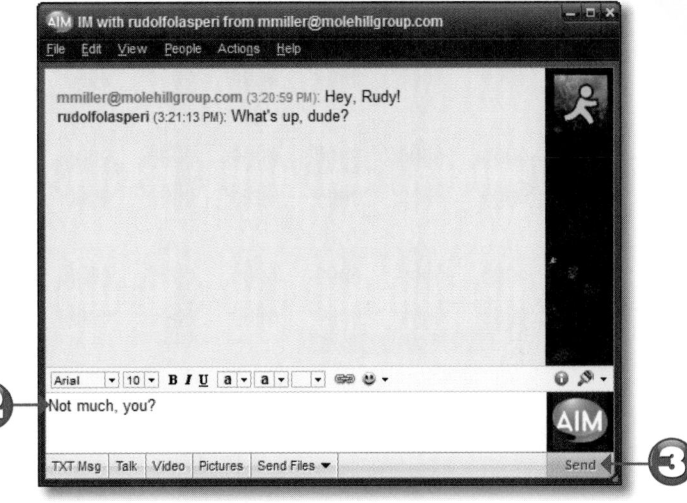

1. Double-click a name in your Buddies list to open the IM window.
2. Enter your message in the lower part of the window.
3. Click the **Send** button (or press **Enter**).

End

CAUTION

Interoperability Most IM services only let you talk to other users of that service. So, for example, if you're using AIM, you can't message someone using Windows Live Messenger. You both need to be on the same service to talk. ■

NOTE

Messages in the Window Your message text appears in your IM window—and in the Conversation window of your recipient. Messages sent by your recipient also appear in your IM window. ■

ADDING BUDDIES IN AOL INSTANT MESSENGER

Before you can send an instant message to another user, that person has to be on your AIM Buddies list. Fortunately, adding buddies is easy—as long as you know their screen names.

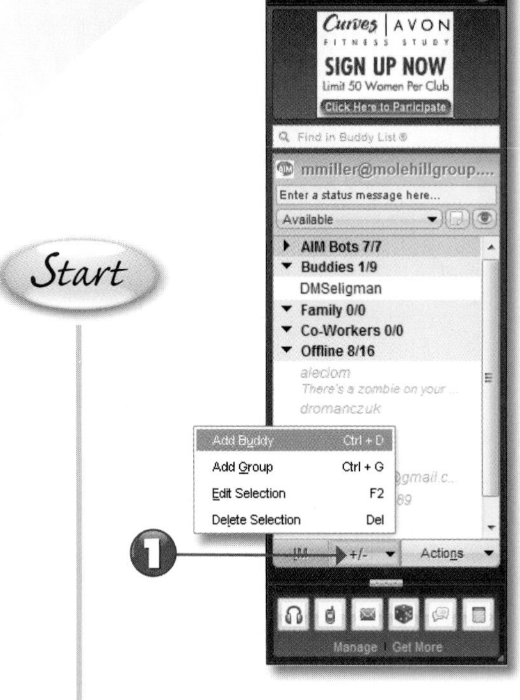

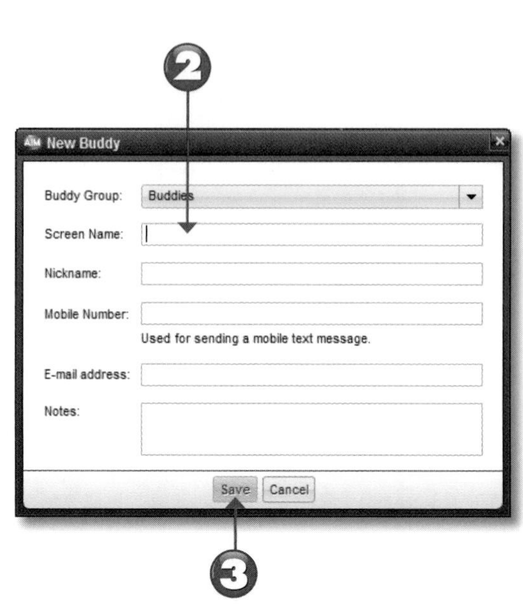

Start

1. Click the **Buddy List Setup** button and then click **Add Buddy**.
2. Enter your friend's screen name and other information.
3. Click **Save**.

End

CAUTION

Don't Accept Files Don't accept any unexpected files sent to you during instant messaging sessions. These files are likely to contain computer viruses, which can damage your computer system. ■

MICRO-BLOGGING WITH TWITTER

Twitter is a *micro-blogging* service that lets you create short (up to 140 characters in length) text posts that keep your friends and family informed of your latest activities. Anyone subscribing to your posts receives updates via the Twitter site.

1. From within Internet Explorer, go to **www.twitter.com**.
2. Enter up to 140 characters into the What Are You Doing box.
3. Click **Update**.

End

NOTE

Micro-Blogging A *blog* (short for "web blog") is a means of sharing personal observations over the Internet, kind of like a web-based diary. While a normal blog post can be of any length, a *micro-blog* is limited to very short messages—like the text message you send via mobile phone. ■

FOLLOWING OTHER TWITTER USERS

Twitter lets you "follow" what other users are doing on Twitter. Once you've registered and signed in, the Twitter home page displays "tweets" from users you've decided to follow.

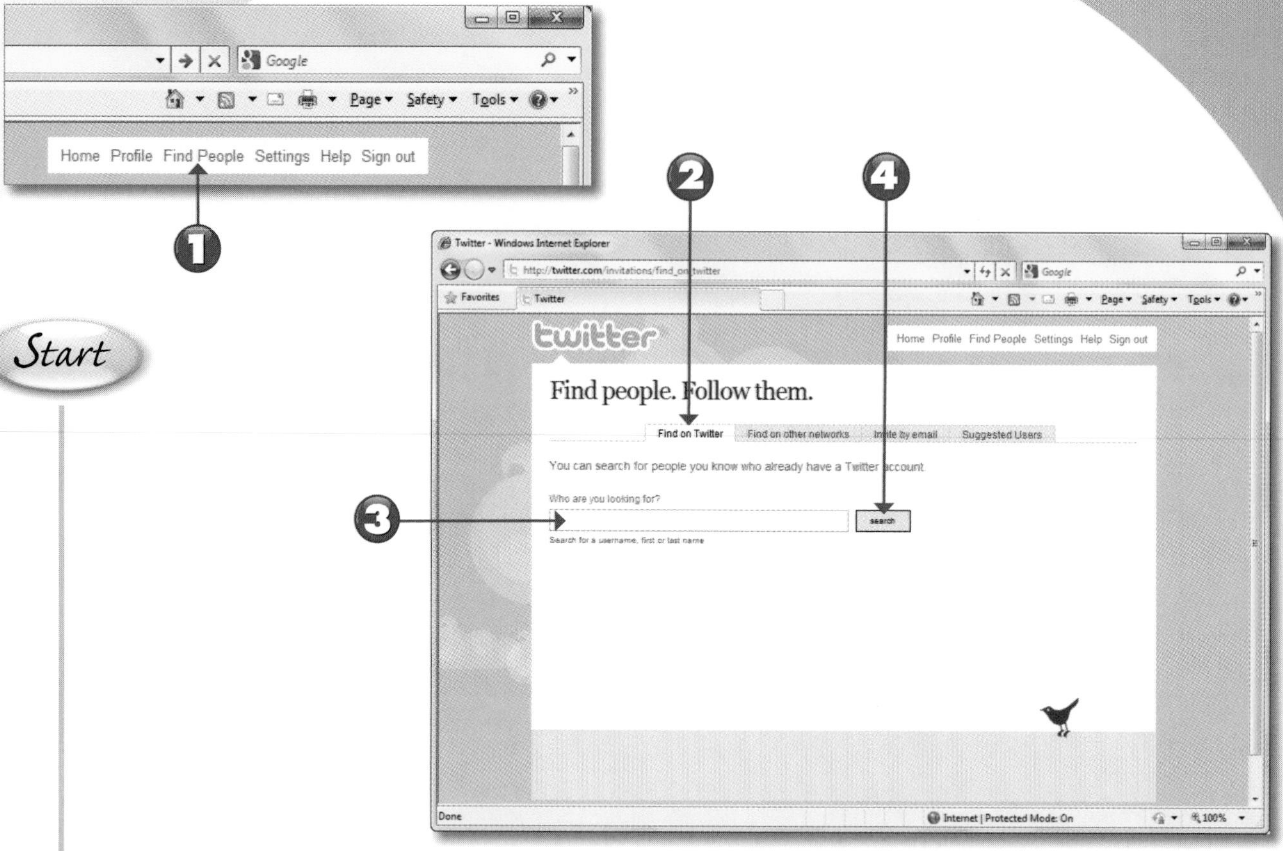

Start

1. From the Twitter home page, click **Find People**.
2. Click the **Find on Twitter** tab.
3. Enter the user's Twitter username or first and last name.
4. Click **Search**.

Continued

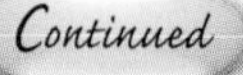

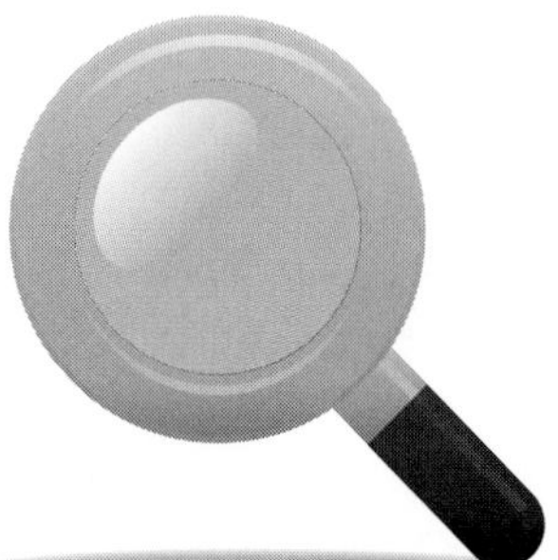

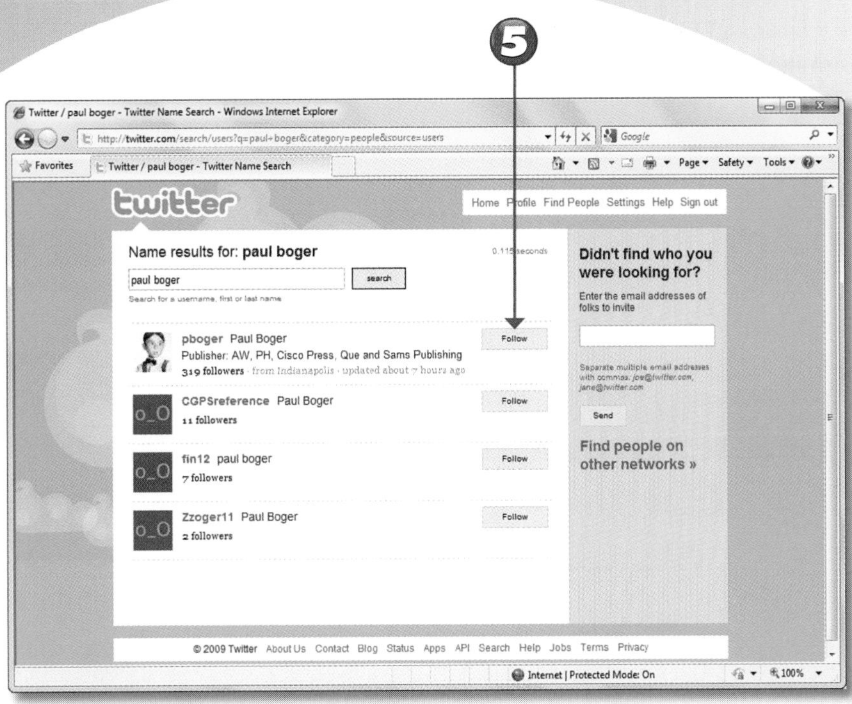

5. When you find a person you want to follow, click the **Follow** button next to that person's name.

End

NOTE

Other Ways to Search You can also search for Twitter users on other email networks (such as Gmail, Yahoo!, and Hotmail), invite nonusers to join Twitter, and view a list of suggested users you might want to follow. ■

SETTING UP A FACEBOOK ACCOUNT

Social networking enables people to share experiences and opinions with each other via community-based websites. The most popular social network today is Facebook, with more than 200 million users.

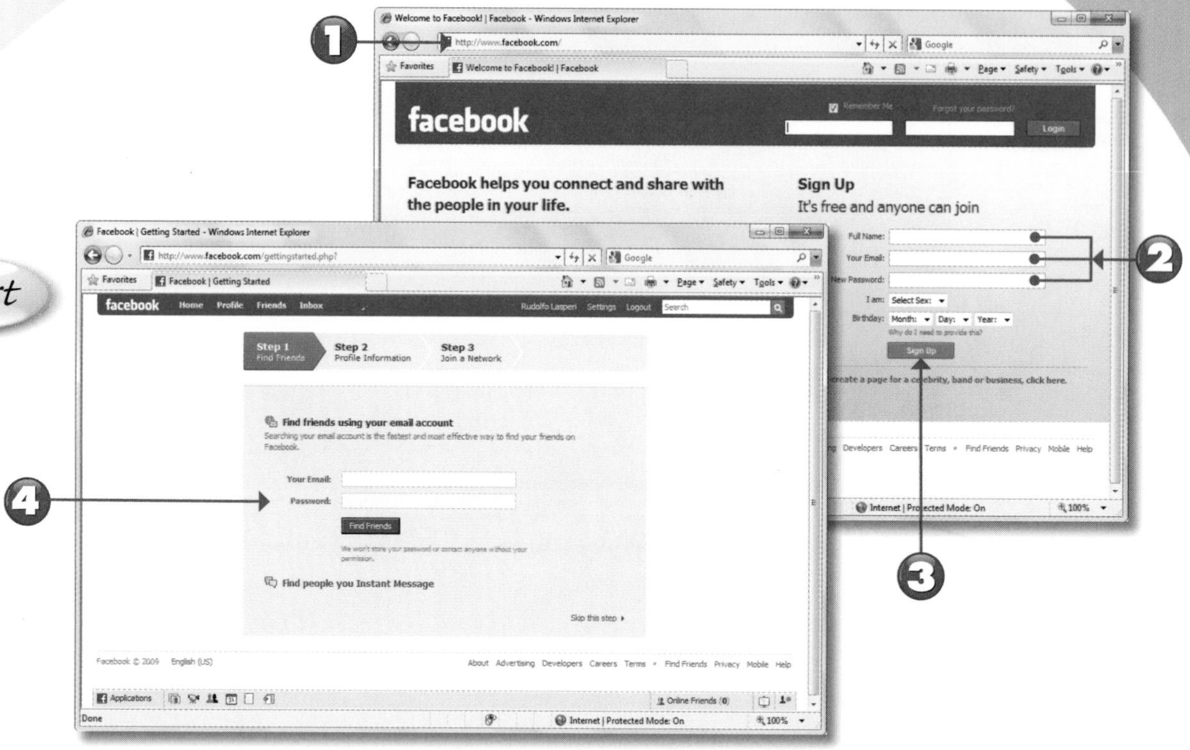

Start

1. From within Internet Explorer, go to **www.facebook.com**.

2. Enter your name, email address, desired password, and other information.

3. Click the **Sign Up** button.

4. After you've confirmed your account, complete the signup process to find friends and create your own Facebook profile.

End

NOTE

MySpace The other big social networking site in the United States is MySpace (www.myspace.com). It's typically visited by younger users, as well as musicians and other performers.

CAUTION

Social Networking Safety Make sure you and your kids don't post overly personal information or incriminating photographs on Facebook or MySpace; you could attract online stalkers. Similarly, don't broadcast your every move on your profile page—and don't automatically accept friend requests from people you don't know.

MANAGING YOUR FACEBOOK PROFILE PAGE

Click **Profile** on the toolbar to view your profile page—the hub for all your social networking activity on Facebook. From here you can view messages from your friends, as well as update your Facebook status.

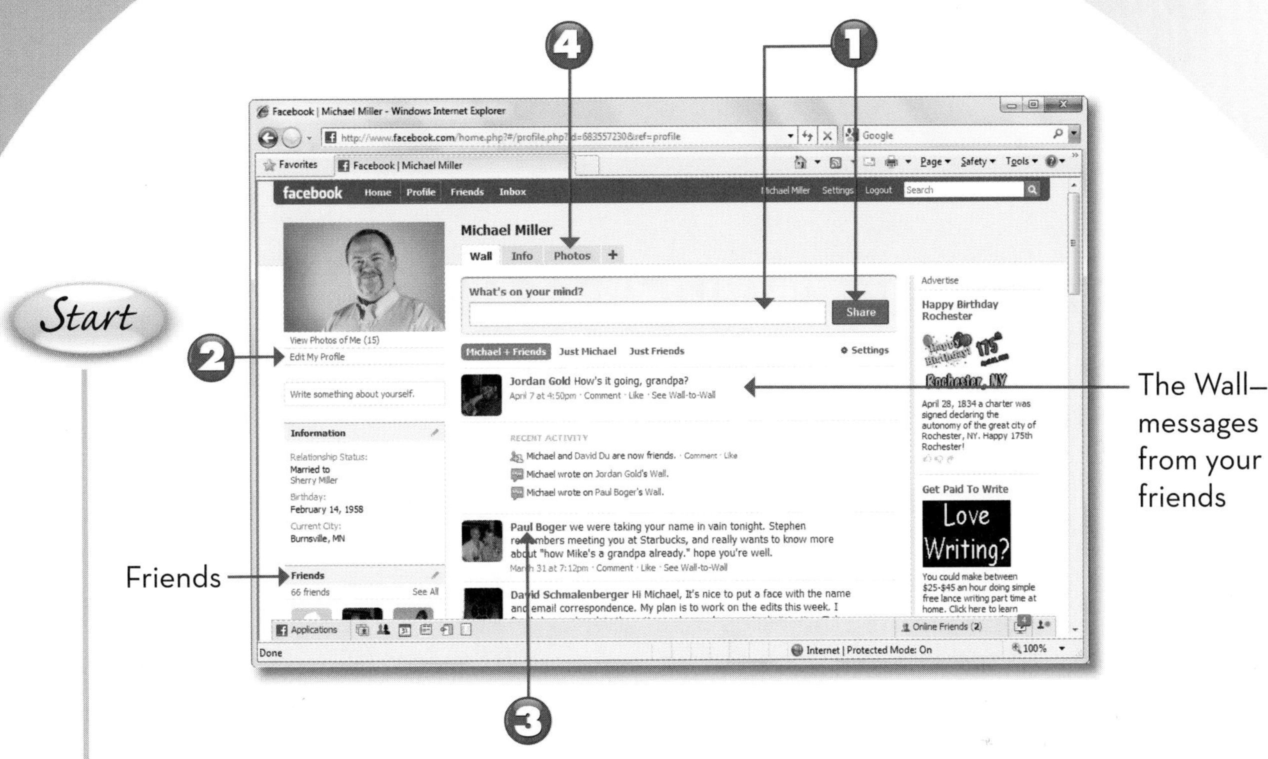

1. Enter what you're doing (or thinking) into the What's on Your Mind box; then click the **Share** button.

2. Click **Edit My Profile** to edit your Facebook profile.

3. Click a friend's name to visit his or her profile page.

4. Click the **Photos** tab to create a photo album and upload personal photos.

End

TIP

Home Page Go to the Facebook home page (click **Home** on the toolbar) to view status updates from all your friends. ■

TIP

Send Messages To send private email-like messages to other Facebook users (through the Facebook website), click **Inbox** on the toolbar and then click **Compose New Message**. ■

SETTING UP A WIRELESS HOME NETWORK

When you want to connect two or more computers, you need to create a computer *network*. A network is all about sharing; you can use your network to share files, share peripherals (such as printers), and share a broadband Internet connection.

There are two ways to connect your network—wired or wireless. A wireless network is more convenient (no wires to run), which makes it the network of choice for most home users. Wireless networks use radio frequency (RF) signals to connect one computer to another. The most popular type of wireless network uses the Wi-Fi standard and can transfer data at 11Mbps (802.11b), 54Mbps (802.11g), or 248Mbps (802.11n).

HOW A WIRELESS NETWORK WORKS

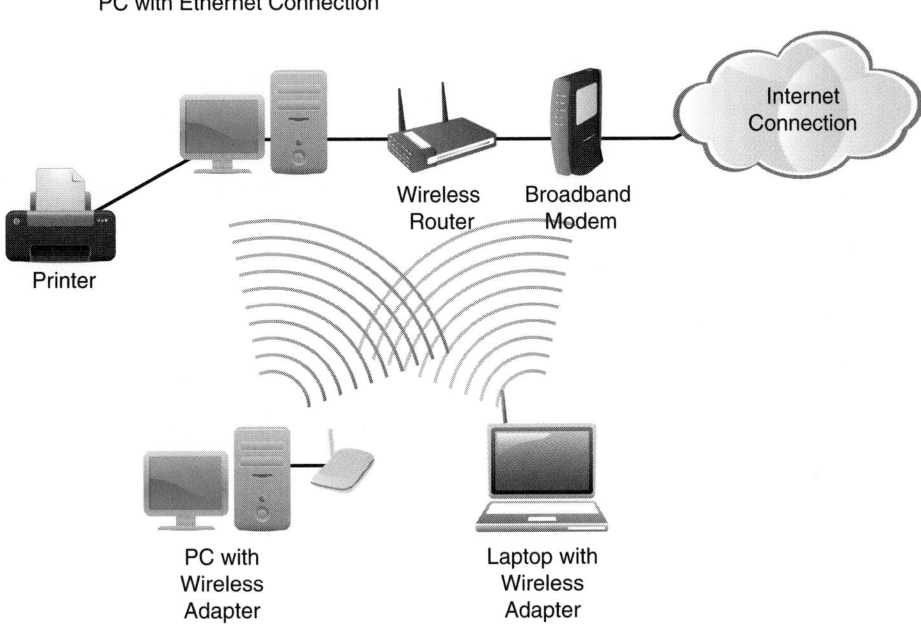

SETTING UP YOUR NETWORK'S MAIN PC

The focal point of your wireless network is the *wireless router*. The wireless PCs on your network must be connected to or contain *wireless adapters*, which function as mini-transmitters/receivers to communicate with the base station.

Start

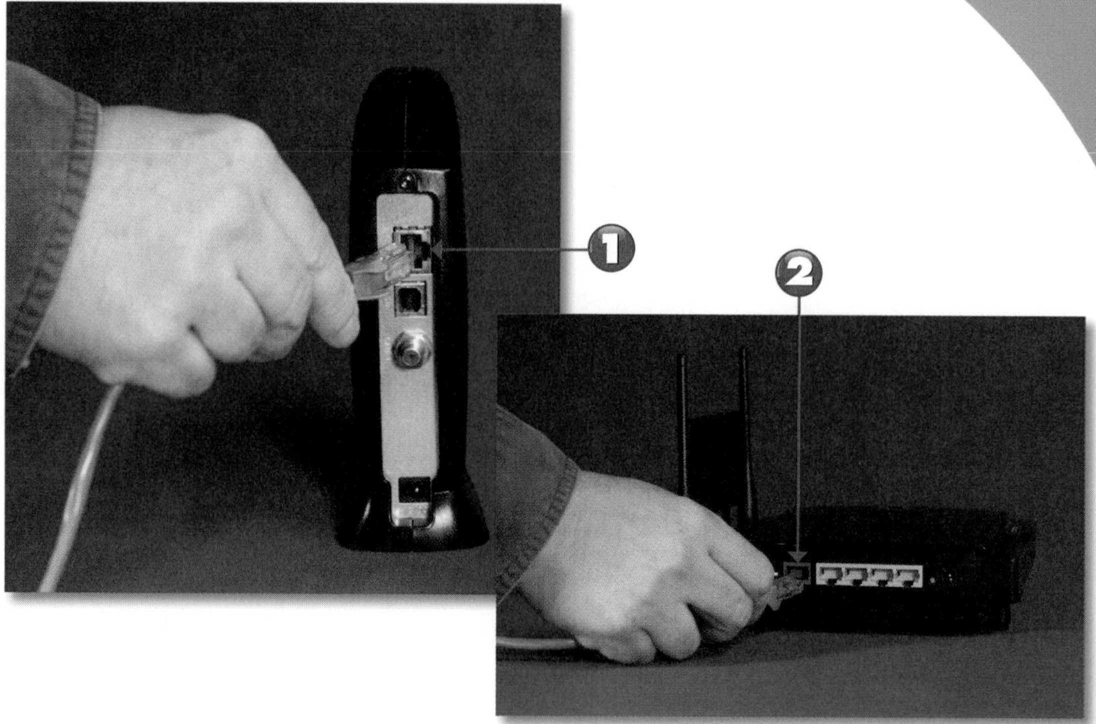

1. Connect one end of an Ethernet cable to the Ethernet port on your broadband modem.
2. Connect the other end of the Ethernet cable to one of the Ethernet ports on your wireless router—preferably the one labeled "Internet."

Continued

TIP

Internet Port Most routers have a dedicated input for your broadband modem, sometimes labeled "Internet"—although the modem can be connected to any open Ethernet input on the router. ■

TIP

Broadband Routers Some ISPs provide broadband modems that include built-in wireless routers. If you have one of these, you don't need to buy a separate router. ■

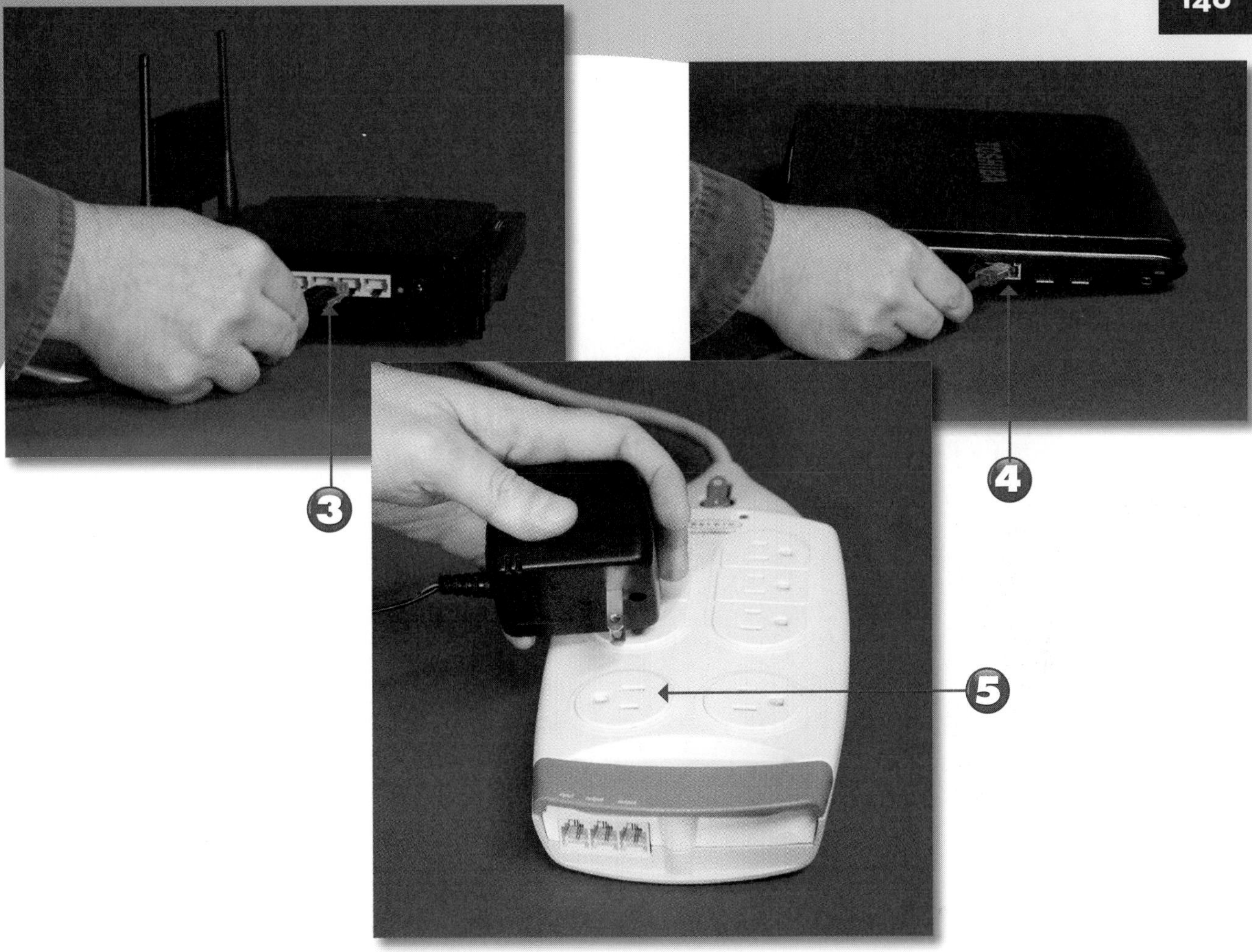

3 Connect one end of an Ethernet cable to another Ethernet port on your wireless router.

4 Connect the other end of the Ethernet cable to the Ethernet port on your main PC.

5 Connect your wireless router to a power source and, if it has a power switch, turn it on. Your computer should now be connected to the router and your network.

End

TIP

Router Configuration When you first connect a new router, you should configure the router using the software that came with the device. Follow the manufacturer's directions to configure the network and wireless security. ■

TIP

Wireless Security To keep outsiders from tapping into your wireless network, you need to enable wireless security for the network. This adds an encrypted key to your wireless connection; no other computer can access your network without this key. ■

CONNECTING ADDITIONAL PCS TO YOUR WIRELESS NETWORK

Each additional PC on your network requires its own wireless adapter. Most notebook PCs come with a wireless adapter built-in; a desktop PC might require an external adapter.

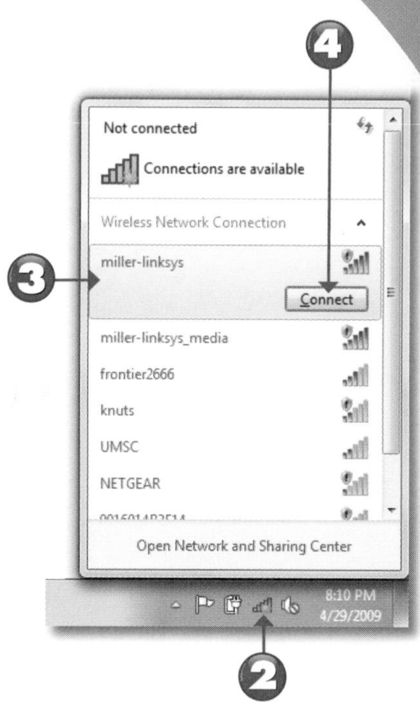

Start

1. Connect the wireless adapter to a USB port on your PC.
2. Click the **Network** icon in the notification area of the Windows taskbar.
3. Click your home network.
4. Click **Connect**.

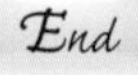

End

TIP

Wireless Adapters A wireless adapter can be a small external device that connects to the PC via USB, an expansion card that installs inside your system unit, or a PC card that inserts into a laptop PC's card slot. ■

TIP

Connecting Securely If you've enabled wireless security on your wireless router, you may be prompted to enter the passphrase or security key assigned during the router setup. ■

MANAGING YOUR NETWORK WITH THE NETWORK AND SHARING CENTER

Just because your network is up and running doesn't mean you're finished with it. In Windows 7, all network management is accomplished from the Network and Sharing Center.

Start

1. Click the **Network** button on the taskbar, and then click **Open Network and Sharing Center**.

2. To view a larger and more complete map of your entire network, click the **See Full Map** link in the Network and Sharing Center window.

End

TIP

Configuration Options The Network and Sharing Center lets you configure network discovery (to see other PCs on your network), file sharing, public folder sharing, printer sharing, password protected sharing, and media sharing (for music, video, and picture files). ■

ENABLING PUBLIC FOLDER AND PRINTER SHARING

To share files, folders, and printers between multiple PCs on your network, you first need to enable file and printer sharing in Windows.

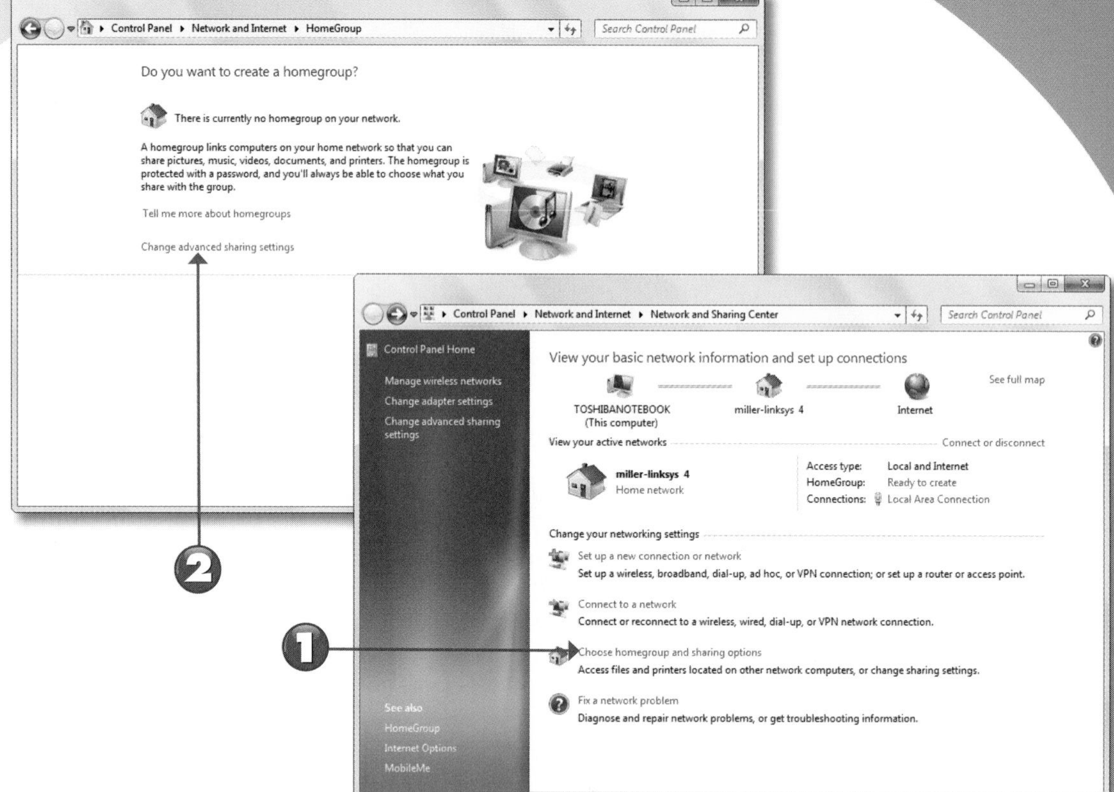

1. From the Network and Sharing Center, click **Choose Homegroup and Sharing Options**.

2. Click **Change Advanced Sharing Settings**.

CAUTION

Share Carefully Be cautious about turning on public folder sharing and file sharing. When you allow a folder to be shared, anyone accessing your network can access the contents of the folder. ■

TIP

File Sharing To share files from any folder on your PC, you need to enable file sharing from the Network and Sharing Center. You can then choose to share any individual folder. ■

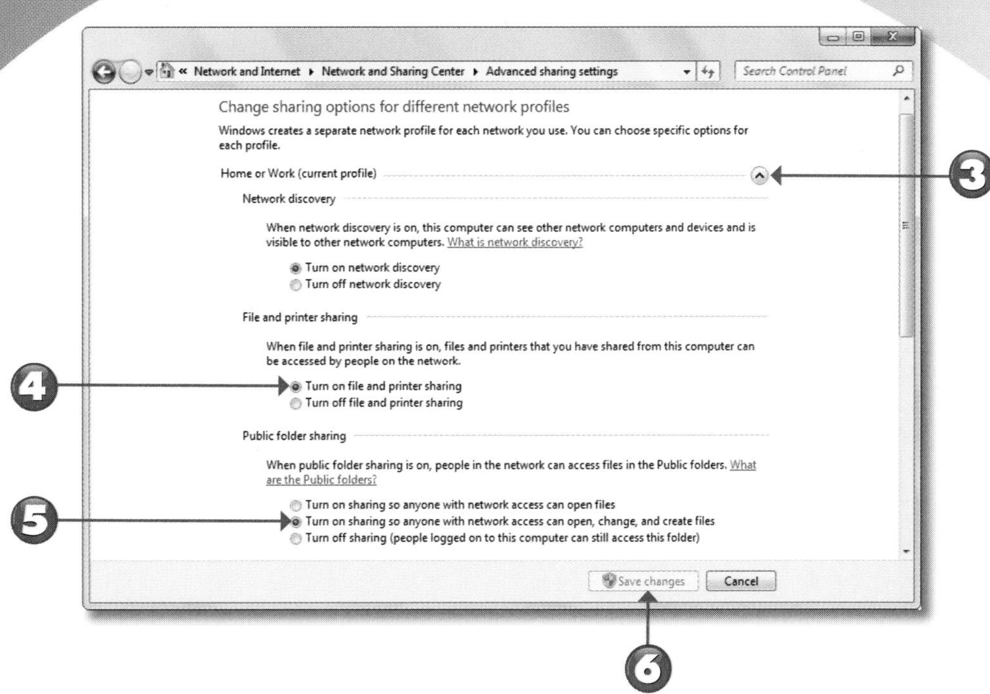

3 If it isn't already open, click the down arrow next to **Home or Work**.

4 Click **Turn on File and Printer Sharing**.

5 Click **Turn on Sharing So Anyone with Network Access Can Open, Change, and Create Files**.

6 Click **Save Changes**.

End

NOTE

Printing to a Network Printer When you use any program's print function on another network computer, all installed network computers should appear in the program's Print dialog box. ■

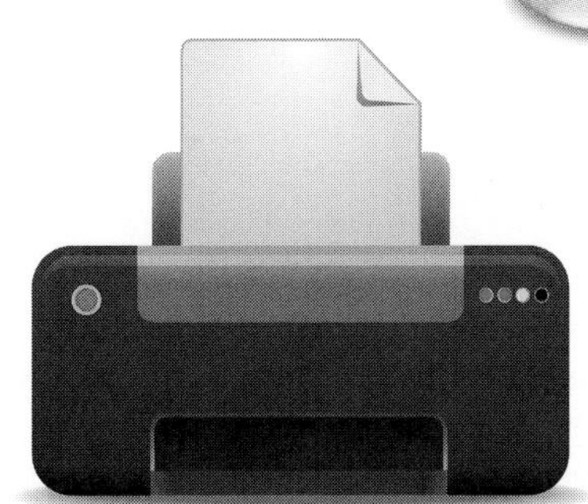

ADDING A COMPUTER TO A HOMEGROUP

Just because a computer is connected to your wireless network doesn't mean that you can share files and folders with that computer. In addition to activating public file sharing, you need to add that computer to your *HomeGroup*.

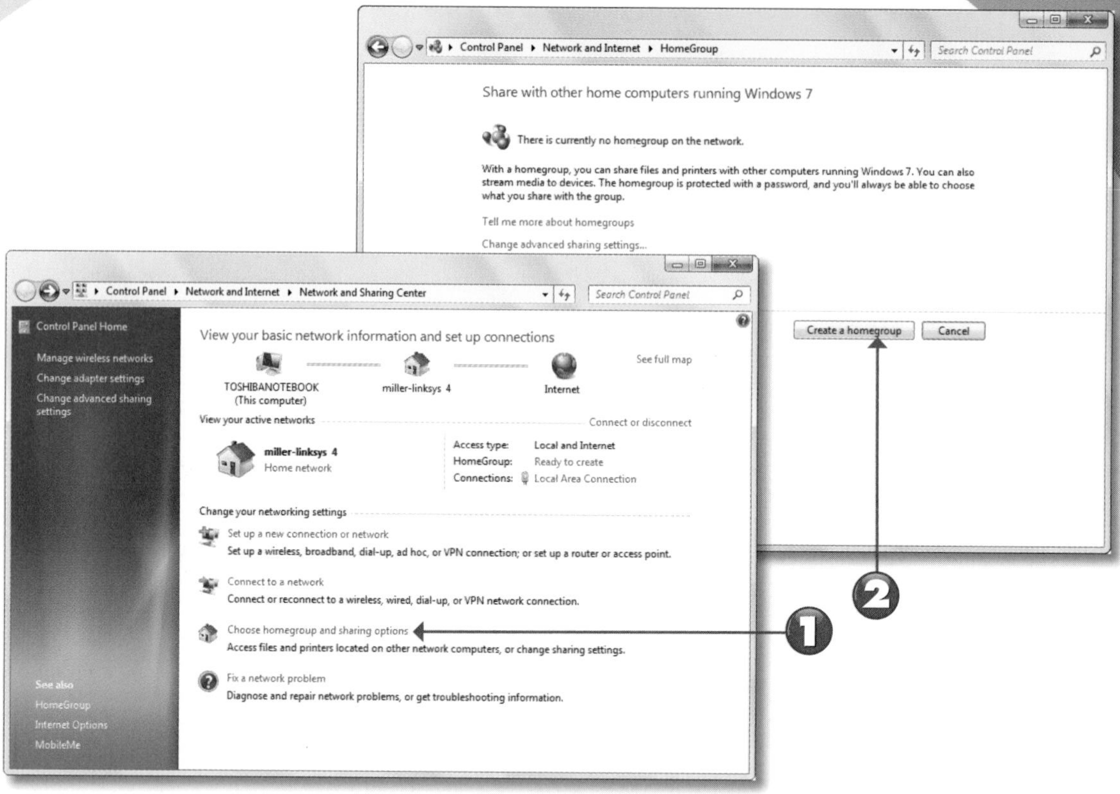

Start

1. From the Network and Sharing Center, click **Choose Homegroup and Sharing Options**.
2. Click **Create a Homegroup**.

Continued

NOTE

Windows 7 HomeGroups A HomeGroup is a new feature in Windows 7 that makes it easier to network multiple home computers. Only PCs running Windows 7 can be part of a HomeGroup, however; PCs running older versions of Windows do not have the HomeGroup feature. ■

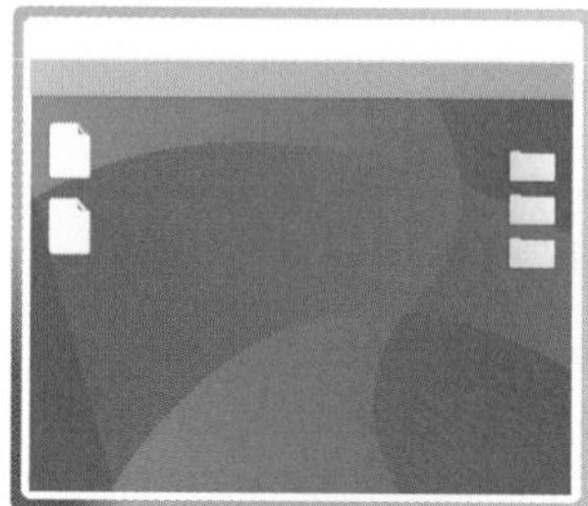

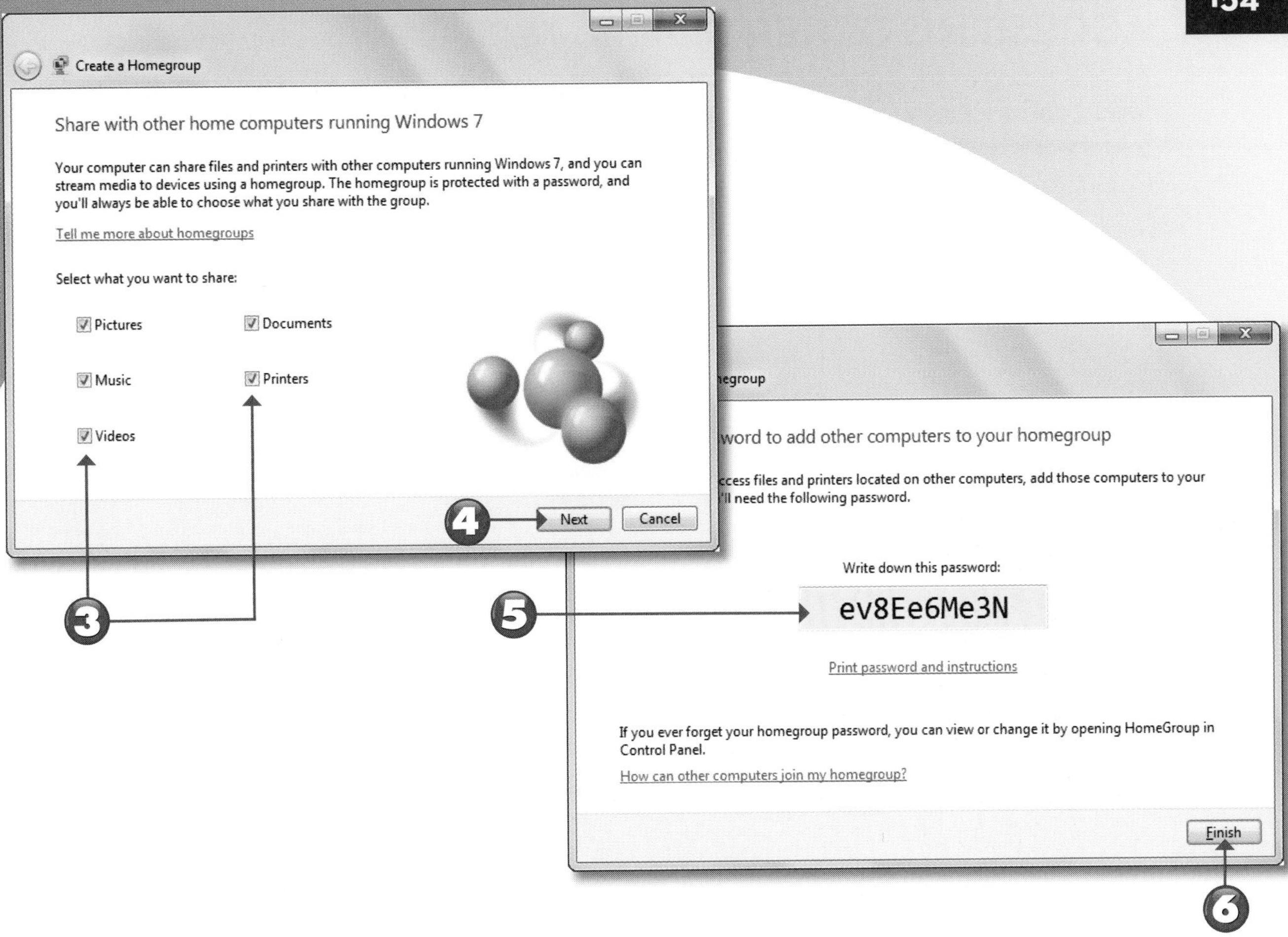

Create a Homegroup

Share with other home computers running Windows 7

Your computer can share files and printers with other computers running Windows 7, and you can stream media to devices using a homegroup. The homegroup is protected with a password, and you'll always be able to choose what you share with the group.

Tell me more about homegroups

Select what you want to share:

Pictures
Documents
Music
Printers
Videos

Next
Cancel

...egroup

...word to add other computers to your homegroup

...ccess files and printers located on other computers, add those computers to your ...'ll need the following password.

Write down this password:

ev8Ee6Me3N

Print password and instructions

If you ever forget your homegroup password, you can view or change it by opening HomeGroup in Control Panel.

How can other computers join my homegroup?

Finish

3. Check those types of items you wish to share across your network: **Pictures**, **Music**, **Videos**, **Documents**, or **Printers**.

4. Click **Next**.

5. Write down the HomeGroup password so that you can enter it when configuring other computers on the network.

6. Click **Finish**.

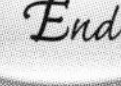

NOTE

Configuring Other PCs You'll need to configure each Windows 7 computer on your network to join your new HomeGroup. Enter the original Home-Group password as instructed. ■

ACCESSING OTHER COMPUTERS ON YOUR NETWORK

After your network is set up and properly configured, it's easy to share files between different computers on the network. In Windows 7, all your network computers and shared folders are found in the Network window; shared files should be stored in that computer's Public folder.

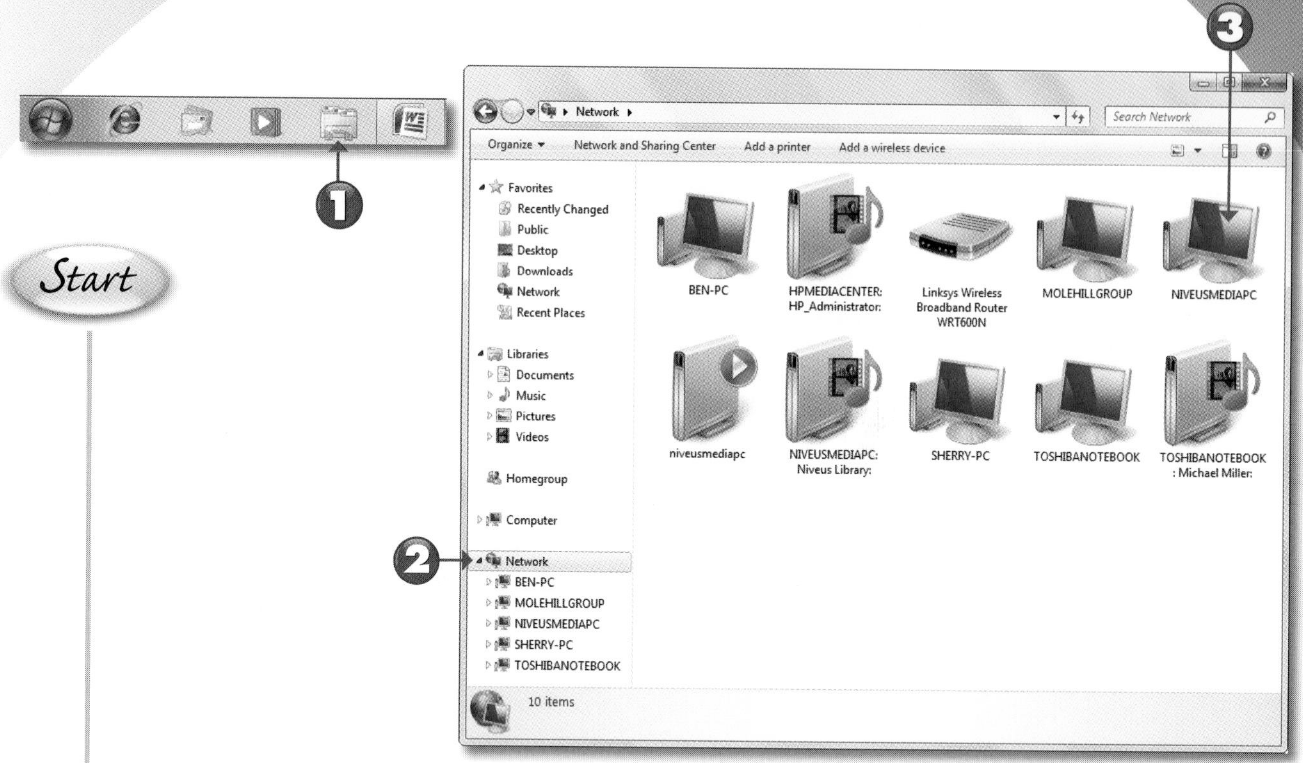

Start

1. Click the **Windows Explorer** button on the taskbar.
2. Click **Network** in the Favorites list.
3. Double-click any networked computer to view its shared folders.

Continued

TIP

Sort Network Computers To sort your network computers by name, category, workgroup, or network location, right-click in an open area of Windows Explorer and select Sort By. ■

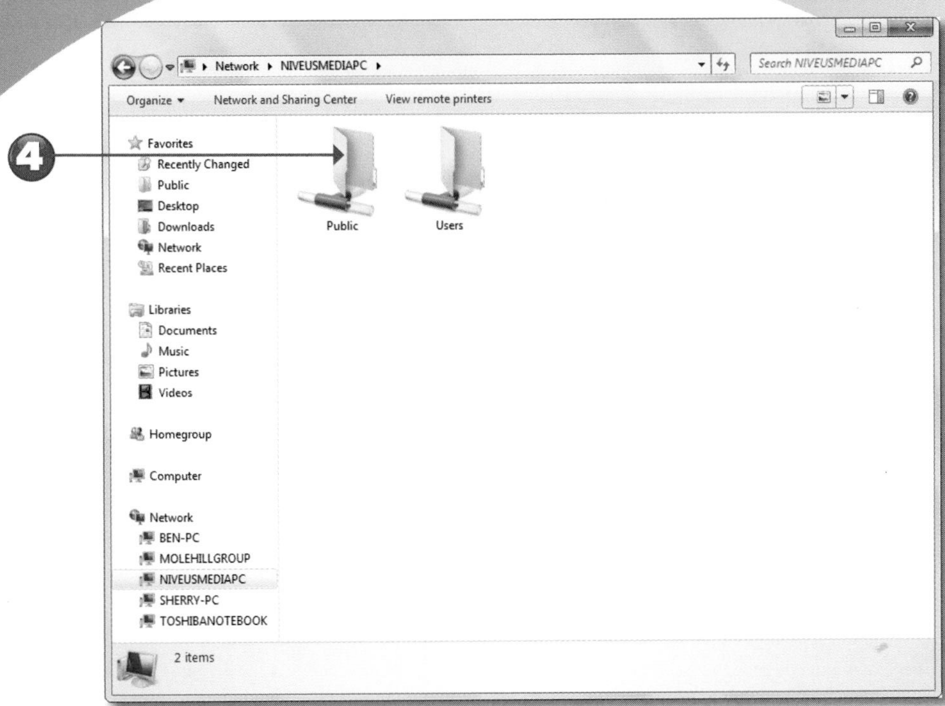

4 Double-click any shared folder to access the subfolders and files stored within.

End

TIP

Look for the Public Folder On most systems, shared files are stored in the Public folder. Look in this folder first for the files you want. ■

INSTALLING A NETWORK PRINTER

One of the advantages of a home network is that you can share a single printer between multiple PCs. To do so, you have to install that printer on each computer on the network.

1. Click **Start** and select **Devices and Printers**.
2. Click **Add a Printer**.

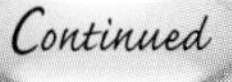

TIP

Enable Printer Sharing To share a printer, you first have to enable printer sharing on the computer to which the printer is physically connected. See the “Enabling Public Folder and Printer Sharing” task for more details. ■

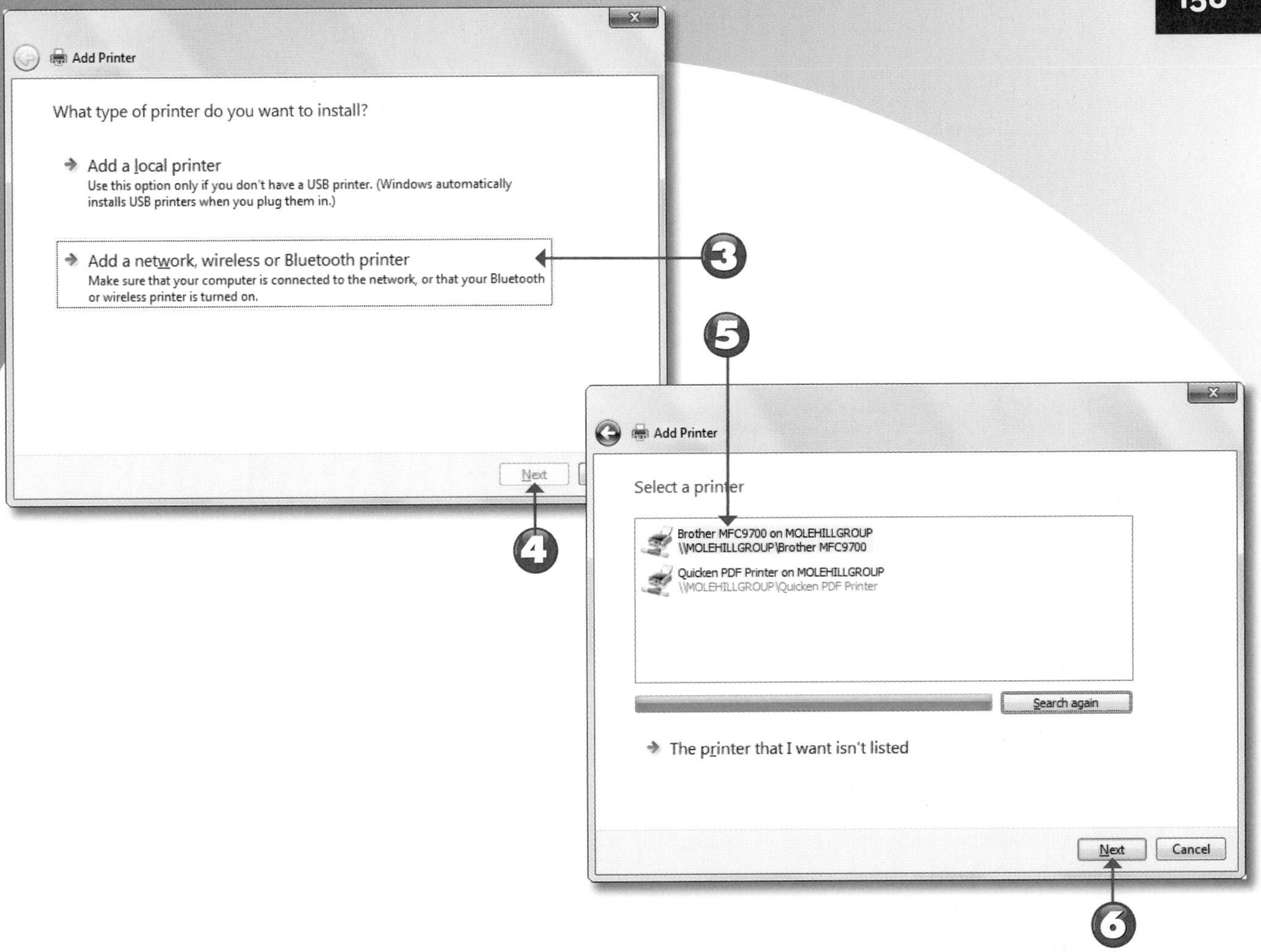

Add Printer

What type of printer do you want to install?

Add a local printer
Use this option only if you don't have a USB printer. (Windows automatically installs USB printers when you plug them in.)

Add a network, wireless or Bluetooth printer
Make sure that your computer is connected to the network, or that your Bluetooth or wireless printer is turned on.

Next

Add Printer

Select a printer

Brother MFC9700 on MOLEHILLGROUP
\\MOLEHILLGROUP\Brother MFC9700

Quicken PDF Printer on MOLEHILLGROUP
\\MOLEHILLGROUP\Quicken PDF Printer

Search again

The printer that I want isn't listed

Next Cancel

3 Click **Add a Network, Wireless or Bluetooth Printer**.

4 Click **Next**.

5 Select your printer from the list.

6 Click **Next**.

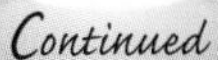

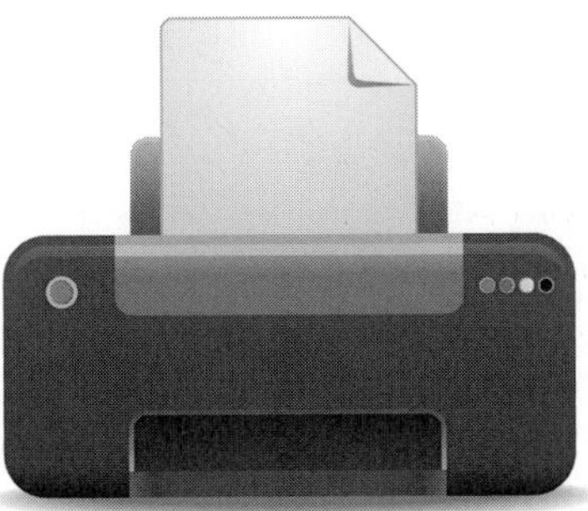

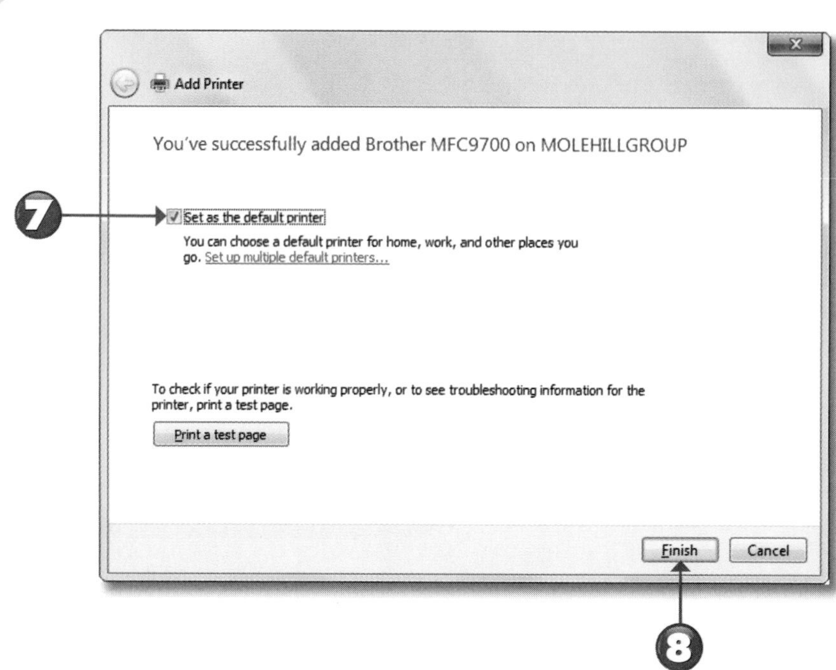

7. If you want this printer to be your default printer, click **Set as the Default Printer**.
8. Click **Finish**.

PRINTING TO A NETWORK PRINTER

Once you've installed the network printer, you can print to it from any computer connected to your home network.

Start

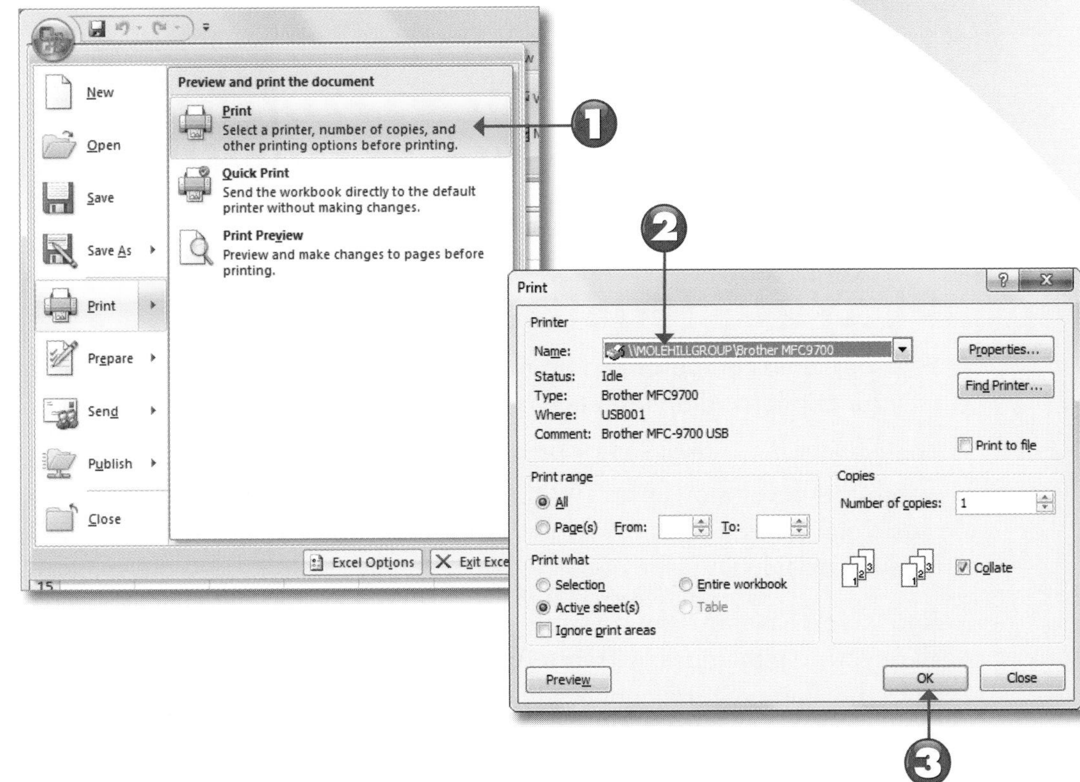

1. Click the **Print** button or menu item within an application.

2. Select the network printer from the list of printers.

3. Click **OK**.

End

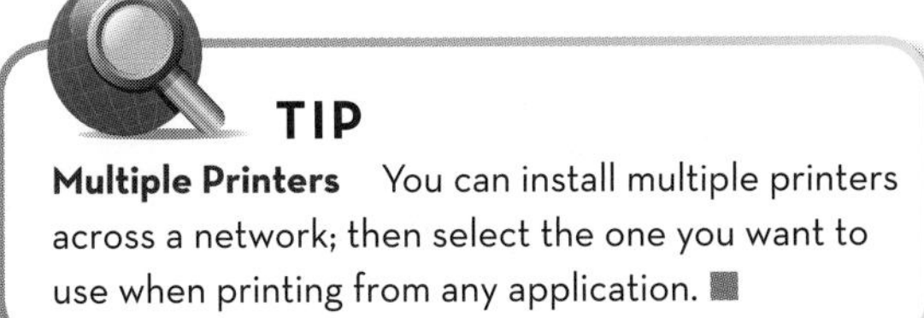

TIP

Multiple Printers You can install multiple printers across a network; then select the one you want to use when printing from any application.

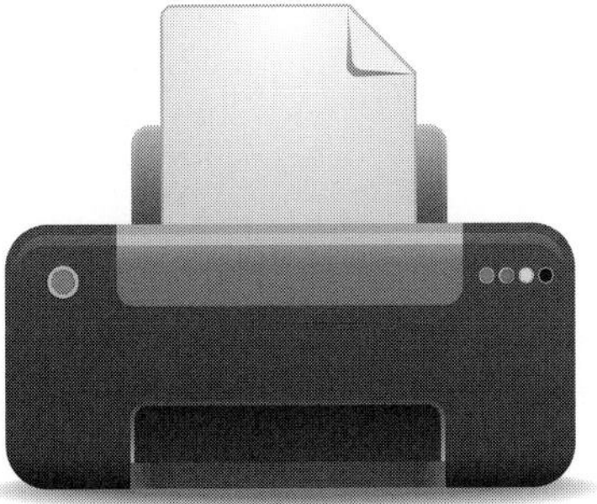

PLAYING MUSIC AND MOVIES

Your personal computer can do more than just compute. It can also serve as a fully functional audio/video playback center!

That's right, you can use your PC to listen to your favorite audio CDs and to watch the latest movies on DVD. The Windows Media Player software is a great music player program, and Windows Media Center is a terrific full-screen interface for playing DVD movies. They're both easy to use.

And, if you have an iPod portable music player, you can use your PC to manage all of your digital music with the iTunes software. It's easy to download music from the iTunes Store, connect your iPod to your computer, and then transfer your music to your iPod. You can even use the iTunes software to burn your own music CDs!

WINDOWS MEDIA PLAYER

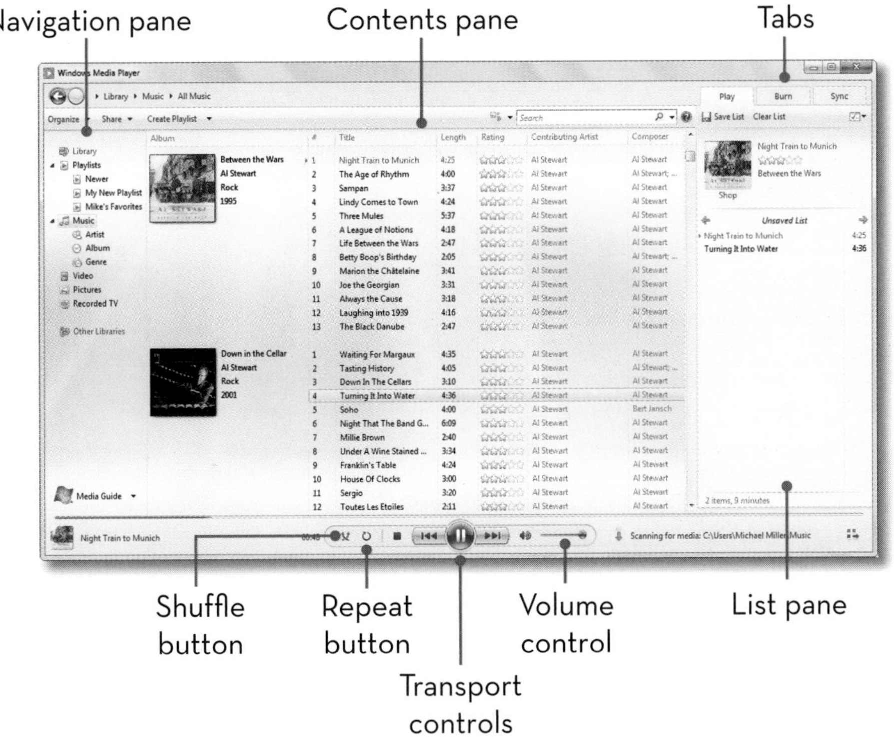

PLAYING A CD WITH WINDOWS MEDIA PLAYER

You play audio CDs using your PC's CD-ROM drive and Windows Media Player (WMP). You can also use WMP to play songs you've downloaded to your PC from the Internet and (if your PC has a DVD drive) to play DVD movies.

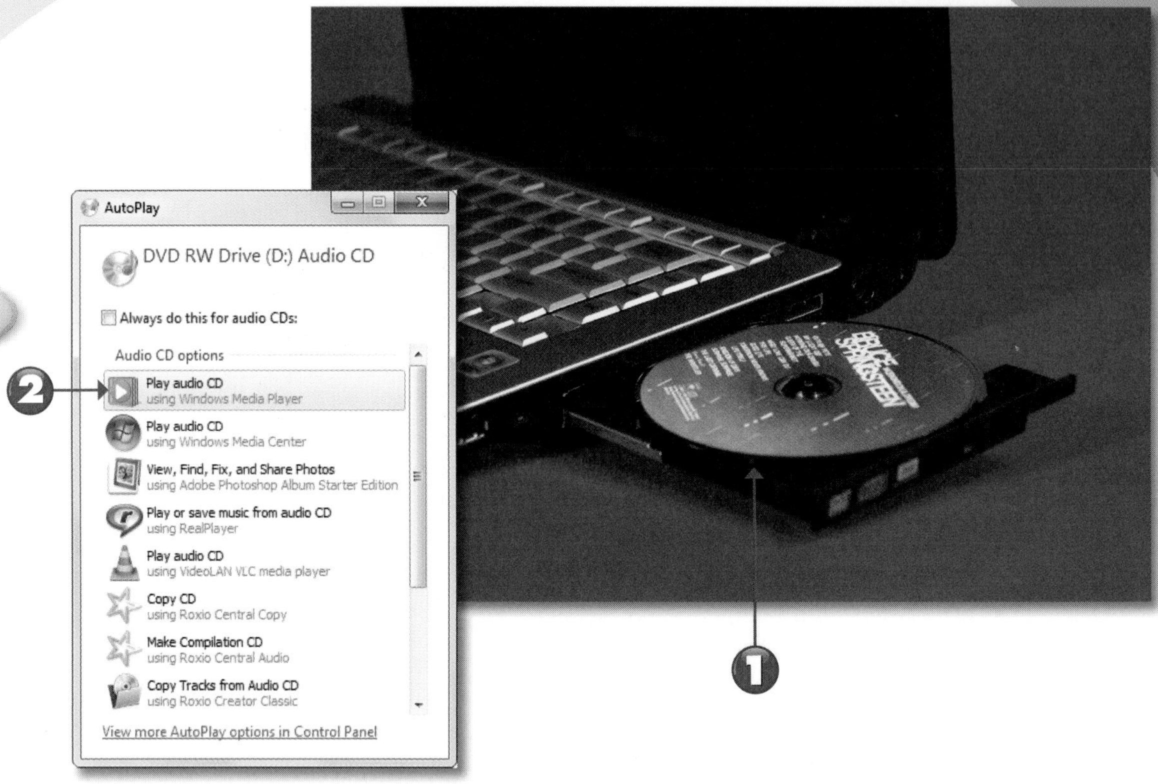

Start

1. Insert a CD into your PC's CD-ROM drive.
2. Windows will ask what you want to do; click **Play Audio CD Using Windows Media Player**.

Continued

TIP

Online Music Stores You can buy downloadable music at many online music stores, including Amazon MP3 Downloads (www.amazonmp3.com), Rhapsody (www.rhapsody.com), and Napster (www.napster.com). Some stores charge by the song, whereas others charge a monthly fee with unlimited downloads. ■

TIP

Download the Latest Version This book covers Windows Media Player version 12, included with Windows 7. To download the latest version of Windows Media Player, go to www.microsoft.com/windows/windowsmedia/. ■

3. The CD should start playing automatically the Now Playing window. To pause the CD, click the **Pause** button; then click **Play** to resume playback.
4. To skip to the next track, click the **Next** button.
5. To replay the last track, click the **Previous** button.
6. To stop playback completely, click the **Stop** button.

End

TIP

Switch to Larger Window To switch from the Now Playing window to the larger Windows Media Player window, click the **Switch to Library** button in the lower-right corner. ■

NOTE

Launching Windows Media Player If WMP doesn't start automatically when you load a CD into your PC's CD-ROM drive, you can launch it manually from the Windows Start menu. ■

RIPPING A CD TO YOUR HARD DISK

Windows Media Player lets you copy music from your CDs to your PC's hard drive. You can then listen to these digital audio files on your computer, transfer the files to a portable music player, or burn your own custom mix CDs. This process of copying files from a CD to your hard disk is called *ripping*.

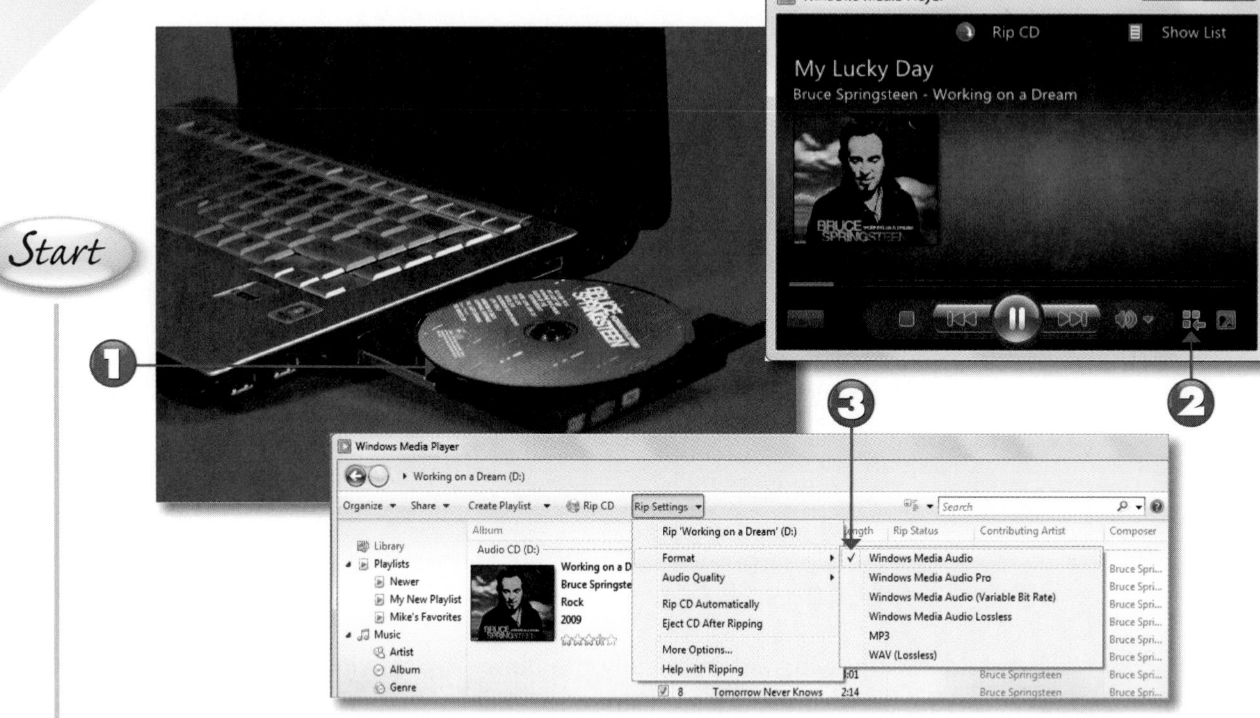

1. Insert the CD you want to rip into your PC's CD-ROM drive.
2. Switch to the larger WMP window by clicking **Switch to Library**.
3. Make sure the CD is selected in the navigation pane. Then set the recording format by clicking **Rip Settings**, **Format**, and then selecting either **Windows Media Audio** or **MP3**.

Continued

TIP

File Format For near-universal compatibility with other music player software and hardware, rip to the MP3 format. For slightly better audio quality with smaller file sizes, rip to the Windows Media Audio (WMA) format. ■

TIP

Bit Rate The higher the bit rate you select for audio quality, the better the sound. For WMA format files, 128Kbps is the default; 192Kbps is a good setting for MP3 files. ■

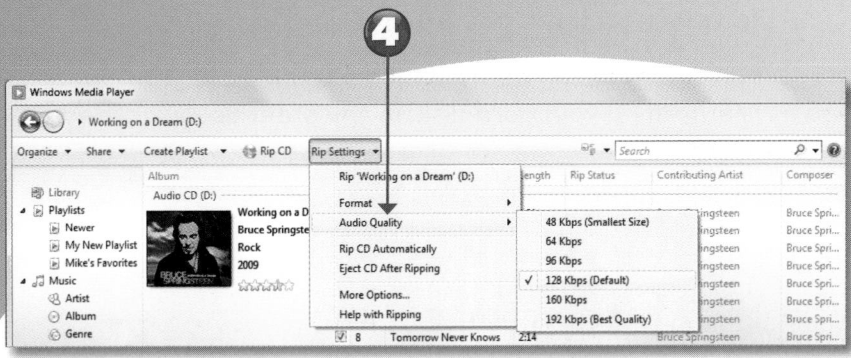

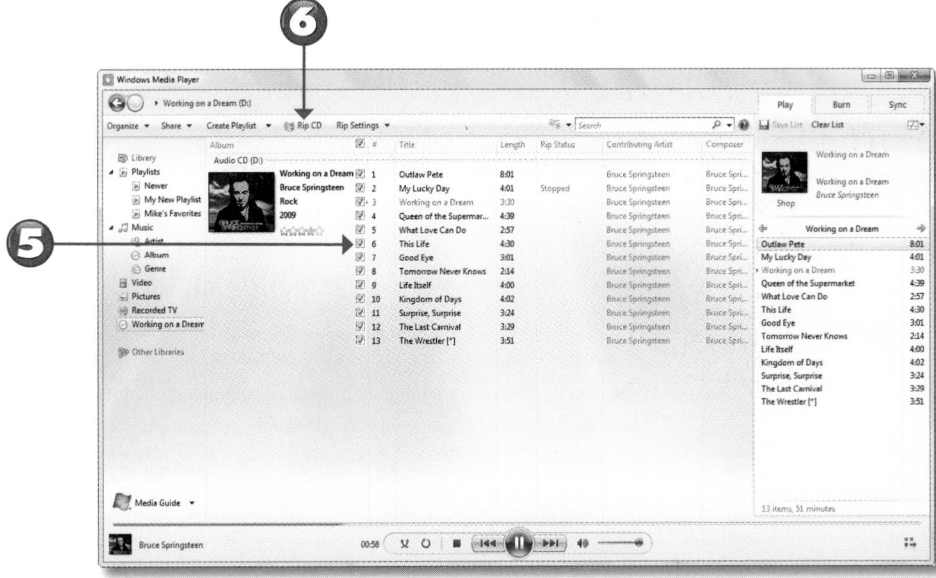

4 Select the recording quality by clicking **Rip Settings**, **Audio Quality** and then selecting the desired bit rate.

5 Put a check mark by the tracks you want to copy.

6 When you've selected which tracks to rip, click **Rip CD**.

End

TIP

Connect to the Internet Before you rip a CD, you should make sure your PC is connected to the Internet. This lets WMP download track names and CD cover art for the songs you're ripping. ■

TIP

Quick Rip After you've first set the rip settings for your recordings, you can rip directly from the Now Playing window by clicking **Rip CD**. ■

CREATING A PLAYLIST

Files in your Windows Media Player library can be combined into *playlists*. You can create playlists from the files you have stored on your hard disk, in any order you want—just like listening to a radio station's playlist.

1. Click the **Play** tab.
2. Click **Create Playlist**.
3. Enter a title for your new playlist.

Continued

NOTE

Understanding Playlists When you create a playlist, you don't actually make copies of the individual songs. Instead, the playlist points to the songs where they continue to reside on your hard disk. When you play a playlist, Windows Media Player accesses each song file in turn on the hard drive. ■

TIP

Auto Playlists Windows Media Player also includes a feature called auto playlists, which are automatically generated based on criteria you specify. To create a new auto playlist, click the down arrow next to the **Create Playlist** button and select **Create Auto Playlist**. ■

4 Use the Navigation pane to navigate to albums or songs you want to add to the playlist.

5 Click and drag songs or complete albums from the Contents pane to the playlist's name in the Navigation pane.

End

TIP

Editing Playlists To edit a playlist, click the **Playlists** item in the Navigation pane; this displays all your playlists in the Content pane. Right-click the playlist you want to edit and select **Edit in List Pane** from the pop-up menu. ■

PLAYING A PLAYLIST

After you've created a playlist, you can play back any or all songs in that playlist—in any order.

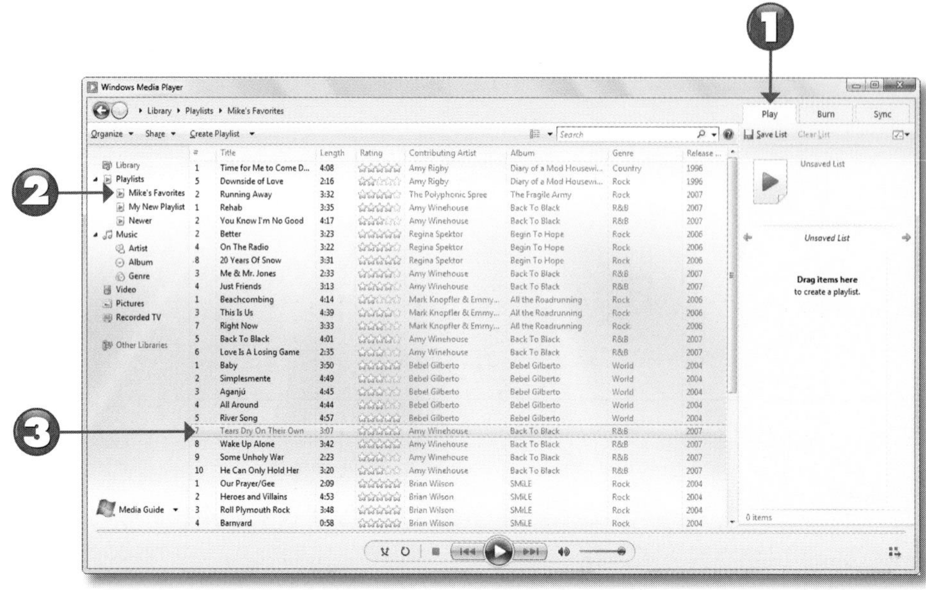

Start

1. Click the **Play** tab.

2. In the Navigation pane, double-click the playlist name to play the entire playlist.

3. Double-click an individual song to play that song.

End

TIP

Random Play To play the songs in a playlist in random order, click the **Shuffle** button next to the transport controls. ■

BURNING A MUSIC CD

If you have a recordable CD drive (called a *CD burner*) in your PC, you can make your own audio mix CDs. You can take any combination of songs on your hard disk; "burn" them onto a blank CD; and then play that CD in your home, car, or portable CD player.

Start

1. Insert a blank CD-R disc into your computer's CD-R/RW drive.
2. From within WMP, select the **Burn** tab.
3. Click and drag the songs you want to burn from the Contents pane to the List pane.
4. Click the **Start Burn** button.

End

TIP

Use CD-R Discs To play your new CD in a regular (non-PC) CD player, record in the CD-R format and use a blank CD-R disc specifically labeled for audio use. (CD-RW discs will not play in most home CD players.) ■

TIP

Burn a Playlist A quicker way to select songs to burn is to create a playlist first and then drag that playlist onto the List tab. ■

CONNECTING AN IPOD TO YOUR PC

To use an iPod or iPhone with your PC, you first have to install Apple's iTunes software from Apple's website (www.apple.com/itunes/download/). When you connect your iPod to your PC, your computer automatically launches the iTunes software and copies any new songs and playlists you've added since the last time you connected.

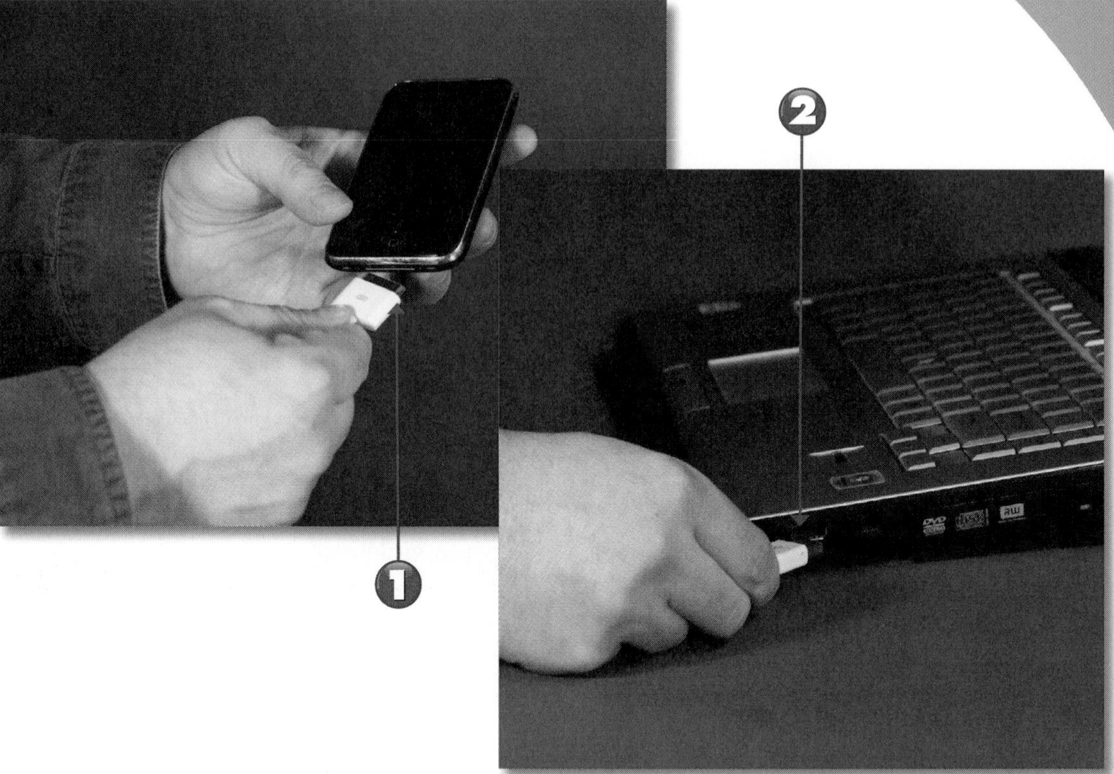

Start

1. Connect one end of the USB cable to your iPod.

2. Connect the other end of the USB cable to a USB port on your PC.

Continued

TIP

Manually Syncing You can also manually select which tunes are copied to your iPod. Just access the Music tab on the connection screen and opt to sync only selected tracks and playlists—those items checked in your iTunes library. ■

TIP

Autofill and the iPod Shuffle If you have an iPod shuffle, iTunes offers an Autofill option. This lets the software automatically choose songs to sync to your iPod—which is useful if you have more songs on your hard disk than you have storage capacity on your shuffle. ■

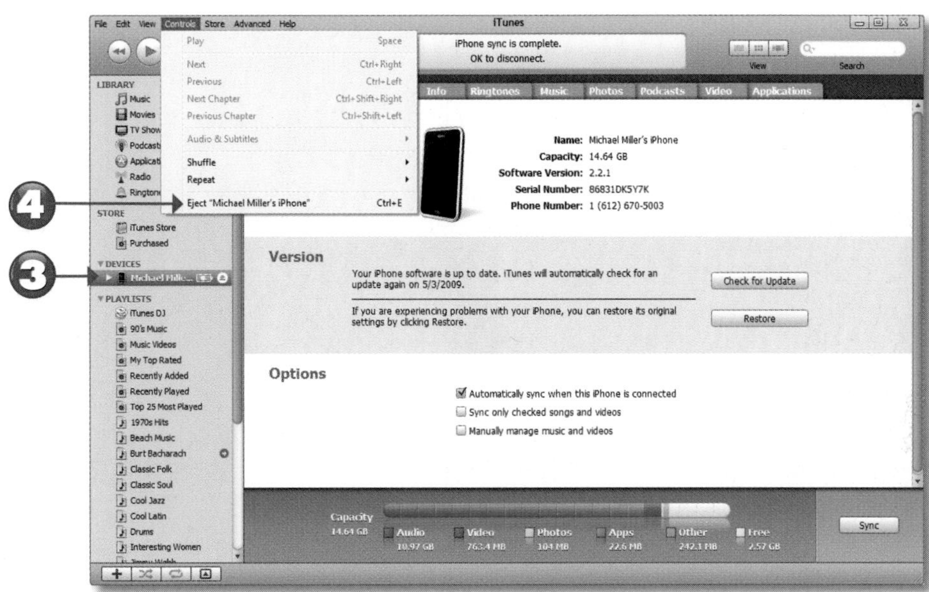

3. The iTunes software will now launch on your PC and automatically sync its songs and playlists to your iPod.

4. When the sync is complete, iTunes will display a message that it's safe to disconnect your iPod. Click the **Controls** menu and select **Eject**; then disconnect your iPod.

End

TIP

Syncing Videos If you have an iPod with video capability, you can configure which movies and videos are synced from the Video tab. From here you can choose to sync all videos, selected videos, or a selected number of unwatched videos. ■

CREATING IPOD PLAYLISTS

You can store thousands of songs on your iPod, which makes it a little difficult to find the music you want. One way to organize your music is to create playlists of your favorite songs.

Start

1. From within iTunes, pull down the **File** menu and select **New Playlist**.
2. Enter a name for the new untitled playlist.

Continued

1. Click **Music** in the Library pane.

2. Click and drag songs from the Contents pane onto the name of the new playlist in the Playlists pane.

End

TIP

Smart Playlists You can also create smart playlists (File, New Smart Playlist) that let you automatically select songs by artist, album, genre, and so on. ■

TIP

Playing a Playlist To play an iTunes playlist on your computer, just double-click the playlist name in the Playlists pane. ■

DOWNLOADING MUSIC FROM THE ITUNES STORE

If you want the latest music for your iPod, it's easy to purchase and download your favorite tunes from Apple's iTunes Store. All you need is an Internet connection and your credit card, and you're ready to shop!

Start

1. In the iTunes software, click **iTunes Store** in the Navigation pane.

2. The iTunes software now connects to the Internet and displays the iTunes Store's main page. To view music for purchase, click **Music** in the iTunes Store box.

3. To search for a specific song or artist, enter your query into the **Search iTunes Store** box and press **Enter**.

Continued

TIP

Browsing by Genre You can also browse the iTunes store by type of music—Alternative, Country, Classical, and so on. Just scroll down to the **Genres** section and click the genre you're interested in. ■

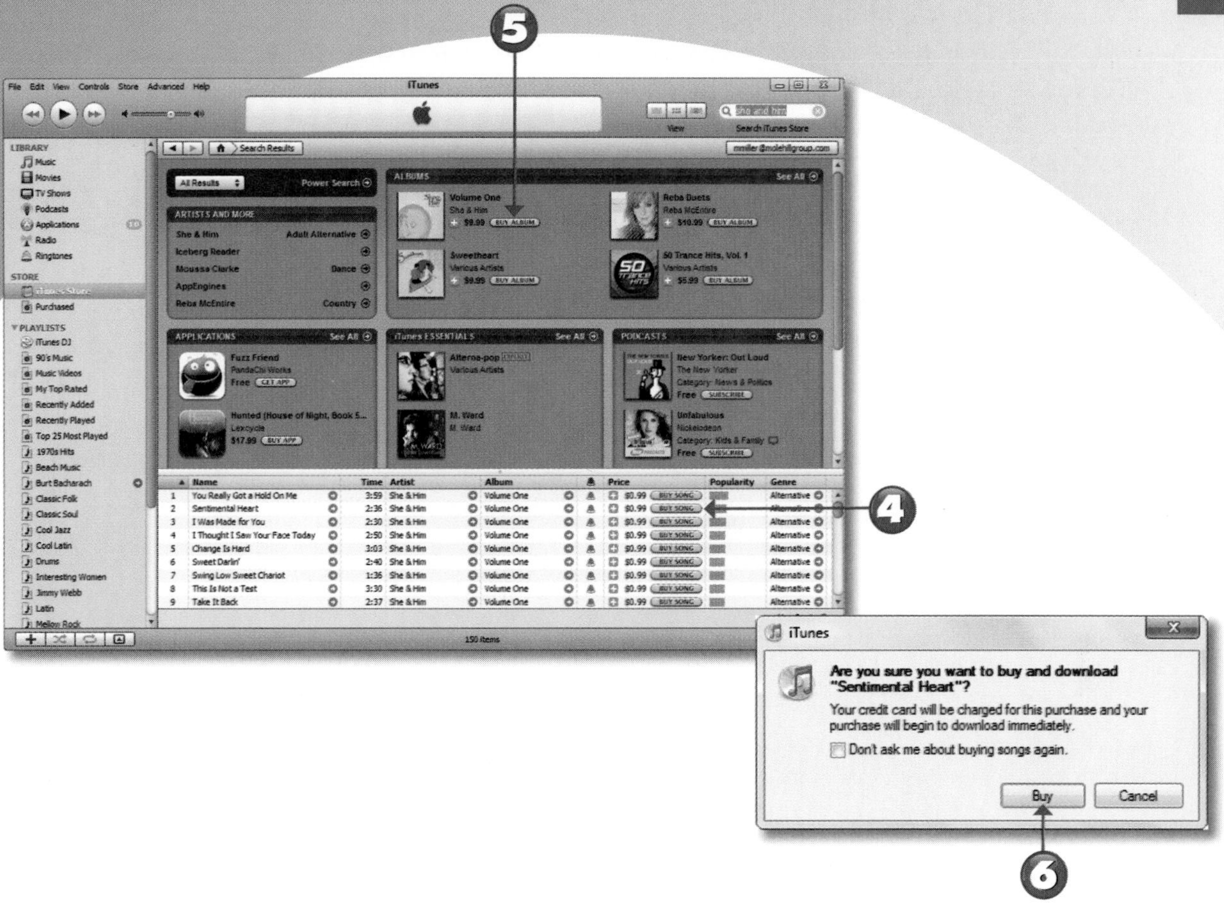

4 The iTunes Store now displays all the music that matches your search. To purchase an individual track, click the **Buy Song** button.

5 To purchase an entire album, click the **Buy Album** button.

6 When prompted if you're sure you want to purchase this item, click the **Buy** button.

End

TIP

Credit Card Required Before you purchase items from the iTunes Store, you need to enter your credit card information. Pull down the **Store** menu, select **View My Account**, and then click the **Edit Payment Information** button and enter the necessary data.

PLAYING A DVD

If your PC has a DVD drive, you can use your PC to watch prerecorded DVD movies via Windows Media Center, a full-screen interface for playing digital media.

Start

1. Insert the DVD into your PC's DVD drive.

2. When prompted, click **Play DVD Movie Using Windows Media Center**.

Continued

3. The movie should start playing automatically. To pause the movie, click the **Pause** button; then click **Play** to resume playback.

4. Click the **Next** button to go to the next chapter on the DVD, or click the **Previous** button to go to the previous chapter.

5. Click the **Fast Forward** or **Rewind** buttons to speed forward and backward through the movie.

End

TIP

DVDs in Windows Media Player You can also play DVD movies in Windows Media Player and other media player programs.

CREATING A HOME MOVIE DVD

If you have a digital video camcorder, you can transfer your home movies to your PC and burn them to DVDs for playback on any DVD player. All you need is the Windows DVD Maker program—included free with Windows 7.

Start

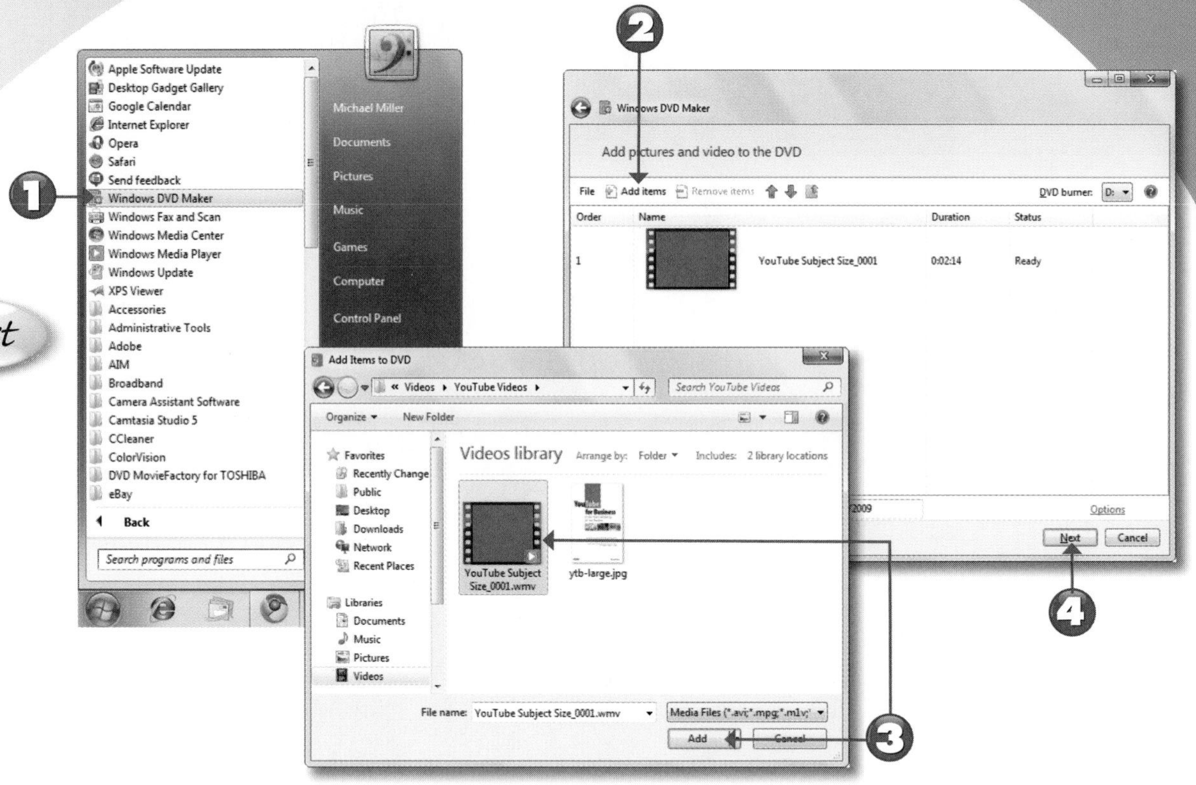

1. Click the Windows **Start** button, click **All Programs**, and then click **Windows DVD Maker**.
2. Click the **Add Items** button.
3. Select the movies you want to include on your DVD, and then click **Add**.
4. Click **Next**.

TIP

Change the Order To change the order of movie clips on your DVD, select a clip and click the up or down arrows in the program's toolbar. ■

TIP

Add a Slideshow To include a slideshow of still photos on your DVD, select JPG-format files from the Add Items to DVD dialog box. You can then click the new Slideshow item to change the order of photos in the slideshow. ■

5 Click the desired menu style.

6 Insert a blank DVD into your computer's DVD drive.

7 Click the **Burn** button.

End

TIP

Change DVD Title To change the title of the DVD, click the **Menu Text** button and enter the new text into the DVD Title field. ■

TIP

Slideshow Music To add music to a photo slideshow, click the **Slide Show** button and then click the **Add Music** button. You can also change the length of time each photo displays, as well as the transition effect between photos. ■

WORKING WITH DIGITAL PHOTOS

More and more people are trading in their old film cameras for new digital cameras—and connecting those cameras to their PCs. You can use your digital camera and PC together to transfer all the photos you take to your hard disk and then edit your pictures to make them look even better.

Windows 7 not only stores your digital photos, it also helps you edit and display them. It's all possible due to the Windows Photo Gallery program, which can be downloaded for free as part of Microsoft's Windows Live Essentials suite at download.live.com.

Want to view your photos in a slideshow? Windows Photo Gallery will do it. Want to organize your photos—by date taken, rating, or keyword? Windows Photo Gallery will do that, too. How about printing your photos or ordering prints online? Also a job for Windows Photo Gallery. Or maybe you need to crop a poorly composed photo, remove a stubborn case of red eye, or adjust brightness or color? These are also things you can do with Windows Photo Gallery; all you need to know is how.

WINDOWS PHOTO GALLERY

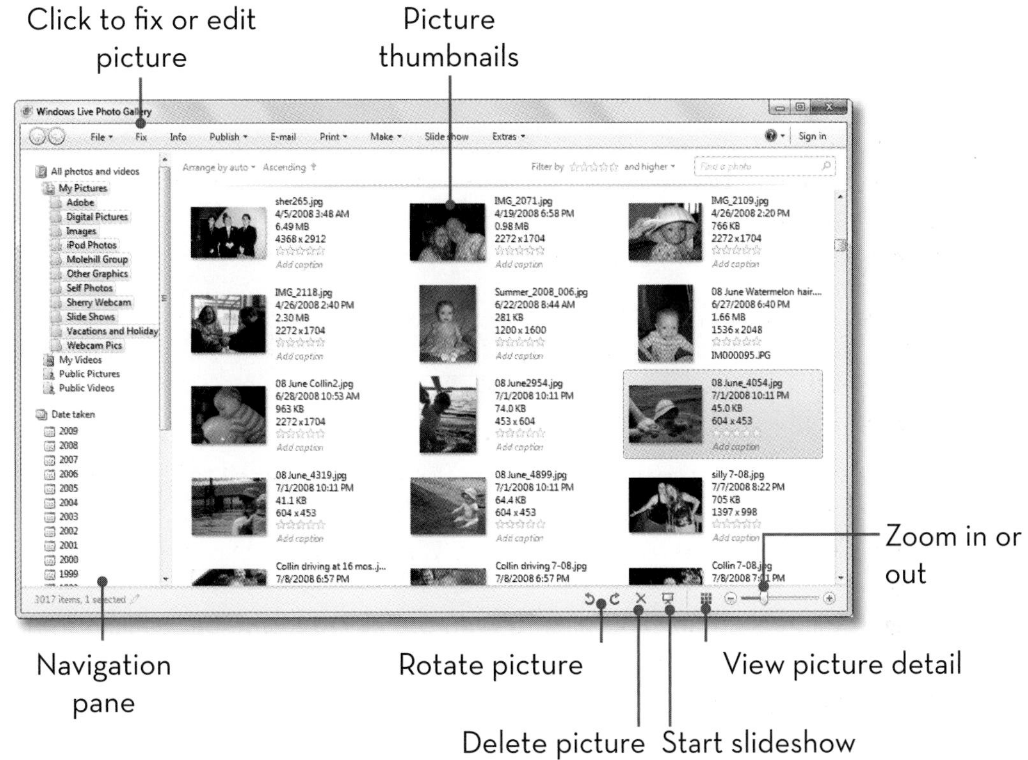

TRANSFERRING PICTURES FROM A DIGITAL CAMERA

Connecting a digital camera to your PC is extremely easy; all you have to do is connect a USB cable between your camera and your computer. With this type of setup, Windows will recognize your camera as soon as you plug it in and will automatically download the camera's contents.

Start

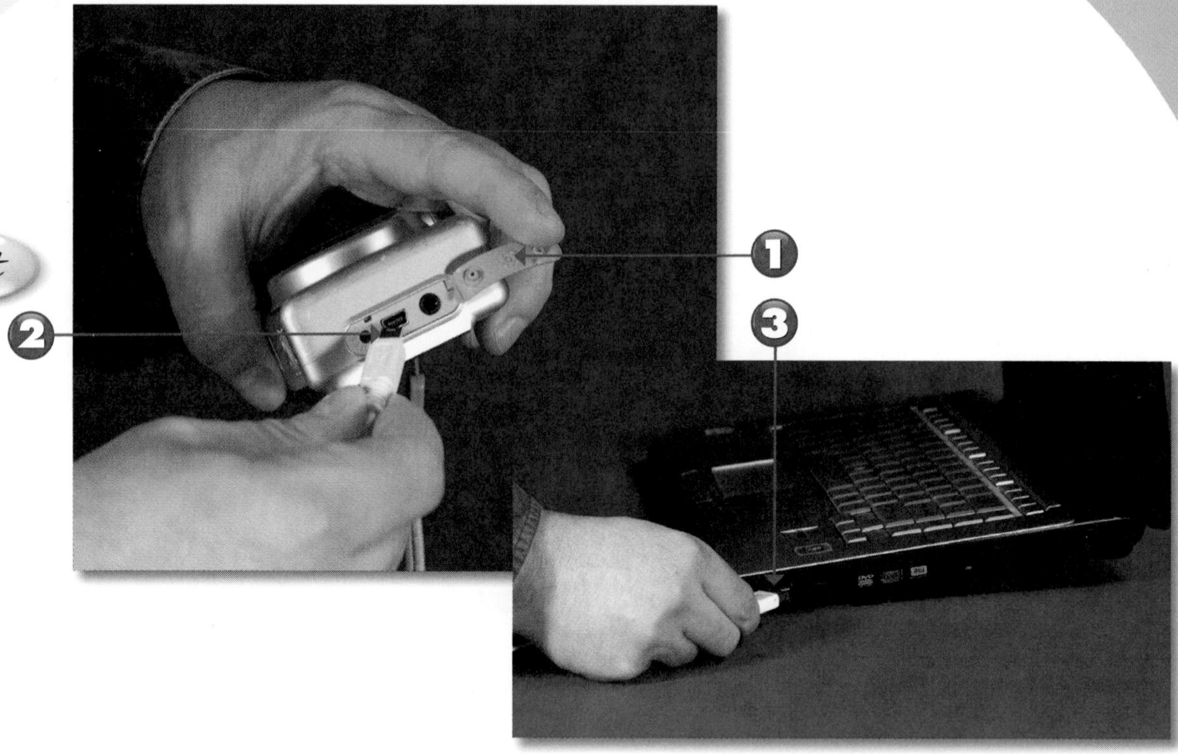

1. On your digital camera, locate and open the cover to the data transfer port.
2. Connect one end of the USB cable to the data transfer port on your digital camera.
3. Connect the other end of the USB cable to a USB port on your PC.

Continued

NOTE

Other Photo-Downloading Software Connecting your camera to your PC may launch other image transfer programs that may be installed on your computer. This may be a program that came with your digital camera, or perhaps a photo-editing program. You can use any of these programs to transfer pictures from your camera. ■

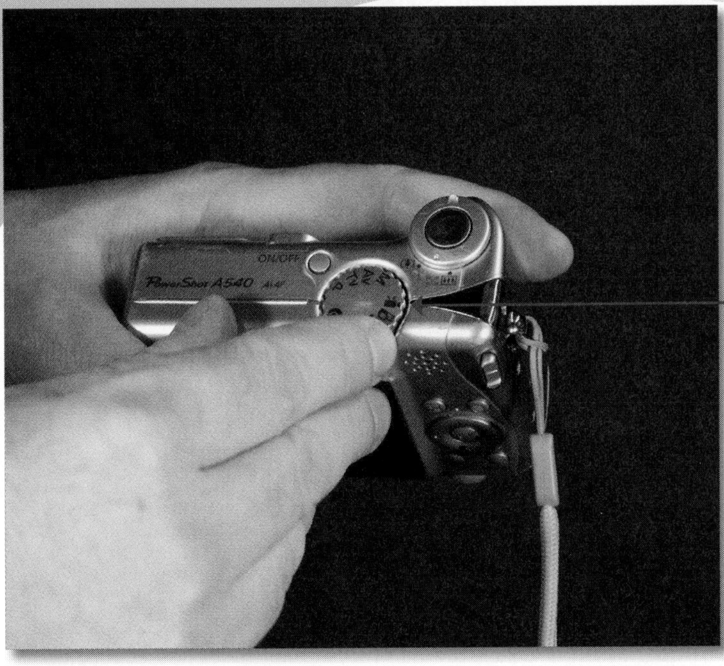

4. Turn on your digital camera and (if necessary) move the selection dial or switch to the transfer pictures setting.

5. When the AutoPlay window appears, click **Import Pictures and Videos Using Windows**.

End

CAUTION

Turn Off Your Camera Don't forget to turn off your camera when you're done transferring pictures. If you leave your camera on, you'll drain your batteries! ■

NOTE

Destination Folder By default, Windows downloads your digital photos to the Pictures folder, in a subfolder labeled by date. ■

TRANSFERRING PICTURES FROM A MEMORY CARD

If your PC includes a memory card reader, it may be easier to copy your digital photos via your camera's memory card. When you insert a memory card, your PC recognizes the card as if it were another disk on your system. You can then copy files from the memory card to your computer's hard disk.

Start

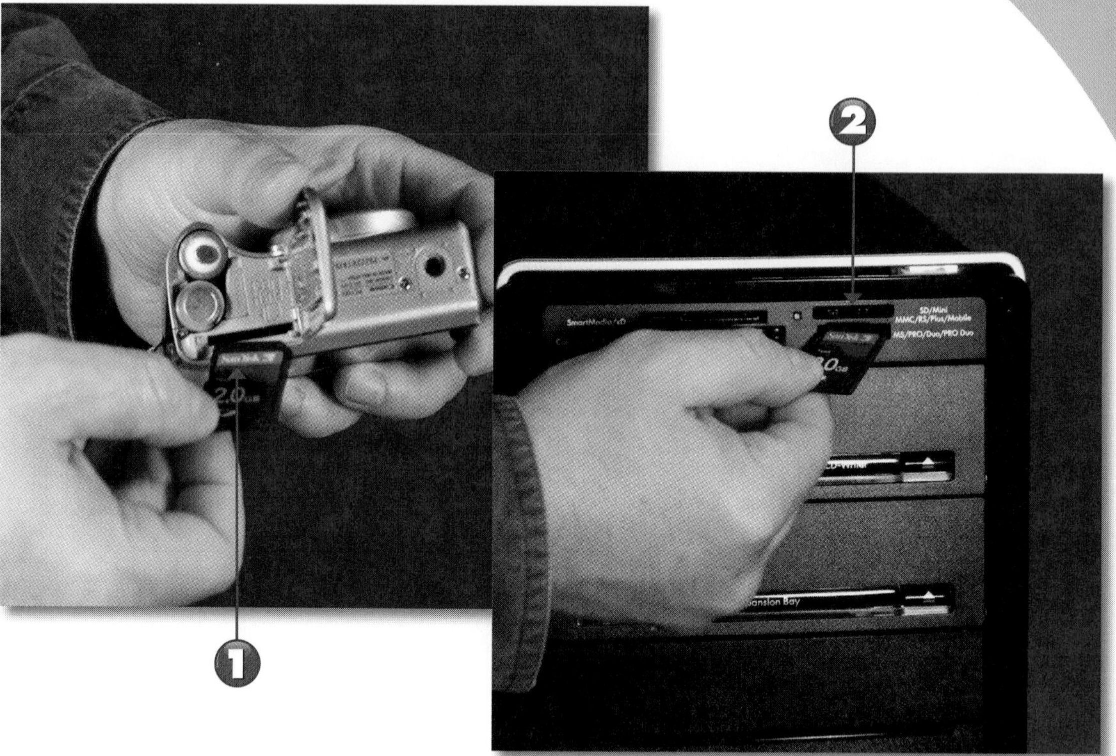

1. Turn off your digital camera and remove the flash memory card.
2. Insert the memory card from your digital camera into the memory card slot on your PC.

Continued

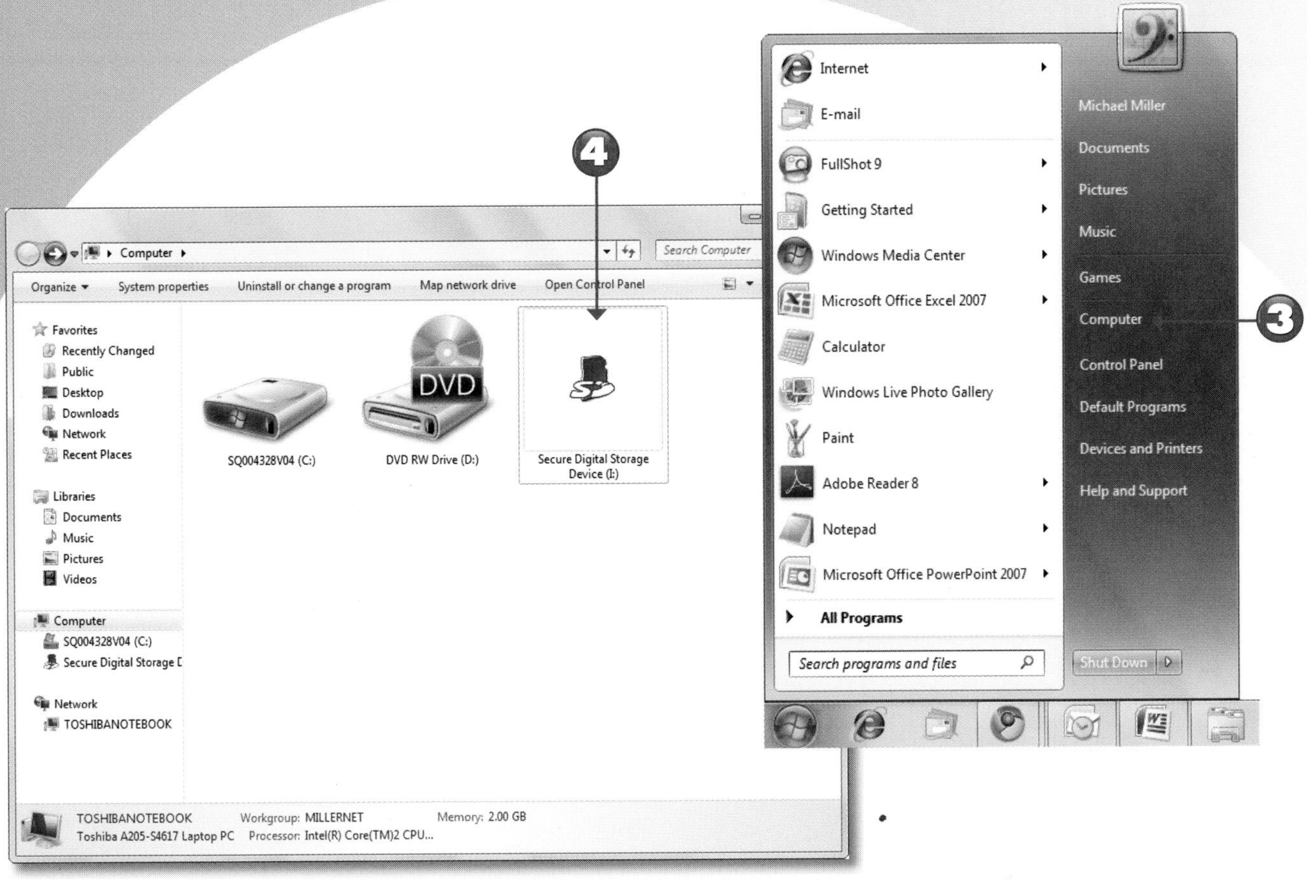

3 Click **Start** and select **Computer**.

4 Double-click the icon for the memory card reader drive.

Continued

NOTE

Copying Automatically In some instances, Windows may recognize that your memory card contains digital photos and start to download those photos automatically—no manual interaction necessary. ■

TIP

Printing from a Memory Card Many color photo printers include memory card slots that let you print directly from your camera's memory card, bypassing your computer entirely. ■

5 Double-click the main folder, typically labeled **DCIM**.

6 Double-click the appropriate subfolder within the DCIM folder to see your photos.

Continued

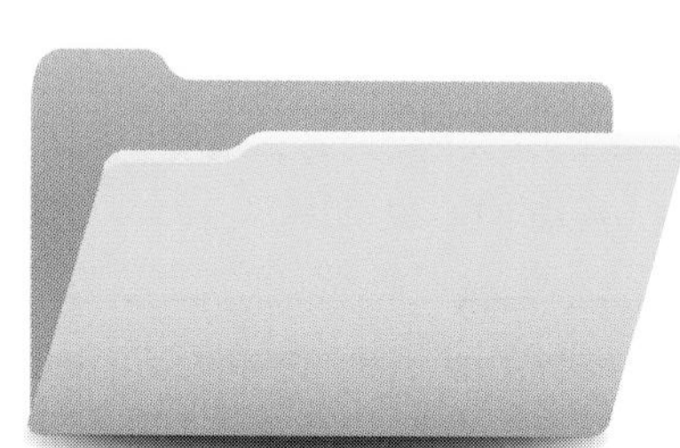

TIP

Different Folder Names Some cameras might use a name other than DCIM for the main folder. ■

7. Hold down the **Ctrl** key and click each photo you want to transfer.

8. Click the **Organize** button and click **Copy**.

9. Navigate to your computer's hard disk and open the desired destination folder for the photos.

10. Click the **Organize** button and click **Paste**.

End

TIP

Buy a Bigger Card To store more pictures (and higher-resolution pictures) on your camera, invest in a higher-capacity flash memory card. The bigger the card, the more photos you can store before transferring to your computer. ■

SCANNING A PICTURE

If your photos are of the old-fashioned print variety, you can still turn them into digital files using a flatbed scanner. You can use Windows 7 to import photos from your scanner and store them in digital format.

Start

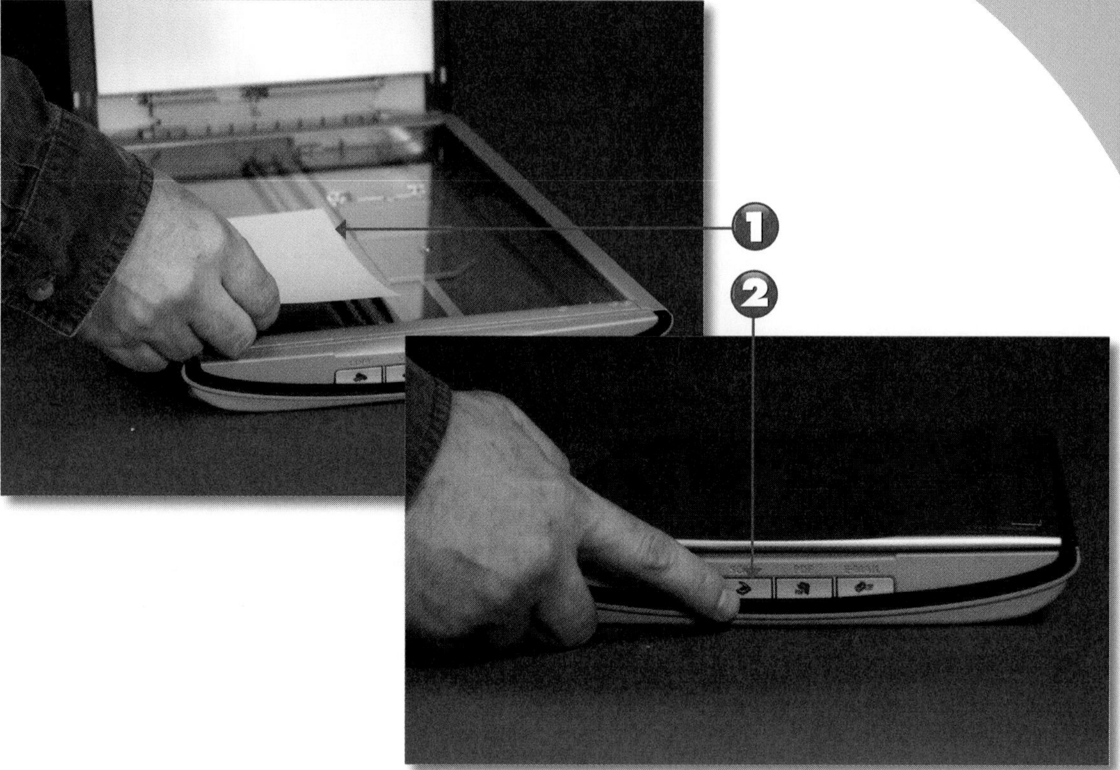

1. Open the scanner lid and place a photo on the scanner glass, face down.
2. Click the **Scan** button on your scanner.

Continued

TIP

Scan Automatically Some scanners launch Windows Live Photo Gallery or some other application automatically when you press the Scan button on the scanner. ■

NOTE

Other Programs for Scanning You can also use other programs to import photos from your scanner. For example, Adobe Photoshop CS and Photoshop Elements both include an "acquire from scanner" feature. ■

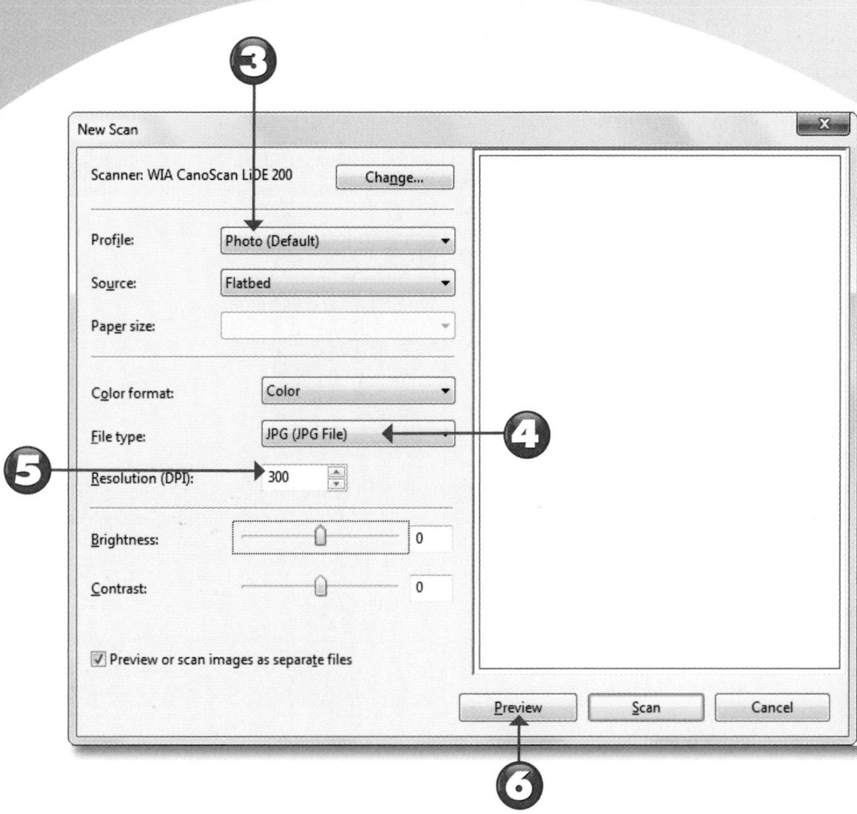

3. Click the **Profile** button and select **Photo**.

4. Click the **File Type** button and select **JPG (JPG File)**.

5. Click the **Resolution** list and select the desired scan resolution, in dots per inch (DPI).

6. Click the **Preview** button to preview how your scan will look.

Continued

TIP

Higher Resolution By default, Windows scans your item at 300dpi (dots per inch). If you plan to print the photo at a large size (8-inch x 10-inch or larger), select a higher resolution. ■

TIP

Scanning Documents If you're scanning a black-and-white text document, click the **Profile** button and select **Documents**. ■

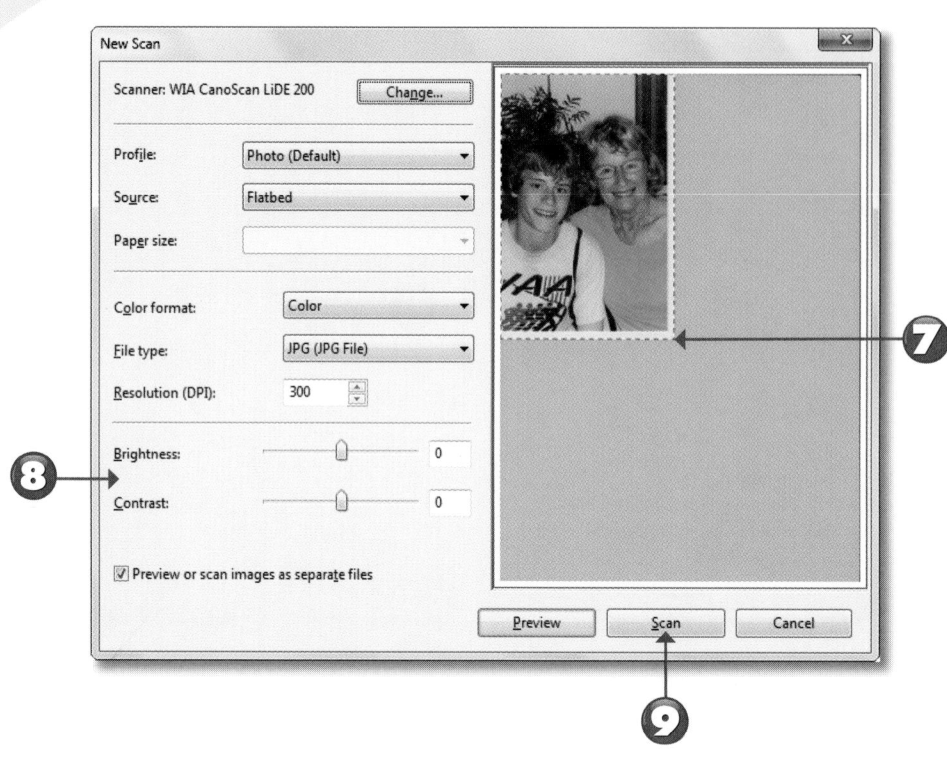

7. Click and drag the border boxes to crop the scan to the size of the picture.

8. If the scan doesn't look right, adjust the **Brightness** and **Contrast** controls as necessary.

9. When you're satisfied with how your scan will look, click the **Scan** button.

Continued

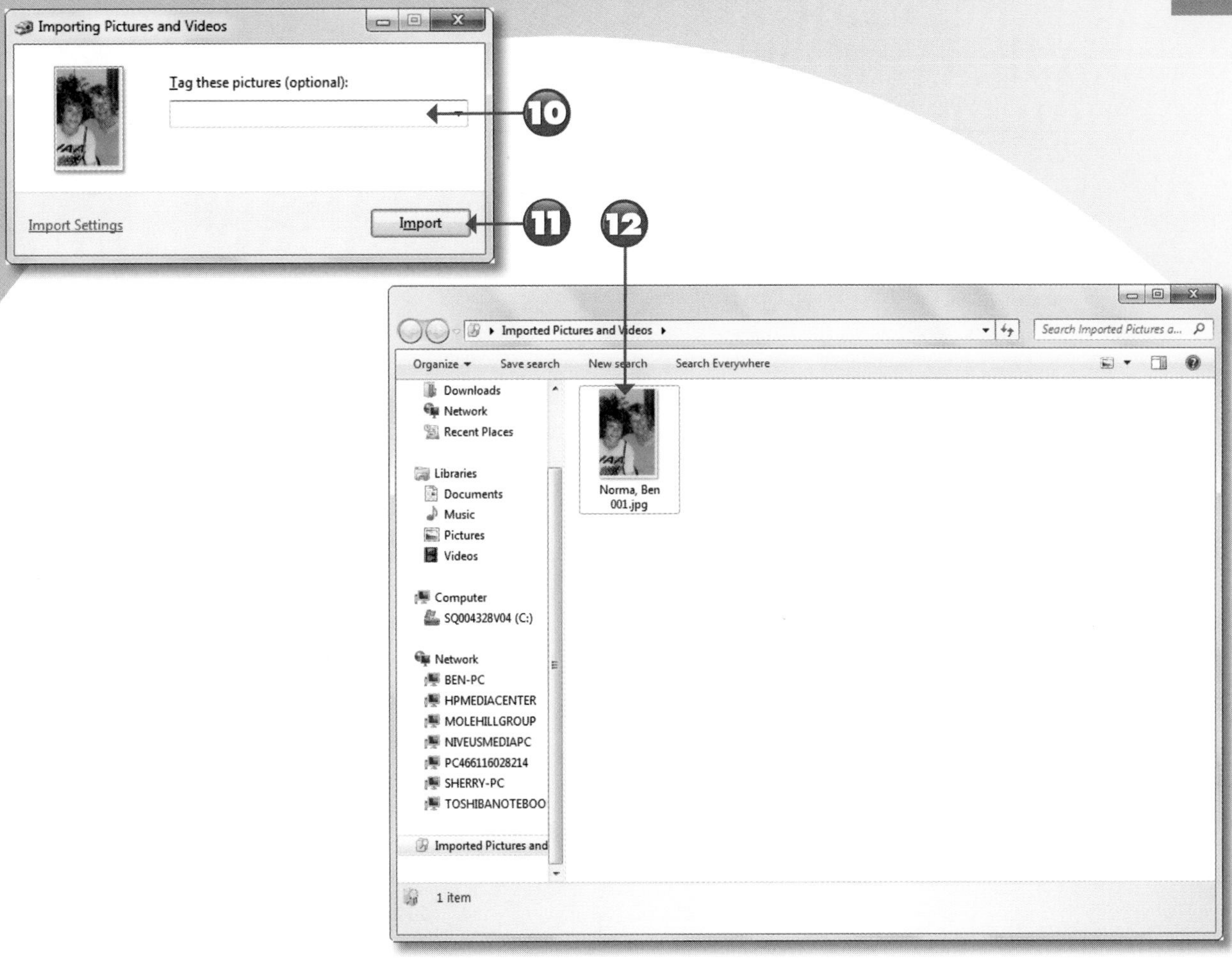

10 Enter any tags (keywords) you want to describe the scanned photo.

11 Click the **Import** button to save the file to your hard disk.

12 The scanned file is now saved in your Imported Pictures and Video folder.

End

TIP

Reposition the Item If you don't like the preview scan, reposition the item on your scanner and click the **Preview** button again to start a new scan. ■

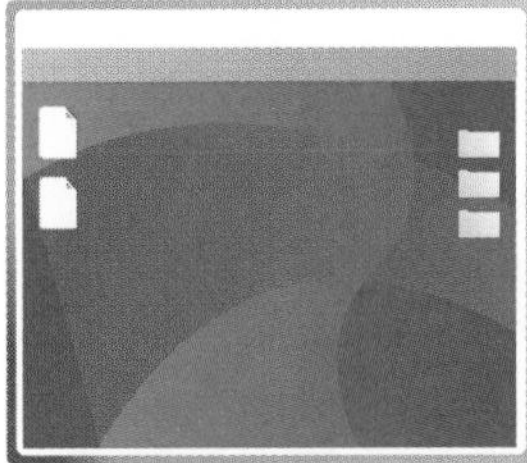

VIEWING PHOTOS WITH WINDOWS LIVE PHOTO GALLERY

You can use Windows Live Photo Gallery to both view and edit your digital photos. You launch Photo Gallery from the Windows Start menu, or by double-clicking any photo in your Pictures folder.

Start

1. Click any folder or subfolder in the Navigation pane to view the photos stored in that folder.
2. Click the **Info** button to view information about the selected photo in the Information pane.
3. Click the **Print** button to print a copy of the selected photo(s).
4. Double-click any photo to view it larger in the Content pane.

Continued

TIP

Organizing Your Photos Use the Navigation pane on the left side of the Photo Gallery window to organize photos by date taken, rating, tag (descriptive keyword), or folder location. ■

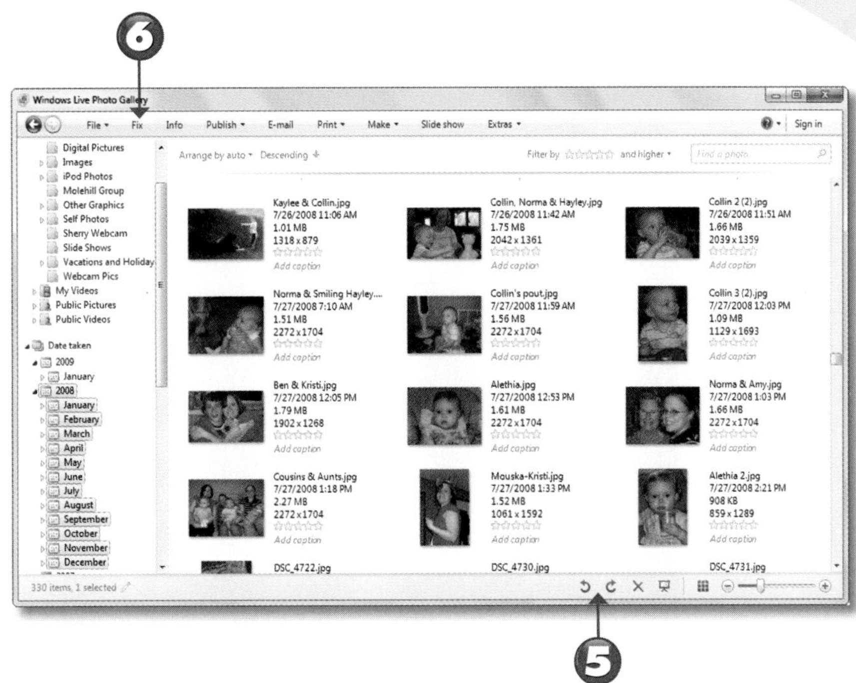

5 Click the left or right **Rotate** buttons to change the photo from landscape to portrait orientation.

6 Click the **Fix** button to edit the selected photo.

End

TIP

Slide Show You can also use Windows Live Photo Gallery to view your photos in a slide show. Just click the **Slide Show** button at the bottom of the window. ■

CROPPING A PHOTO

One of the most common problems with digital photographs is poor composition, where the subject of the picture is either too far away or off center. You can fix this problem in Windows Live Photo Gallery by cropping unwanted areas out of the final picture.

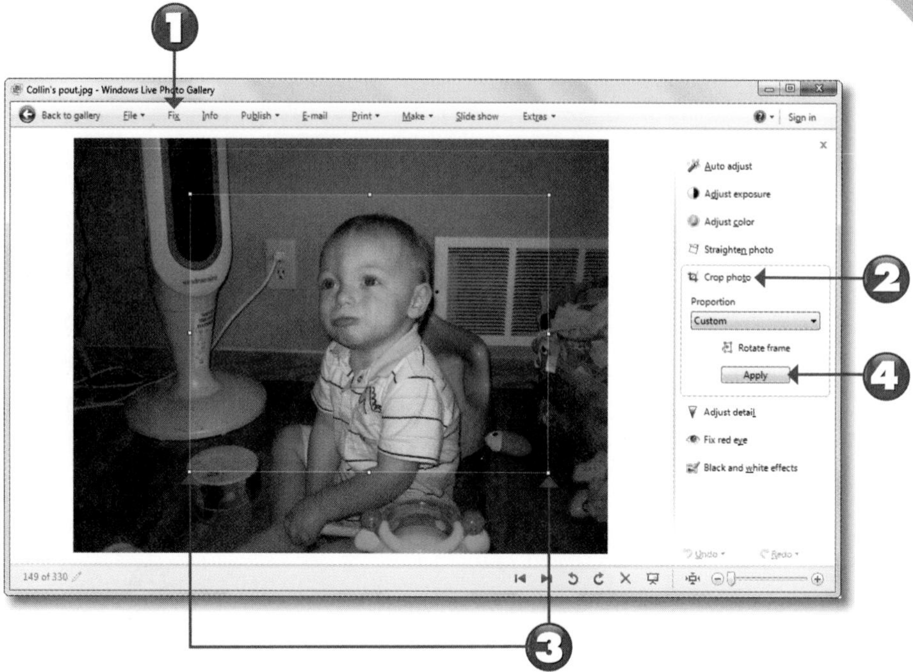

1. Click the **Fix** button.
2. Click **Crop Photo**.
3. Click and drag the corners of the onscreen box until the box frames the part of the area you want to keep.
4. Click the **Apply** button.

End

TIP

Crop for Prints To crop to an exact size, perfect for photo prints, click the **Custom** button and select a print size from the list. ■

REMOVING RED EYE

Another common problem with pictures of people is red eye, which is sometimes caused by using your camera's built-in flash. Fortunately, Windows Live Photo Gallery has a tool that lets you quickly and easily fix all red eye problems.

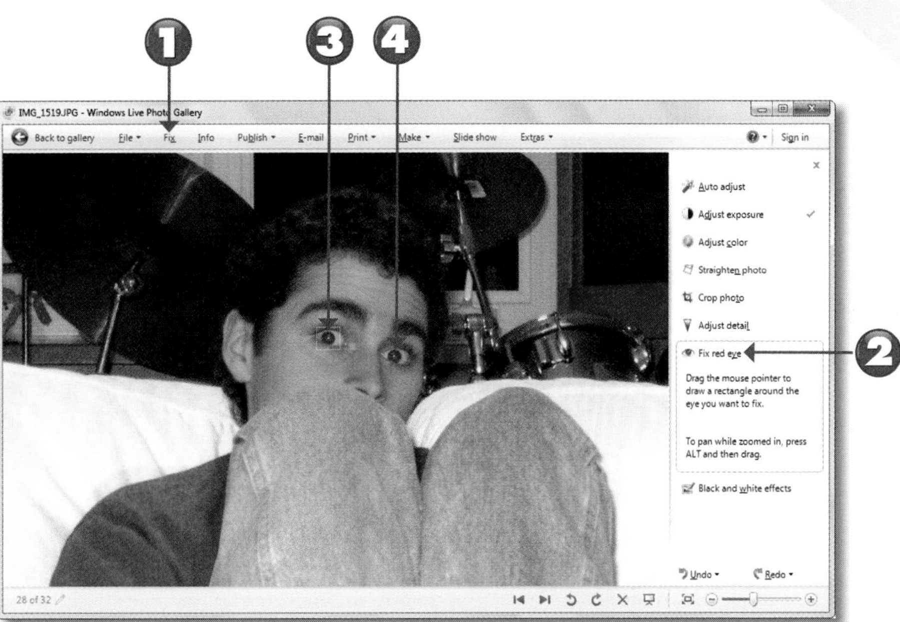

1. Click the **Fix** button.
2. Click **Fix Red Eye**.
3. Click and drag the cursor to draw a rectangle around the first eye you want to fix.
4. Repeat step 3 for the other eye.

End

NOTE

Learn More in Photopedia Learn more about taking and editing digital photos in my companion book, *Photopedia: The Ultimate Digital Photography Resource* (Michael Miller, Que, 2007). ■

TIP

Other Photo-Editing Programs Windows Live Photo Gallery is good because it's free, but you may need the more powerful editing tools found in other programs, such as Adobe Photoshop Elements (www.adobe.com), Paint Shop Pro Photo (www.corel.com), and Picasa (picasa.google.com). ■

ADJUSTING BRIGHTNESS AND CONTRAST

Many digital photos end up too light or dark, due to poor lighting. Fortunately, you can adjust the lightness of your photos using the Brightness and Contrast controls in Windows Live Photo Gallery.

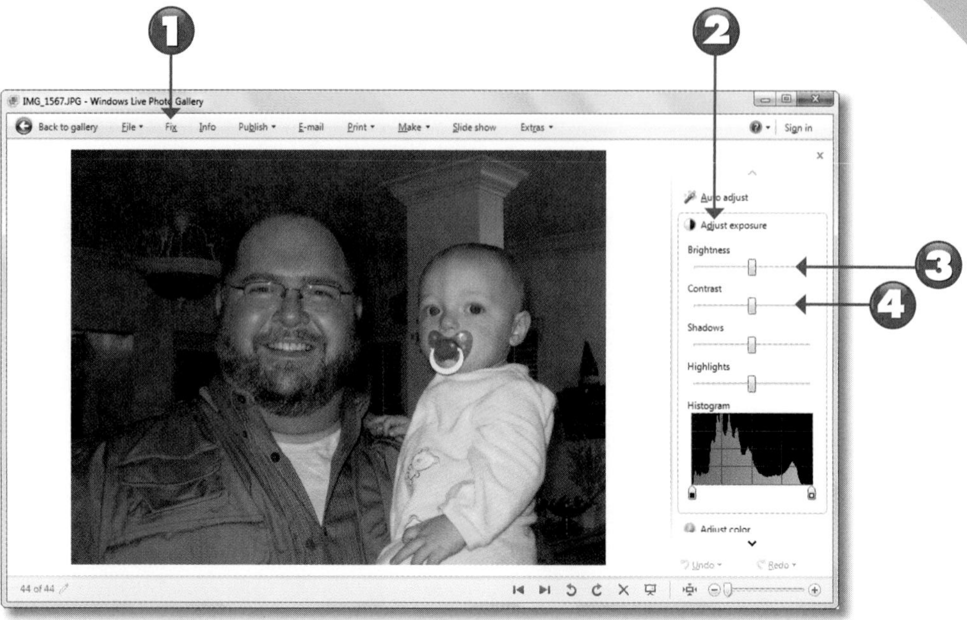

1. Click the **Fix** button.
2. Click **Adjust Exposure**.
3. Click and drag the **Brightness** slider to make the picture darker or lighter.
4. Click and drag the **Contrast** slider to increase or decrease the picture's contrast level.

End

TIP

Shadows and Highlights You can also use the Adjust Exposure pane to increase or decrease the level of a photo's shadows and highlights, using the Shadows and Highlights sliders. ■

TIP

Auto Adjust and Undo For a quick fix for most photos, click the **Auto Adjust** button. If you don't like the automatic adjustment, click the **Undo** button. ■

ADJUSTING COLOR AND HUE

What do you do when the colors don't turn out right in a photograph? The answer is simple—use Windows Live Photo Gallery's Color Temperature, Tint, and Saturation controls to fix the problem.

Start

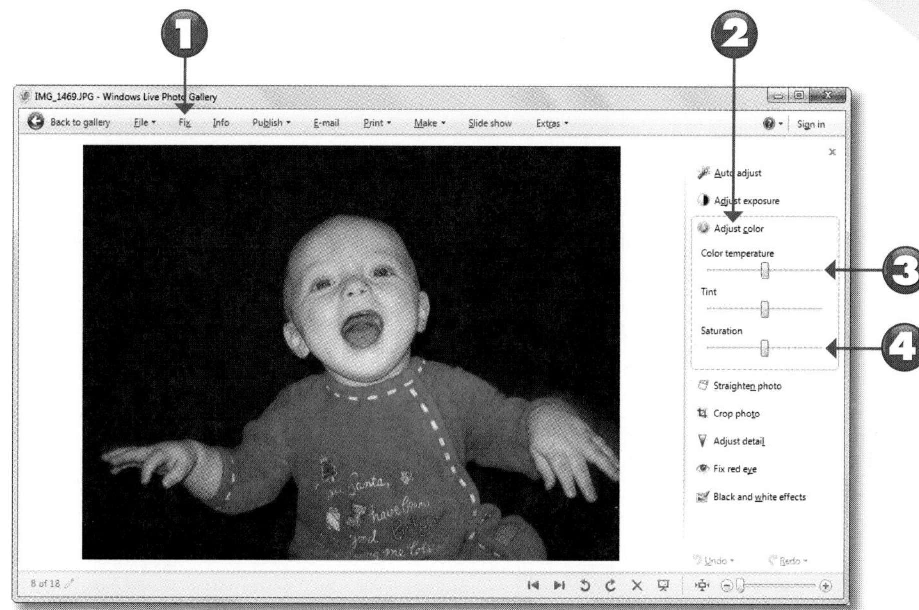

1. Click the **Fix** button.
2. Click **Adjust Color**.
3. Click and drag the **Color Temperature** slider to the left for cooler colors (more blue), or to the right for warmer colors (more orange).
4. Click and drag the **Saturation** slider to the left to decrease the amount of color in the photo, or to the right to increase the amount of color.

End

TIP

Tint Another way to adjust the color of a photo is to use the Tint slider. Slide to the left for a greener tint, or to the right for more red. ■

NOTE

Color and Lighting Poor color is often caused by the type of lighting you use in your photos. Incandescent lighting often creates an orange cast, while fluorescent lighting creates a bluish-green cast. ■

PRINTING A PHOTO

Any photo-editing program will let you print your pictures from within the program. You can also print directly from Windows Live Photo Gallery.

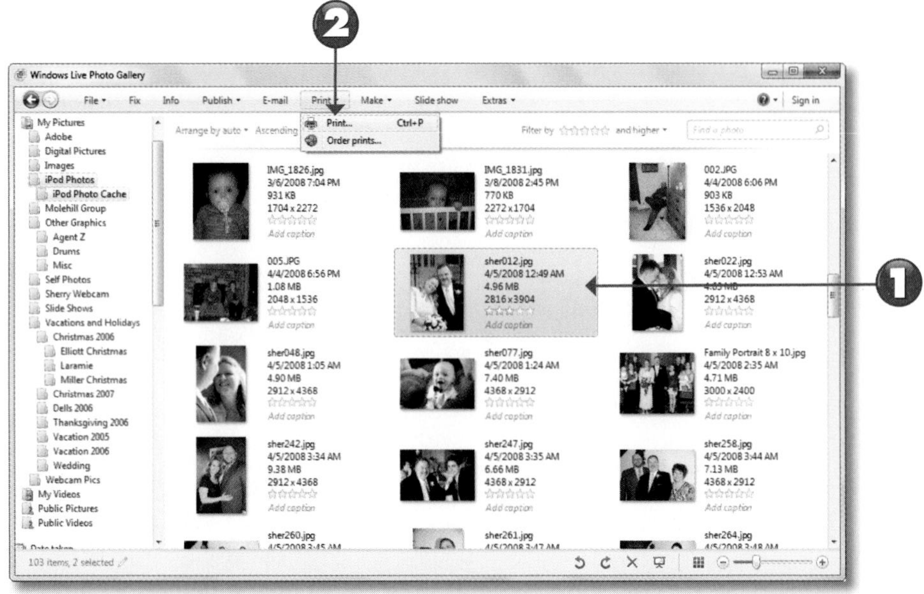

1. Click the pictures you want to print. (To select multiple pictures, hold down the **Ctrl** key while clicking.)

2. Click the **Print** button and click **Print**.

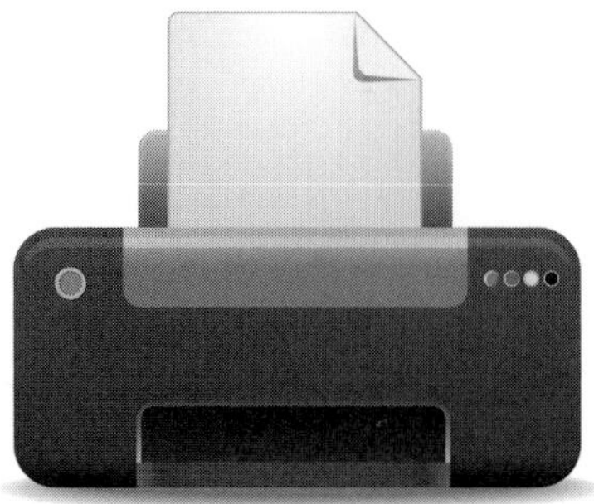

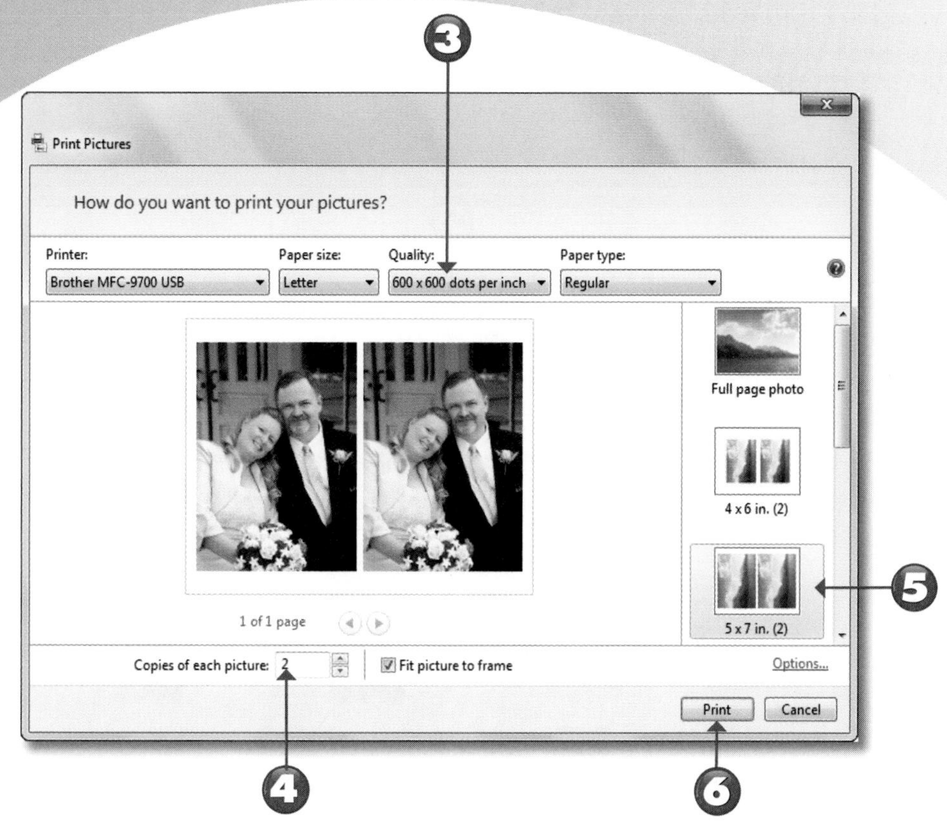

3. Click the **Quality** button and select the quality (DPI) of the print.

4. Select how many copies you want to make of each picture.

5. Scroll down the right-hand list and select what size and type of prints you want—full page photo, two 4-inch x 6-inch prints, four 3.5-inch x 5-inch prints, and so forth.

6. Click the **Print** button.

End

TIP

Different Sizes You can choose to print your photos full-page, at a specific print size, or as multiple prints on a single contact sheet. ■

ORDERING PRINTS ONLINE

If you don't have your own photo-quality printer, you can use a professional photo-processing service to print your photos. You can go directly to one of the Internet's many photo-processing sites, or you can order prints from within Windows Live Photo Gallery.

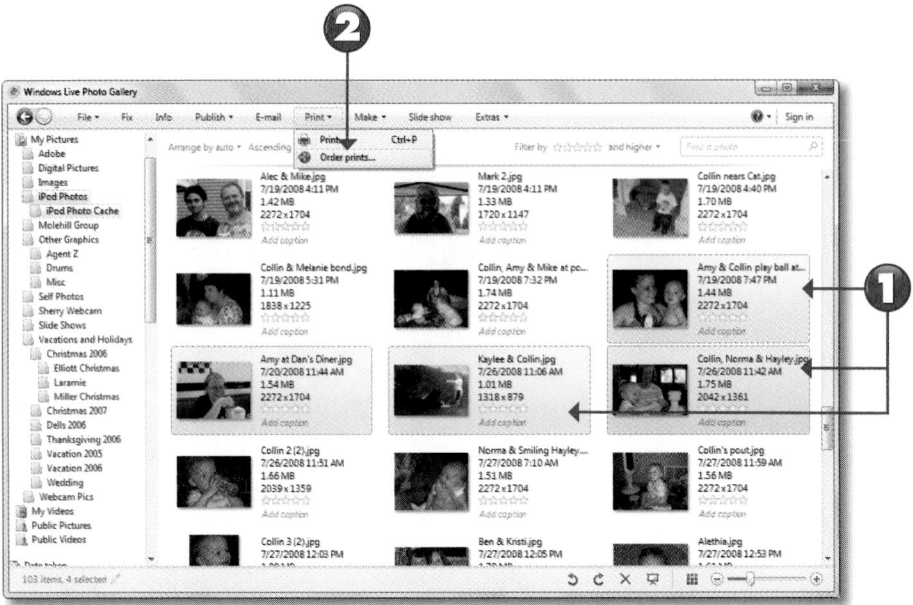

1. Click the pictures you want to print. (To select multiple pictures, hold down the **Ctrl** key while clicking.)

2. Click the **Print** button and click **Order Prints**.

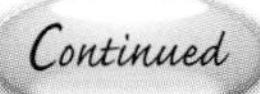

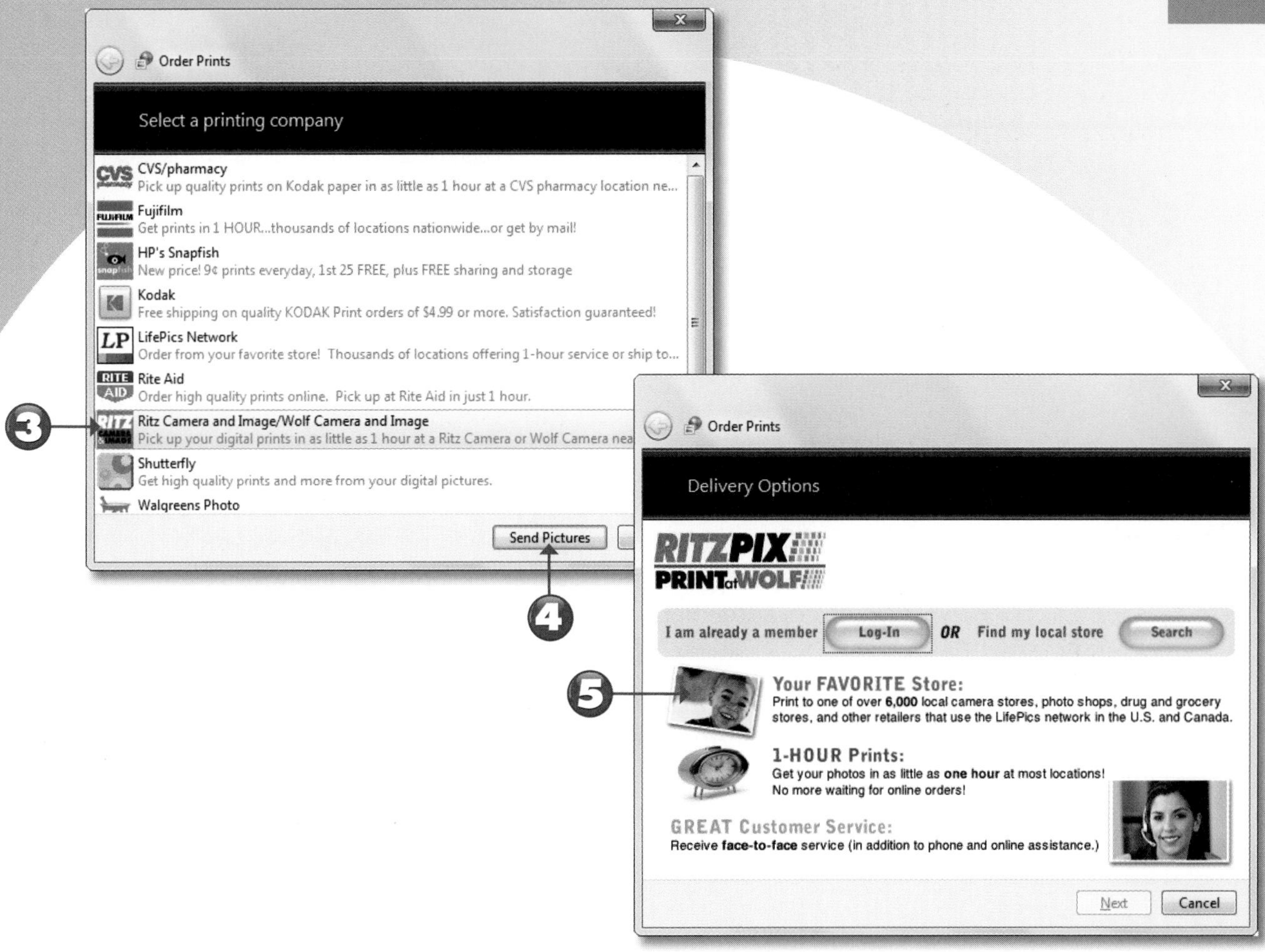

3 Windows now displays a list of online printing companies. Click the company you want to use.

4 Click **Send Pictures**.

5 Complete the rest of the online ordering process from the site you selected. (Each site has its own distinct process!)

End

TIP

Other Online Photo Sites You can also order prints directly from most of the online photo sites listed, by uploading your photos directly to the company's website. ■

TIP

Online Ordering for Local Pickup Some online photo sites, such as Walgreens and CVS, let you order your prints online and pick them up at your nearest local store. ■

PROTECTING YOUR COMPUTER

When you connect your PC to the Internet, you open up a whole new world of adventure and information for you and your family. Unfortunately, you also open up a new world of potential dangers—viruses, spyware, computer attacks, and more.

Fortunately, it's easy to protect your computer and your family from these dangers. Windows 7 includes a built-in firewall and anti-spyware utility, as well as anti-phishing tools. Add a low-cost (or even free) third-party anti-virus program, and you'll be protected against most malicious software (malware) that might come your way.

HOW A FIREWALL WORKS

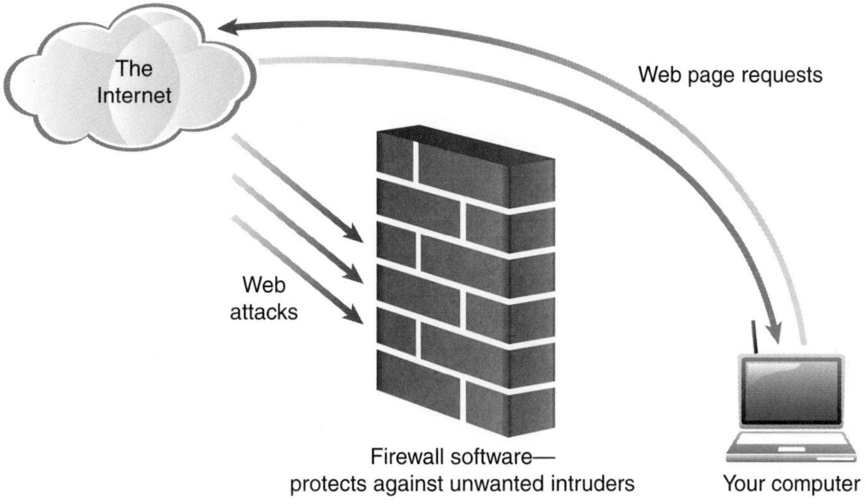

DEFENDING AGAINST COMPUTER ATTACKS WITH WINDOWS FIREWALL

Connecting to the Internet is a two-way street. Not only can your PC access other computers online, but other computers can access *your* PC—to access your private data or damage your system hardware and software. You protect against incoming attacks with a firewall program, such as the Windows Firewall.

Start

1. From the Windows Control Panel, click **System and Security**.
2. Click **Windows Firewall**.

Continued

NOTE

Zombies and Botnets Many computer attacks today are executed using personal computers compromised by a computer virus. These so-called *zombie computers* are operated via remote control in an ad hoc attack network called a *botnet*. A firewall program protects against incoming attacks and botnet controllers. ■

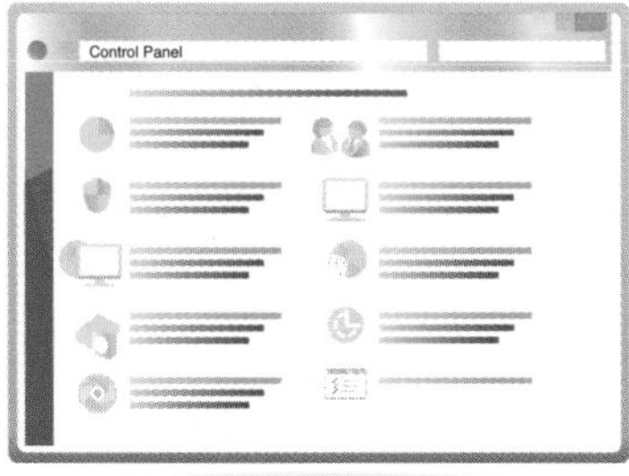

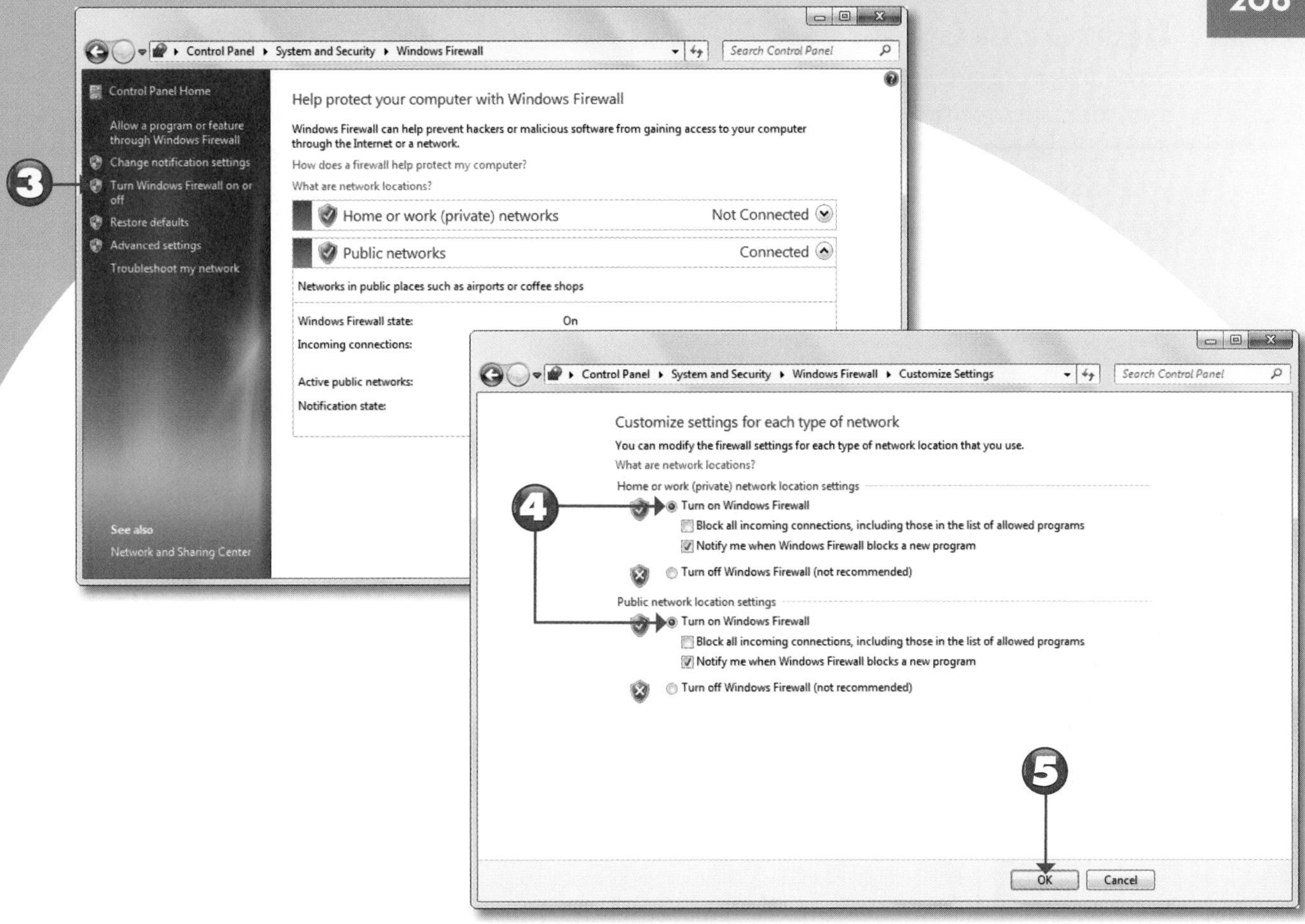

3. To turn on Windows Firewall, click **Turn Windows Firewall On or Off**.

4. Click **Turn On Windows Firewall** in both the Home or Work and Public Network sections.

5. Click **OK**.

End

TIP

Other Firewall Programs Many third-party firewalls offer more protection than the Windows Firewall. These programs include McAfee Total Protection (www.mcafee.com), Norton Internet Security (www.symantec.com), and ZoneAlarm Free Firewall (www.zonealarm.com). ■

REMOVING SPYWARE WITH WINDOWS DEFENDER

Spyware programs install themselves on your computer, typically without your knowledge, and then surreptitiously send information about the way you use your PC to some interested third party—to serve advertising or for other, more nefarious purposes. You can protect your system from spyware and remove spyware from your computer by using an antispyware program, such as Microsoft's Windows Defender.

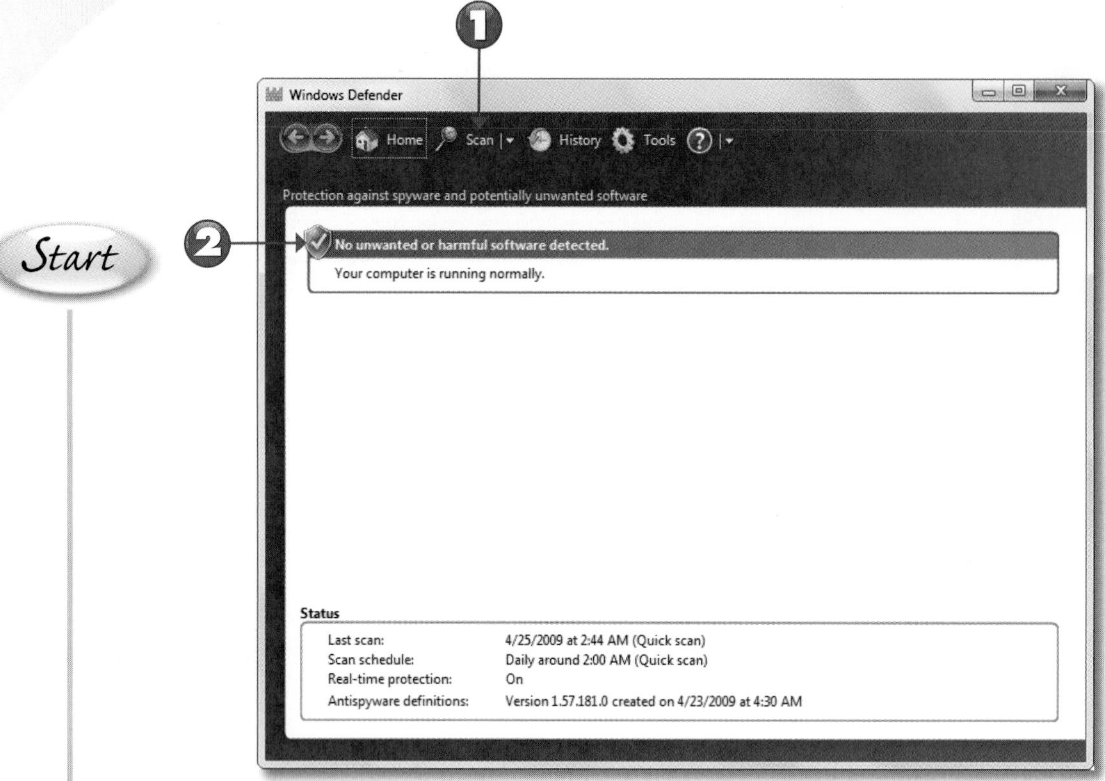

Start

1. To manually scan your system for spyware, click **Scan**.
2. Defender's main screen informs you if any spyware has been detected.

Continued

TIP

Download Windows Defender Windows Defender is a free program included as part of Windows 7. You can also download it for use with other computers from www.microsoft.com/windows/products/winfamily/defender/. ■

TIP

Other Antispyware Utilities Other popular antispyware utilities include Ad-Aware (www.lavasoftusa.com) and Spybot Search & Destroy (www.safer-networking.org). ■

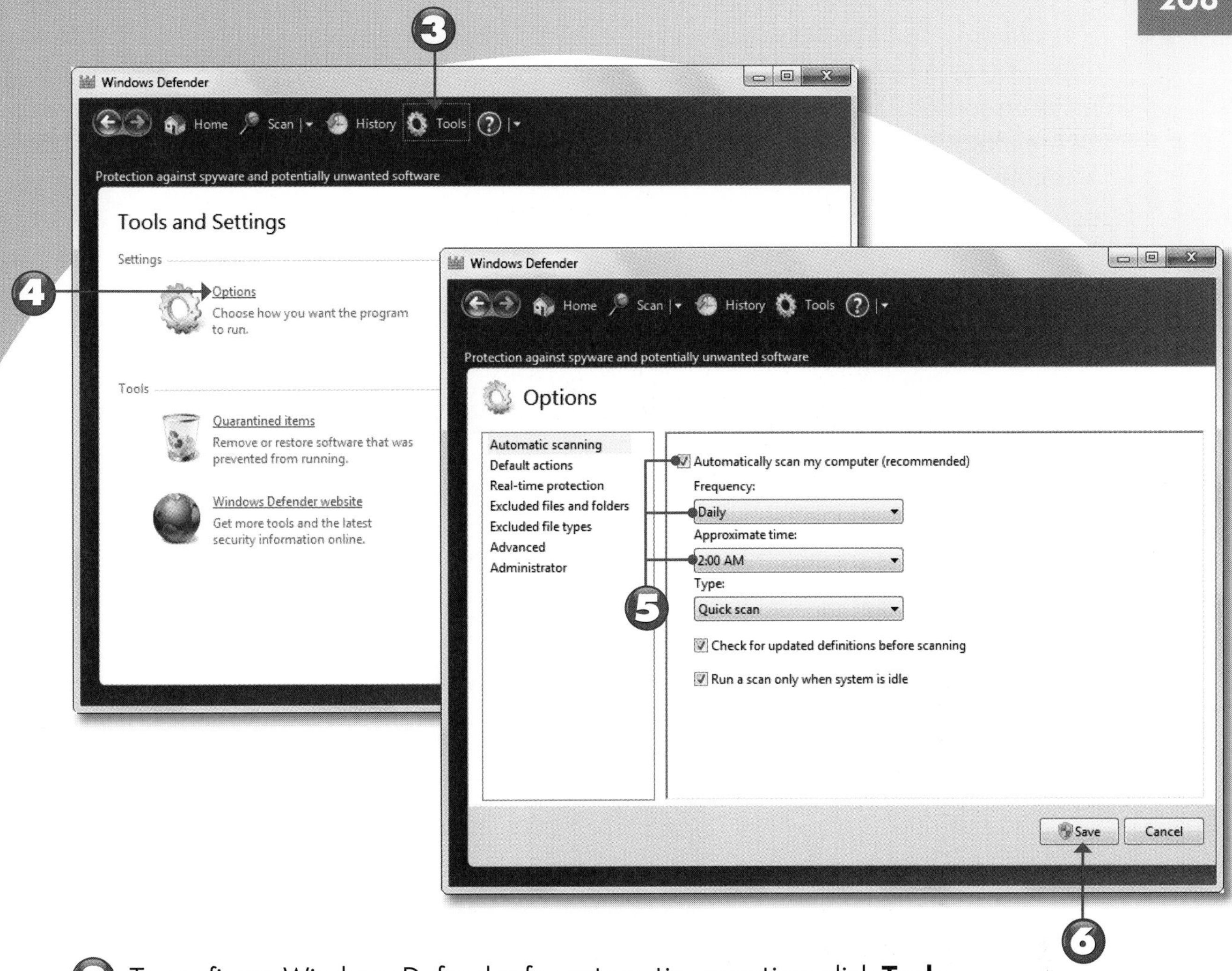

3 To configure Windows Defender for automatic operation, click **Tools**.

4 Click **Options**.

5 Check **Automatically Scan My Computer** and select a frequency and time for the scan.

6 Click **Save**.

End

CAUTION

Avoid File-Sharing Networks One common source of spyware is files downloaded from peer-to-peer file-sharing networks. When you download the software used to download music and movie files, you often download a spyware program, too.

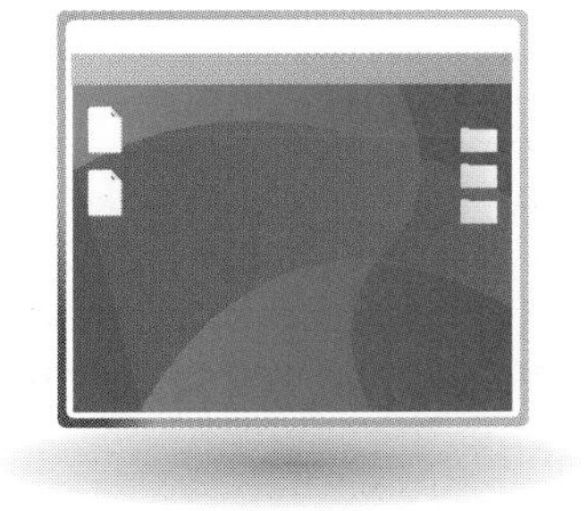

PROTECTING AGAINST COMPUTER VIRUSES

Computer viruses can be even more damaging than spyware. For that reason, you should install on your PC an antivirus program, such as AVG Anti-Virus Free Edition (free.avg.com), McAfee VirusScan Plus (www.mcafee.com), Norton AntiVirus (www.symantec.com), or ZoneAlarm Antivirus (www.zonealarm.com).

Start

1. One of the more popular antivirus programs is AVG Anti-Virus Free Edition, from free.avg.com. Click the Overview tab to view your current protection status.

2. Click the **Computer Scanner** tab and click the **Edit Scan Schedule** button to change when the program scans your computer.

End

CAUTION

Virus Damage Some computer viruses delete critical system files or documents. Other viruses hijack your computer to use in a botnet attack. ■

NOTE

How to Catch a Virus Computer viruses are most commonly transmitted via infected computer files. You can receive virus-infected files via email or instant messaging, or by downloading files from unsecure websites. ■

PROTECTING AGAINST PHISHING SCAMS

Identity theft is a big problem. One way scammers steal your personal information is through a technique called *phishing*. A phishing scam creates official-looking emails and websites that attempt to get you to enter your personal information. If you do so, your information is stolen—and used by the scammer.

Start

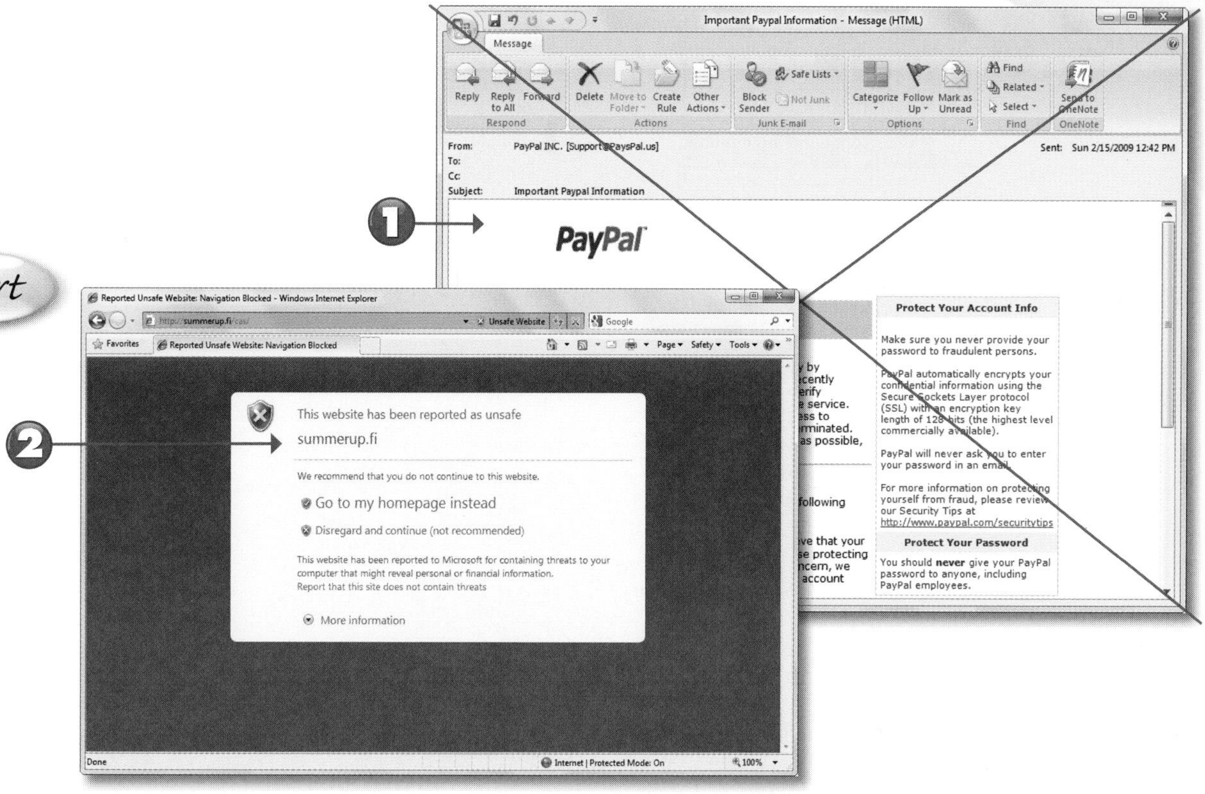

1. A phishing email is designed to look like an official message—but it is an artfully constructed scam.
2. Internet Explorer's SmartScreen Filter alerts you to potential phishing sites. Do not enter any information into these sites—return to your home page, instead!

End

CAUTION

Beware Phishing Emails As a general rule of thumb, never click links in email messages—no matter how official-looking those messages might appear. Links in phishing messages open phishing websites designed to scam you of your personal information. ■

NOTE

Anti-Phishing Filters Internet Explorer 8 includes a SmartScreen Filter that warns you of potential phishing websites. Many email programs, including Windows Live Mail, include similar anti-phishing filters for email messages. ■

REDUCING EMAIL SPAM

If you're like most users, a large portion of the messages delivered to your email Inbox are unsolicited, unauthorized, and unwanted—in other words, *spam*. These spam messages are the online equivalent of the junk mail you receive in your postal mailbox, and they're a huge problem.

Start

1. *Don't* post your primary email address in public forums, on message boards, in blogs, or on your own web page or Facebook/MySpace page.
2. *Do* install and use an anti-spam program, such as MailWasher (www.mailwasher.net) or iHateSpam (www.sunbeltsoftware.com).

TIP

Use a Spamblock To confuse email address-harvesting software, you can insert a spamblock into your email address on any public web page or blog. For example, if your email address is johnjones@ myisp.com, you might change the address to read johnSPAMBLOCKjones@myisp.com. ■

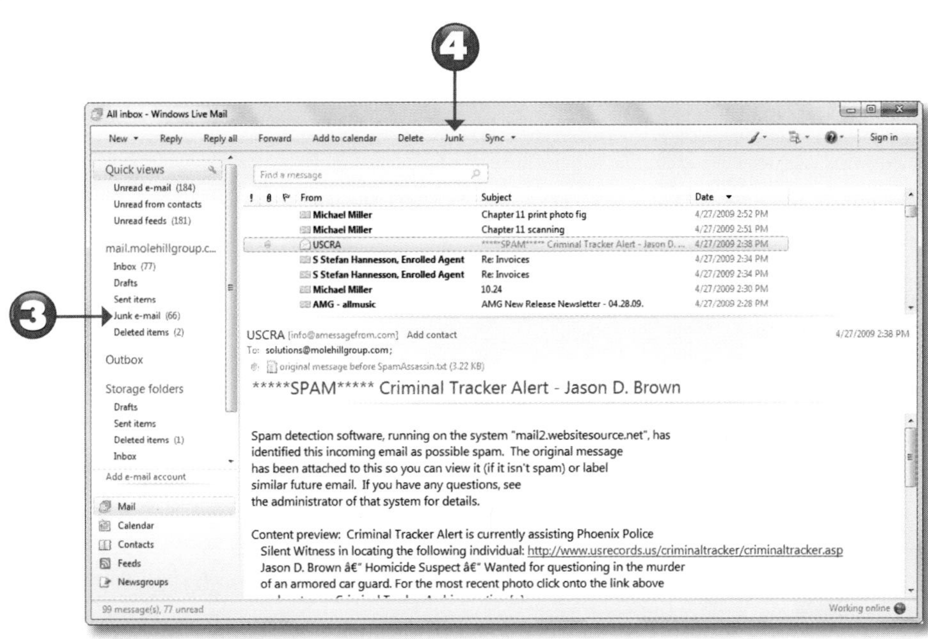

3 Most email programs include some form of spam filter. For example, Windows Live Mail automatically sends suspected spam to the Junk E-Mail folder.

4 If a spam message gets through the filter, select it and click the **Junk** button to send it to the Junk E-Mail folder.

End

NOTE

Windows Live Mail Windows Live Mail is the successor to Microsoft Outlook Express and Windows Mail. It can be downloaded for free from download.live.com. ■

TIP

Viewing Junk Email It's a good idea to review messages in your spam folder periodically, to make sure no legitimate messages have been accidentally sent there. To review these messages in Windows Live Mail, click the Junk E-Mail folder in the Folders list. ■

CONFIGURING USER ACCOUNT CONTROL

One of the key security features in Windows 7 is User Account Control (UAC). UAC prevents unauthorized people and processes from taking control of your system and installing and running malicious programs. Instead, you're prompted whenever Windows needs to run an administrative-level task, so that these operations aren't executed automatically.

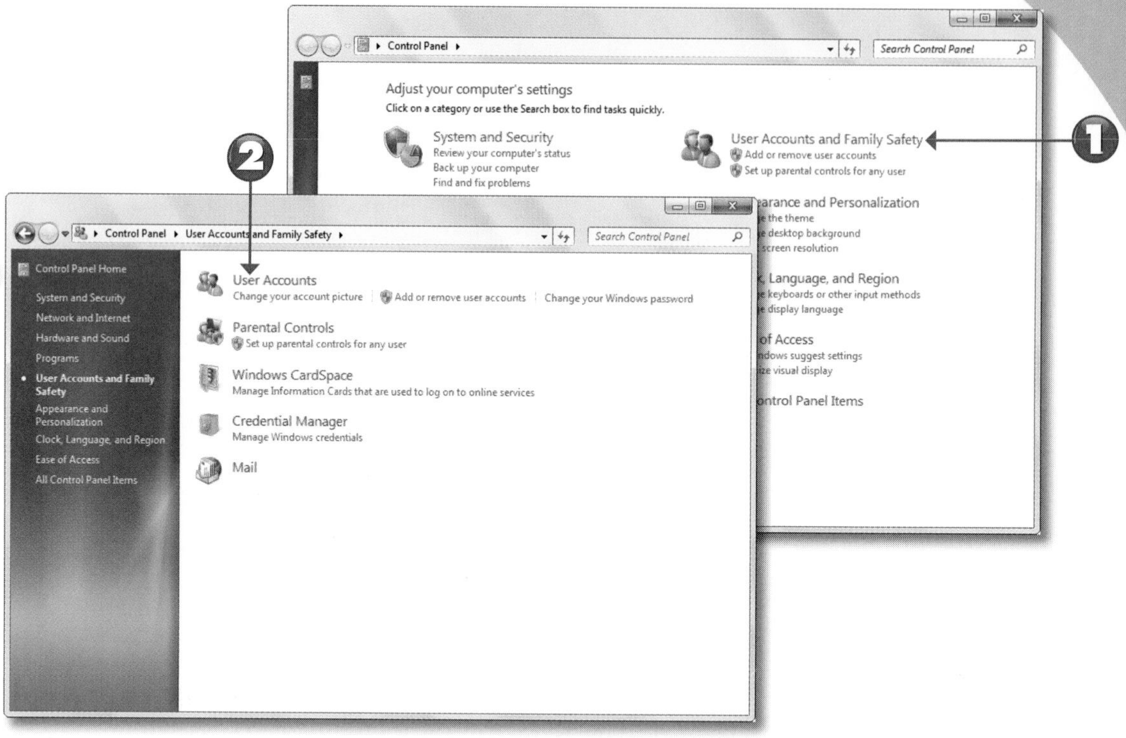

1. To adjust the level of User Account Control, open the Control Panel and click **User Accounts and Family Safety**.
2. Click **User Accounts**.

Continued

NOTE

What Is Unauthorized? What types of operations need UAC authorization? Just about anything that could affect the way your system runs, such as installing a new software program, changing system settings, or deleting a system file. ■

TIP

Providing Authorization When a program or user attempts to perform an administrative-level task, User Account Control presents a dialog box that asks for authorization. Click **OK** to proceed with the task. ■

3. Click **Change User Account Control Settings**.

4. Drag the slider up to increase the UAC level (and generate more warning dialogs), or drag the slider down to decrease the UAC level.

5. Click **OK**.

End

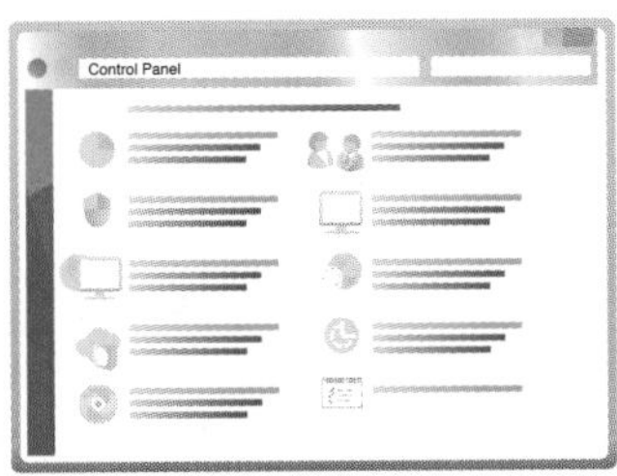

TAKING CARE OF YOUR COMPUTER

"An ounce of prevention is worth a pound of cure" is a bit of a cliché, but it's also true—especially when it comes to your computer system. Spending a few minutes a week on preventive maintenance can save you from costly computer problems in the future.

To make this chore a little easier, Windows 7 includes several utilities to help you keep your system running smoothly. You should use these tools as part of your regular maintenance routine—or if you experience specific problems with your computer system.

The best way to manage your PC's maintenance and security is to open the Windows Control Panel and select **System & Security**, and then **Action Center**. The Action Center will alert you to any action you need to take to protect and maintain your system.

WINDOWS ACTION CENTER

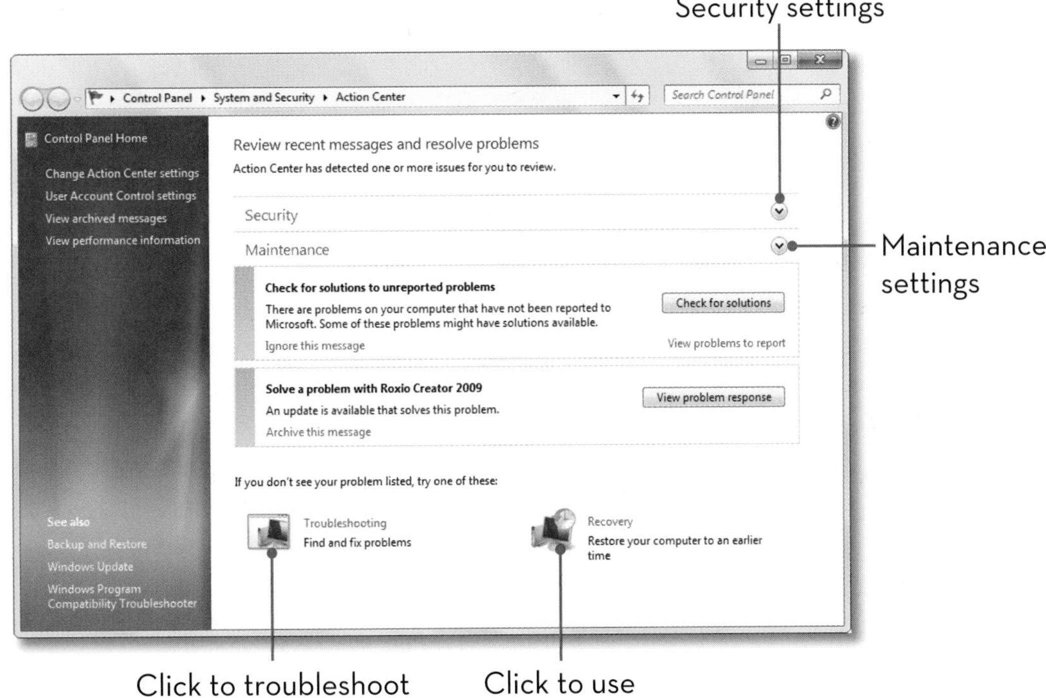

BACKING UP IMPORTANT FILES

The data stored on your computer's hard disk is valuable, and perhaps irreplaceable. That's why you want to keep a backup copy of all these valuable files, preferably on an external hard disk, using Windows 7's Backup utility. You can configure the Backup utility to back up your data automatically, on a predefined schedule.

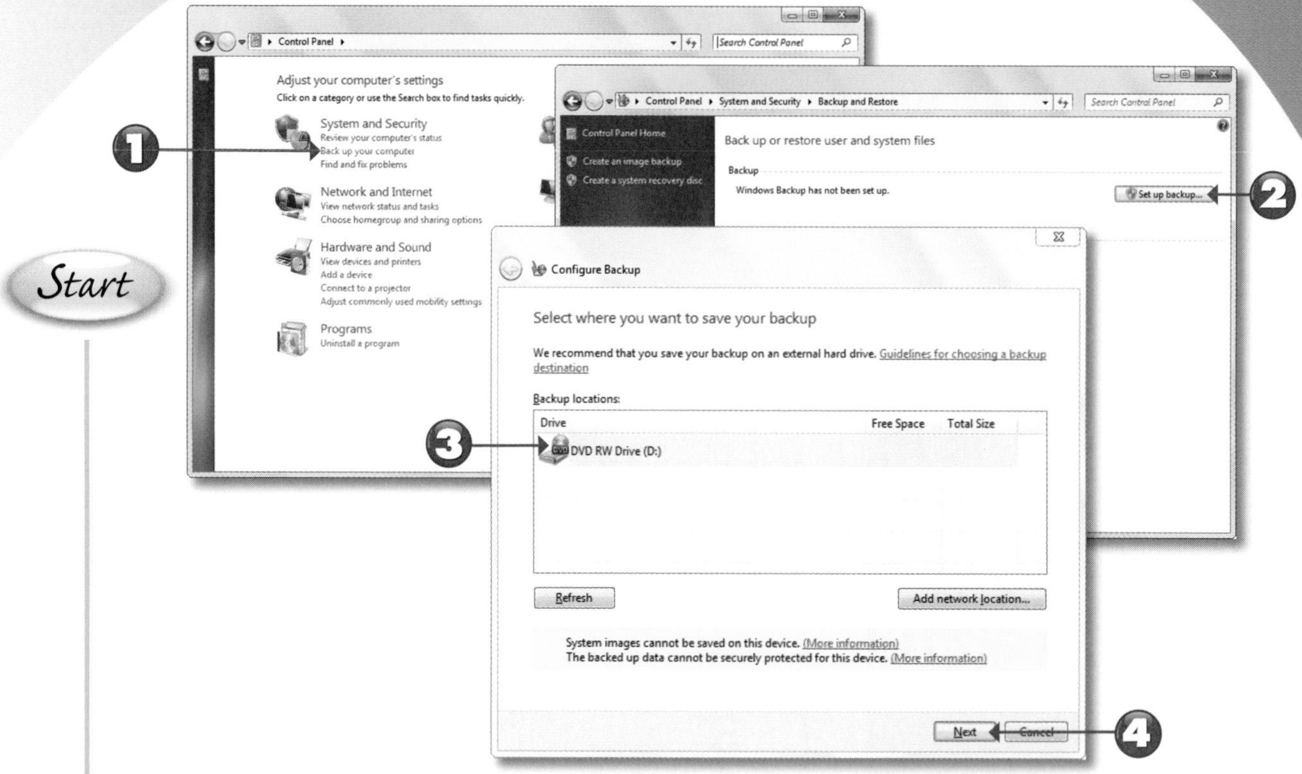

Start

1. From the Windows Control Panel, click **Back Up Your Computer** (in the System and Security section).
2. Click **Set Up Backup**.
3. Select where you want to back up your data—to an external hard disk, to a CD or DVD disc, or to another computer on your network.
4. Click **Next**.

Continued

TIP

Incremental Backup Windows 7's Backup utility performs an incremental backup. That is, it doesn't back up every file every time; it only backs up those files that are new or have changed since the last backup. ■

TIP

External Hard Drives The easiest way to perform a backup is to use an external hard disk drive. These drives provide lots of storage space for a relatively low cost, and they connect to your PC via USB. There's no excuse not to do it! ■

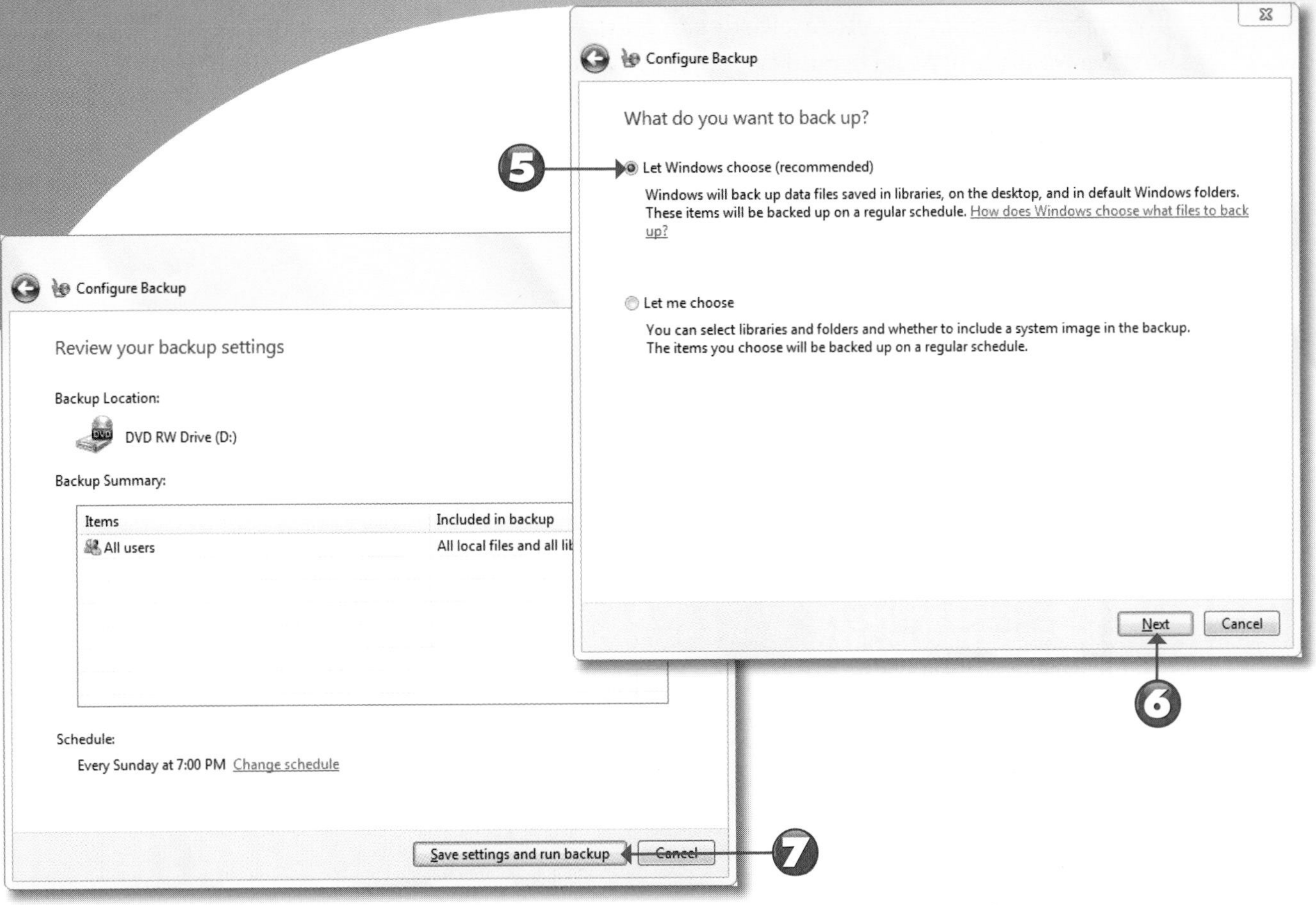

5. Click **Let Windows Choose**.

6. Click **Next**.

7. Click **Save Settings and Run Backup** to perform your first backup.

End

TIP

Change the Schedule By default, Windows will back up your data once a week (Sunday at 7:00 p.m.). To change the backup schedule, click **Change Schedule** and select how often, what day, and what time to back up. ■

TIP

How Often to Back Up? Should you back up your data daily, weekly, or monthly? It depends on how often you use your computer and how valuable your data is. There's no harm in performing daily backups—which means that your backup is never more than 24 hours out of date. ■

RESTORING YOUR COMPUTER AFTER A CRASH

If your computer system ever crashes or freezes, your best course of action is to run the System Restore utility. This utility can automatically restore your system to the state it was in before the crash occurred—and save you the trouble of reinstalling any damaged software programs. It's a great safety net for when things go wrong!

Start

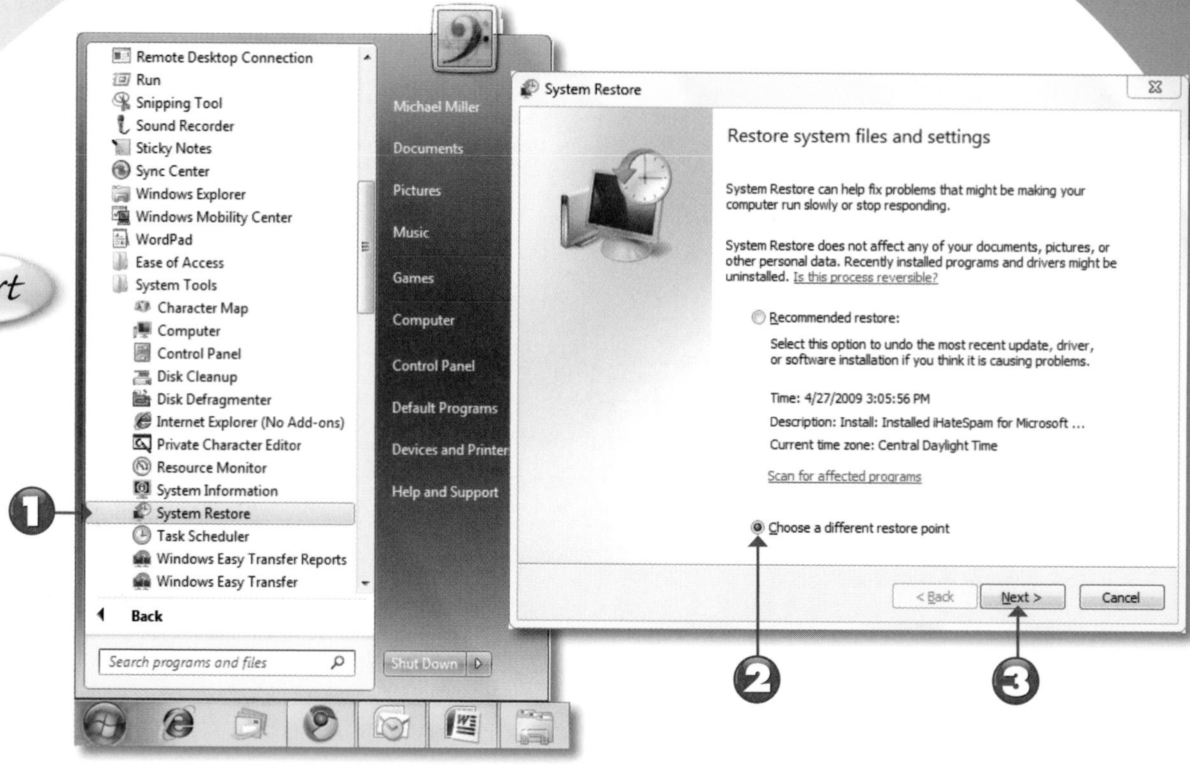

1. Click the **Start** button and select **All Programs**, **Accessories**, **System Tools**, **System Restore**.
2. Click **Choose a Different Restore Point**.
3. Click **Next**.

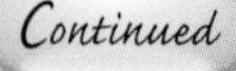

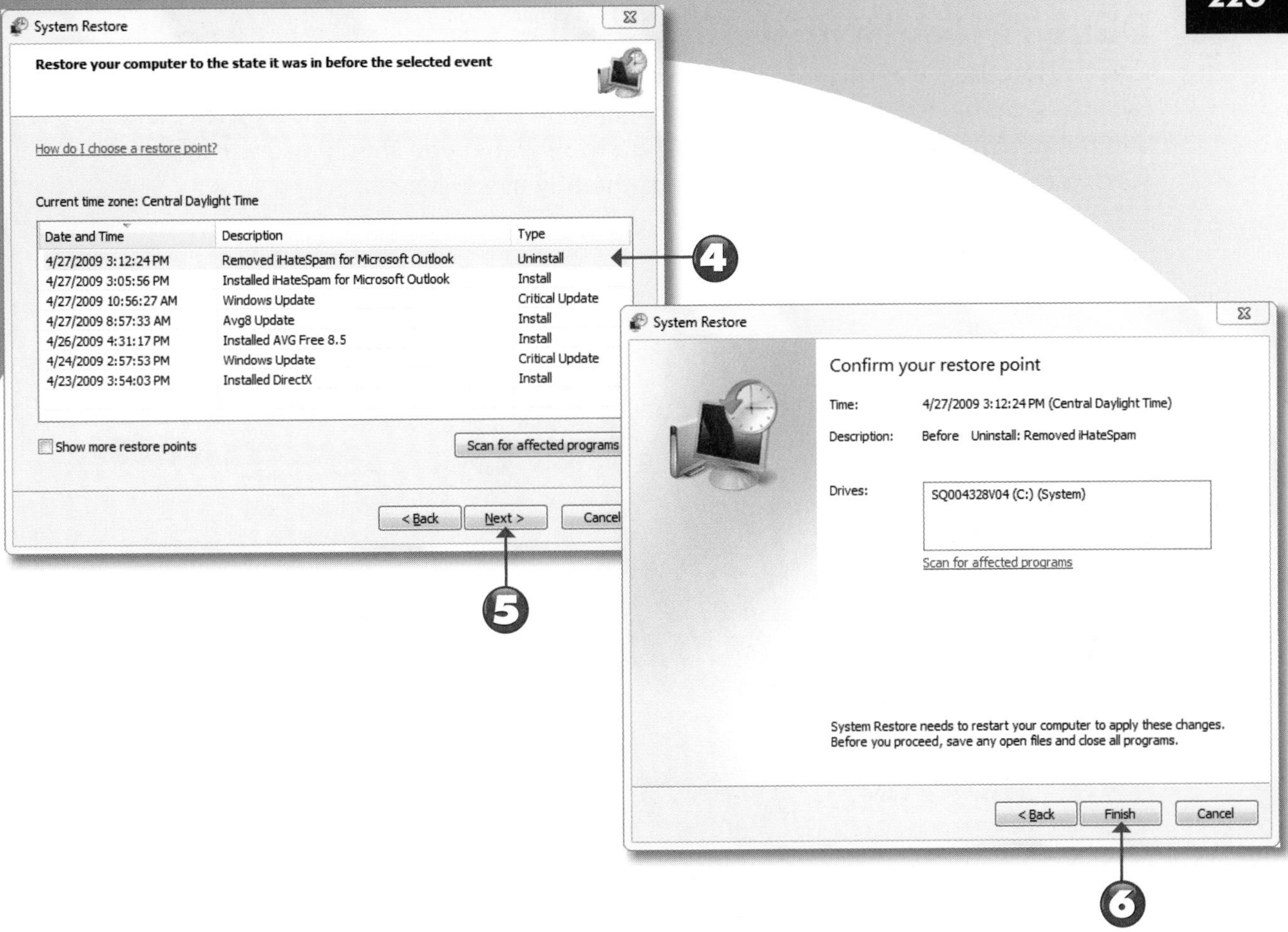

4. Select the restore point you wish to revert to.

5. Click **Next**.

6. When the confirmation screen appears, click **Finish** to begin the restore process.

End

TIP

Restoring Your System Be sure to close all programs before you use System Restore because Windows will need to be restarted when it's done. The full process might take a half-hour or more. ■

CAUTION

System Files Only—No Documents System Restore will help you recover any damaged programs and system files, but it won't help you recover any documents or data files. This is why you need to back up all your data on a regular basis—and restore that backed-up data in the case of an emergency. ■

DELETING UNNECESSARY FILES

Even with today's humongous hard disks, you can still end up with too many useless files taking up too much hard disk space. Fortunately, Windows 7 includes a utility that identifies and deletes unused files. The Disk Cleanup tool is what you should use when you need to free up extra hard disk space for more frequently used files.

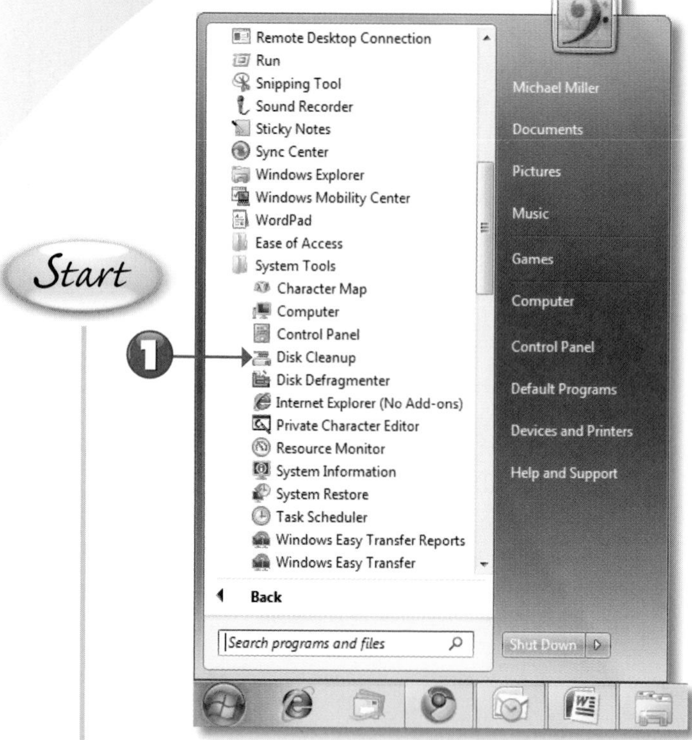

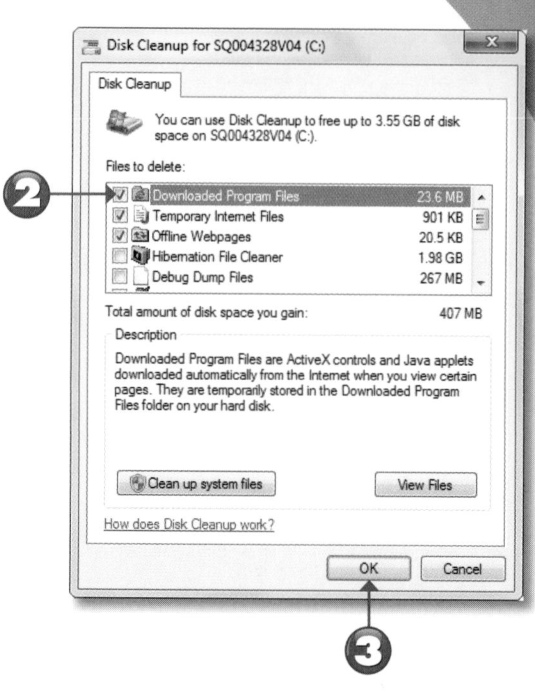

1. Click the **Start** button and select **All Programs**, **Accessories**, **System Tools**, **Disk Cleanup**.
2. Disk Cleanup analyzes the contents of your hard drive and presents its results in the Disk Cleanup dialog box. Check which types of files you want to delete.
3. Click **OK** to delete the files.

TIP

Which Files to Delete? You can safely choose to delete all these files except the setup log files and hibernation files, which are needed by the Windows operating system. ■

DELETING UNUSED PROGRAMS

Another way to free up valuable hard disk space is to delete those programs you never use. This is accomplished using Windows' Uninstall or Change a Program utility.

Start

1. From the Control Panel, click **Uninstall a Program** (in the Programs section).
2. Click the program you wish to delete.
3. Click **Uninstall**.

End

TIP

New PC Bloatware Most brand-new PCs come with unwanted programs and trial versions installed at the factory. Many users choose to delete these "bloatware" programs when they first run their PCs. ■

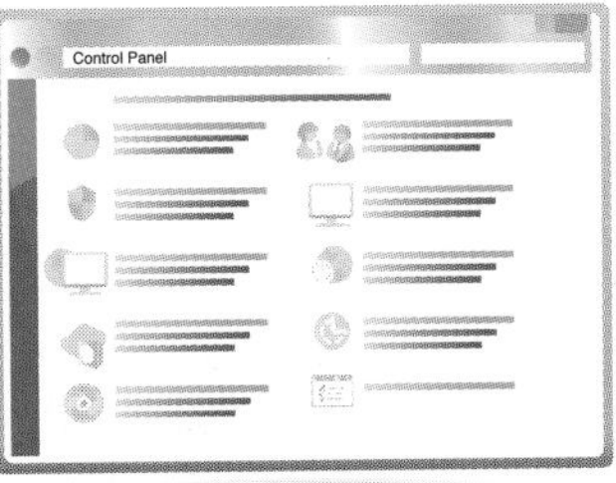

DEFRAGMENTING YOUR HARD DISK

If you notice that your system takes longer and longer to open and close files or run applications, it's probably because little fragments of files are spread all over your hard disk. You fix the problem when you put all the pieces of the puzzle back in the right boxes—which you do by defragmenting your disk.

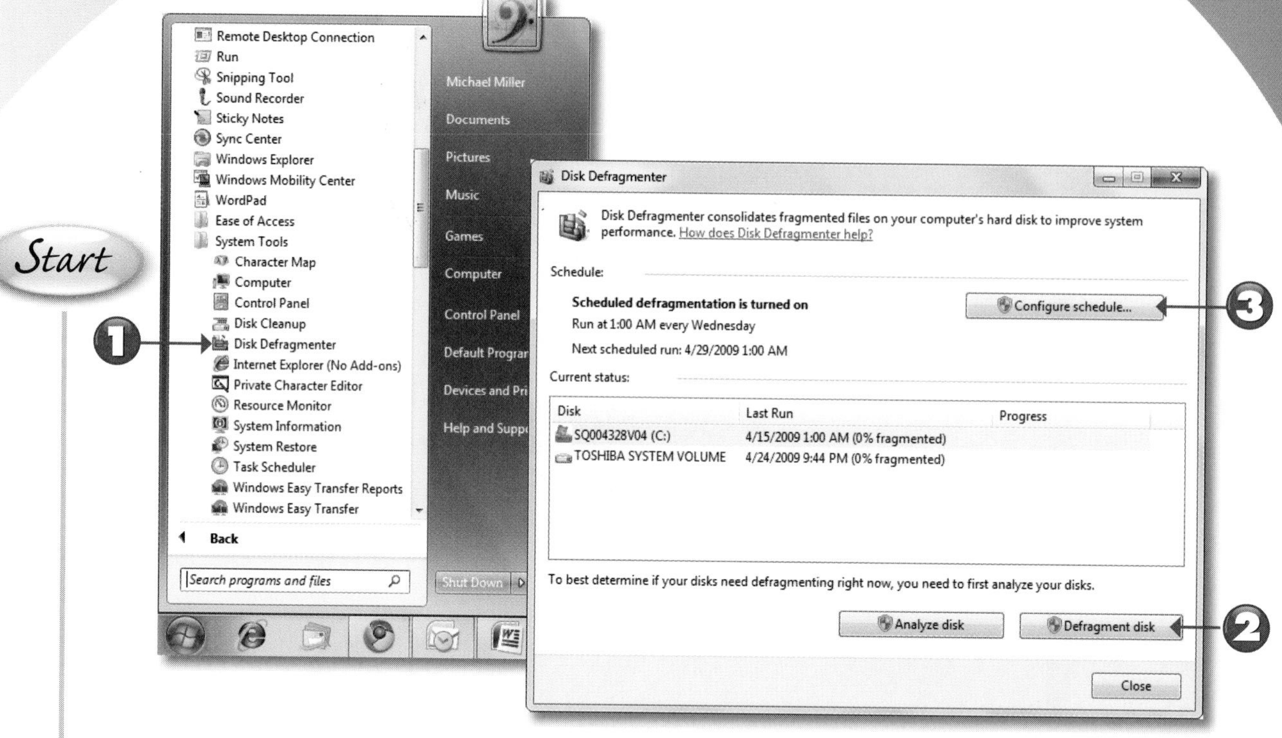

1. Click the **Start** button and select **All Programs**, **Accessories**, **System Tools**, **Disk Defragmenter**.
2. To manually defragment your hard drive, click **Defragment Disk**.
3. To set up automatic disk defragmenting, click **Configure Schedule**.

Continued

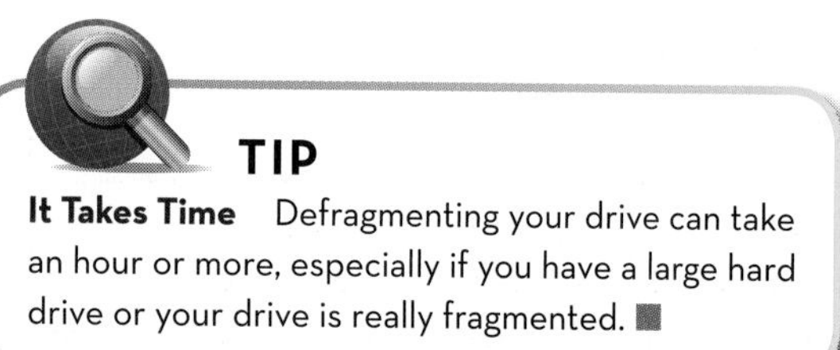

TIP

It Takes Time Defragmenting your drive can take an hour or more, especially if you have a large hard drive or your drive is really fragmented. ■

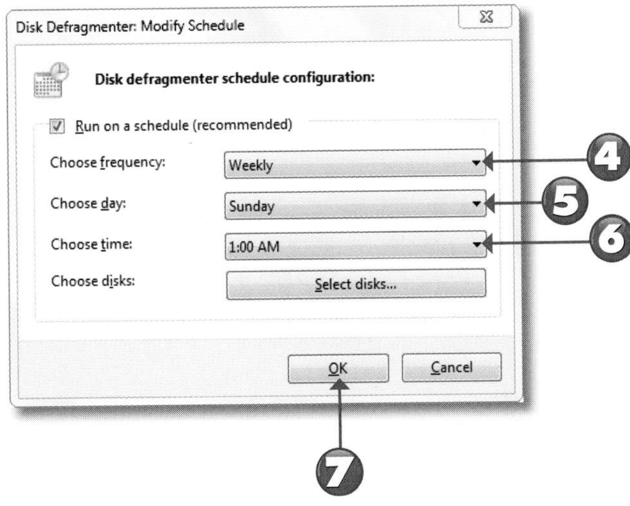

4. Click the **Choose Frequency** button and select how often you want to defragment.

5. Click the **Choose Day** button and select what day of the week you want to defragment your disk.

6. Click the **Choose Time** button and select at what time of day you want to run the defragmenter utility.

7. Click **OK**.

End

NOTE

Pieces of the Puzzle File fragmentation is like taking the pieces of a jigsaw puzzle and storing them in different boxes along with pieces from other puzzles. The more dispersed the pieces are, the longer it takes to put the puzzle together. ■

NOTE

Fragmented Files Files can get fragmented whenever you install, delete, or run an application, or when you edit, move, copy, or delete a file. ■

CHECKING YOUR HARD DISK FOR ERRORS

Any time you move or delete a file or accidentally turn off the power while the system is running, you run the risk of introducing errors to your hard disk. Fortunately, you can find and fix most of these errors directly from within Windows 7, using the ScanDisk utility.

Start

1. Click the **Start** button and select **Computer**.
2. Click the icon for the drive you want to scan.
3. Click **Properties** from the toolbar.

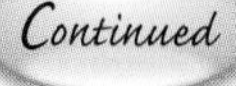

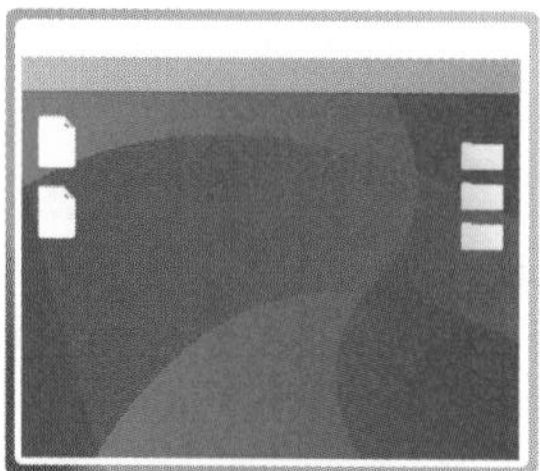

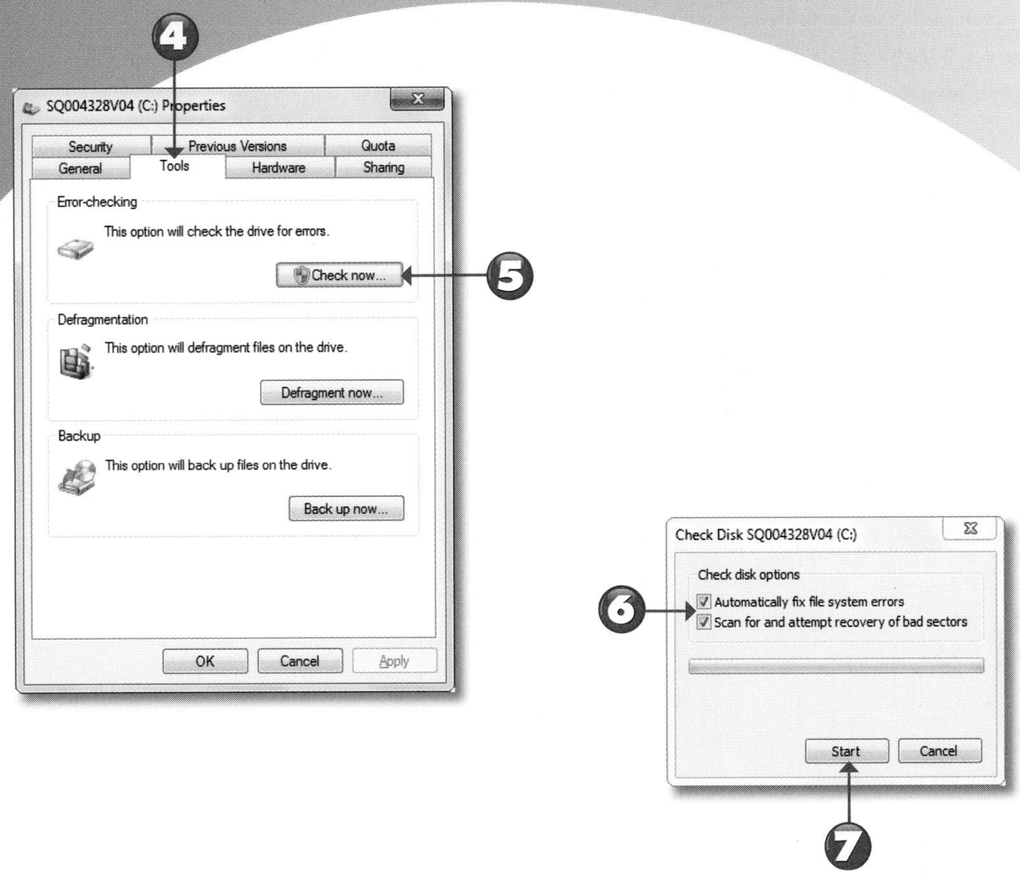

4. When the Properties utility opens, click the **Tools** tab.

5. Click the **Check Now** button in the Error-Checking section.

6. Check **Automatically Fix File System Errors** and **Scan for and Attempt Recovery of Bad Sectors**.

7. Click **Start**.

End

TIP

Scanning and Fixing ScanDisk not only scans your hard disk for errors but also automatically fixes any errors it finds. (If it finds errors, however, you may need to reboot your system.)

TIP

How Often to Run? It's a good idea to run all these system utilities at least once a month, just to ensure that your system stays in tip-top condition.

MANAGING YOUR NOTEBOOK'S MOBILITY SETTINGS

If you own a notebook computer, key settings for portable use can be managed in the Windows Mobility Center. You can monitor or configure such features as display brightness, battery life, presentation settings, and your wireless network.

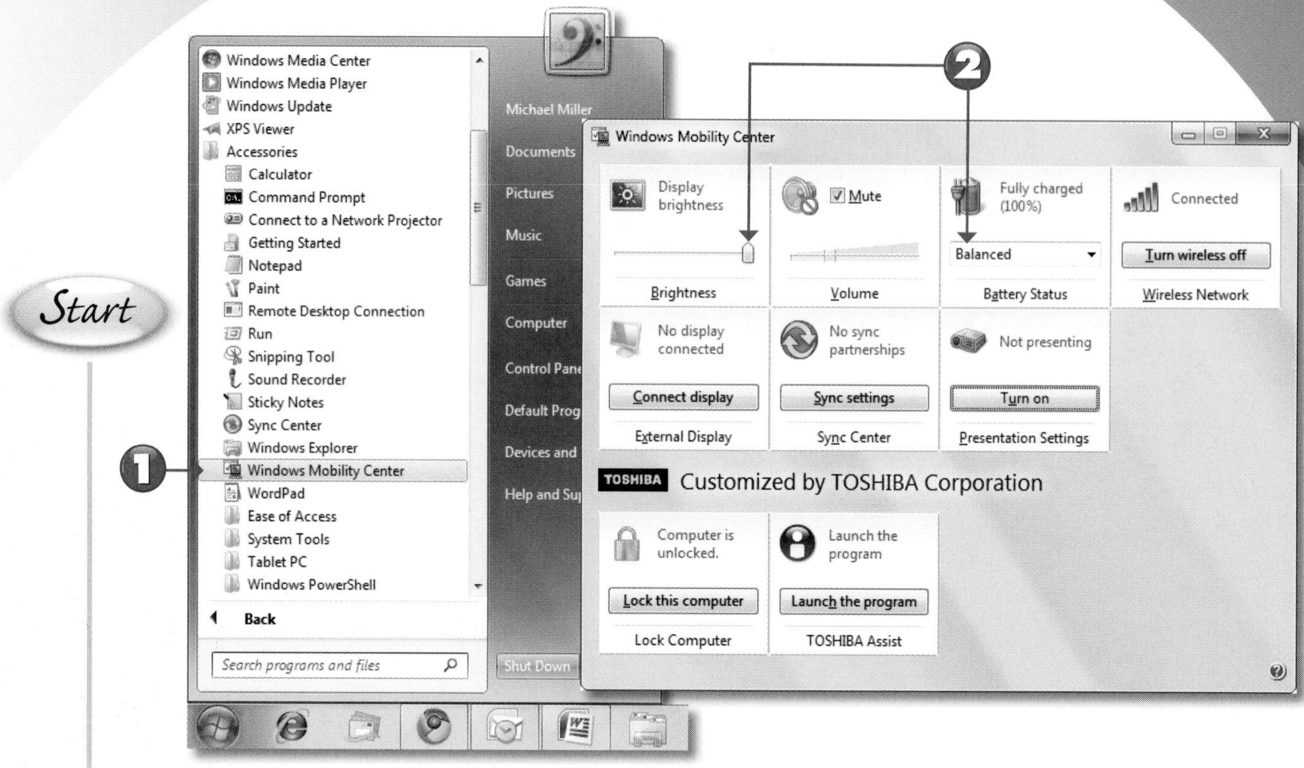

1. Click the **Start** button and select **All Programs**, **Accessories**, **Windows Mobility Center**.
2. Use the appropriate control to adjust any specific settings.

NOTE

Manufacturer Settings Some notebook manufacturers will add their own mobile configuration settings to the Windows Mobility Center. ■

KEEPING YOUR COMPUTER IN TIP-TOP SHAPE

Not all preventive maintenance takes place from within Windows. There are also some physical things you should do to keep your computer operating in tip-top shape.

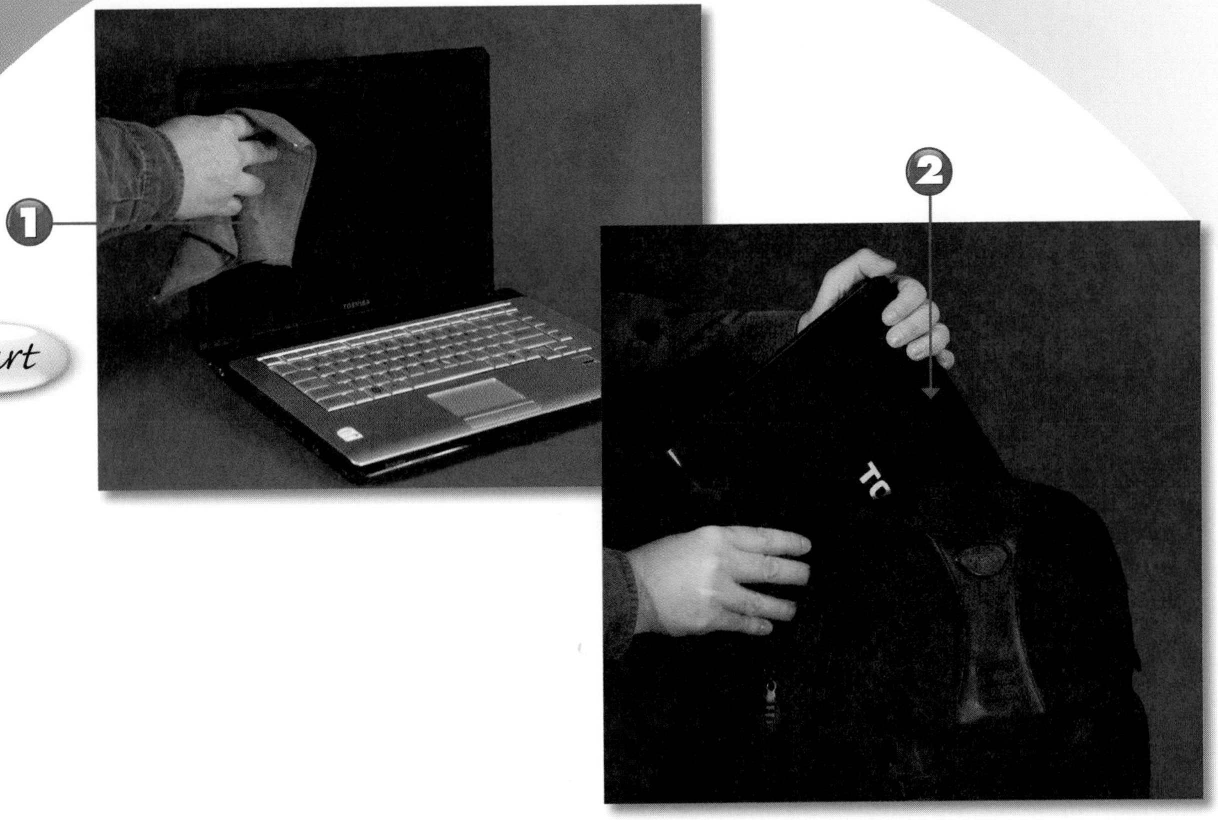

Start

1. Clean your computer's LCD display with plain water or specially formulated display cleaner on a lint-free cloth. Spray the cleaner on the cloth, not directly on the screen.
2. Carry your notebook PC in a well-padded case. Travel with the CD/DVD drive *up*, so as not to jar it when you set down the case.

End

TIP

Keyboard Cleaning Clean your computer keyboard with cotton swabs or a can of compressed air (to blow the dirt away). ■

CAUTION

Avoid Alcohol and Ammonia When cleaning your monitor, do not use any cleaner that contains alcohol or ammonia; these chemicals may damage an LCD screen. You can, however, use commercial cleaning sprays and wipes specially formulated for LCD screens. ■

Glossary

A

add-in board A device that plugs in to a desktop computer's system unit and provides auxiliary functions. (Also called a *card*.)

address The location of an Internet host. An email address might take the form johndoe@xyz.com; a web address might look like www.xyztech.com. See also ***URL***.

Aero The translucent desktop interface in Windows 7 and Windows Vista.

Aero Peek The new Windows 7 feature that lets you "peek" at the desktop beneath all open windows with the click of a button on the toolbar.

Aero Snaps The mouse actions that enable you to maximize and "snap" windows to either side of the screen.

application A computer program designed for a specific task or use, such as word processing, accounting, or missile guidance.

attachment A file, such as a Word document or graphics image, attached to an email message.

B

backup A copy of important data files.

boot The process of turning on your computer system.

broadband A high-speed Internet connection; it's faster than the older dial-up connection.

browser A program, such as Internet Explorer, that translates the Hypertext Markup Language (HTML) of the Web into viewable web pages.

bug An error in a software program or the hardware.

burner A device that writes CD-ROMs or DVD-ROMs.

C

cable modem A high-speed, broadband Internet connection via digital cable TV lines.

card Also called an *add-in board*, this is a device that plugs in to your computer's system unit and provides auxiliary functions.

CD-R (compact disc recordable) A type of CD drive that lets you record only once onto a disc, which can then be read by any CD-ROM drive or audio CD player.

CD-ROM (compact disc read-only memory) A CD that can be used to store computer data. A CD-ROM, similar to an audio CD, stores data in a form readable by a laser, resulting in a storage device of great capacity and quick accessibility.

CD-RW (compact disc rewritable) A type of CD that can be recorded, erased, and rewritten to by the user, multiple times.

computer A programmable device that can store, retrieve, and process data.

CPU (central processing unit) The group of circuits that direct the entire computer system by (1) interpreting and executing program instruction and (2) coordinating the interaction of input, output, and storage devices.

cursor The highlighted area or pointer that tracks with the movement of your mouse or arrow keys onscreen.

D

data Information—on a computer, in digital format.

database A program for arranging facts in the computer and retrieving them—the computer equivalent of a filing system.

desktop The entire screen area on which you display all your computer work. A typical computer desktop can contain icons, a taskbar, menus, and individual application windows.

device A computer file that represents some object—physical or nonphysical—installed on your system.

disk A device that stores data in magnetic or optical format.

disk drive A mechanism for retrieving information stored on a magnetic disk. The drive rotates the disk at high speed and reads the data with a magnetic head similar to those used in tape recorders.

domain The identifying portion of an Internet address. In email addresses, the domain name follows the @ sign; in website addresses, the domain name follows the www.

download A way to transfer files, graphics, or other information from the Internet to your computer.

dpi (dots per inch) A measurement of printer resolution; the more dots per inch, the higher the resolution.

driver A support file that tells a program how to interact with a specific hardware device, such as a hard disk controller or video display card.

DSL (digital subscriber line) A high-speed Internet connection that uses the ultra-high frequency portion of ordinary telephone lines, allowing users to send and receive voice and data on the same line at the same time.

DVD An optical disc, similar to a CD, that can hold a minimum of 4.7GB, enough for a full-length movie.

E

email Electronic mail; a means of corresponding with other computer users over the Internet through digital messages.

encryption A method of encoding files so only the recipient can read the information.

Ethernet The most common computer networking protocol; Ethernet is used to network, or hook together, computers so they can share information.

executable file A program you run on your computer system.

F

favorite A bookmarked site in Internet Explorer.

file Any group of data treated as a single entity by the computer, such as a word processor document, a program, or a database.

firewall Computer hardware or software with special security features to safeguard a computer connected to a network or to the Internet.

FireWire A high-speed bus used to connect digital devices, such as digital cameras and video cameras, to a computer system. Also known as *i.LINK* and *IEEE-1394*.

Flip 3D The display of a three-dimensional stack for all open windows, used to cycle through and select a window in Windows 7 and Windows Vista; you enable Flip 3D by pressing Windows+Tab.

folder A way to group files on a disk; each folder can contain multiple files or other folders (called *subfolders*). Folders are sometimes called *directories*.

freeware Free software available over the Internet. This is in contrast with *shareware*, which is available freely but usually asks the user to send payment for using the software.

G

gadget A small single-purpose utility that resides on the Windows desktop.

gigabyte (GB) One billion bytes.

graphics Pictures, photographs, and clip art.

H

hard disk A sealed cartridge containing a magnetic storage disk(s) that holds much more memory than removable disks—up to 1 terabyte or more.

hardware The physical equipment, as opposed to the programs and procedures, used in computing.

home page The first or main page of a website.

HomeGroup A small network of computers all running Windows 7.

hover The act of selecting an item by placing your cursor over an icon without clicking.

hyperlink A connection between two tagged elements in a web page, or separate sites, that makes it possible to click from one to the other.

I–J

icon A graphic symbol on the display screen that represents a file, peripheral, or some other object or function.

instant messaging Text-based, real-time one-on-one communication over the Internet.

Internet The global network of networks that connects millions of computers and other devices around the world.

Internet service provider (ISP) A company that provides end-user access to the Internet via its central computers and local access lines.

K–L

keyboard The typewriter-like device used to type instructions to a personal computer.

kilobyte (KB) A unit of measure for data storage or transmission equivalent to 1,024 bytes; often rounded to 1,000.

LAN (local area network) A system that enables users to connect PCs to one another or to minicomputers or mainframes.

laptop A portable computer small enough to operate on one's lap. Also known as a *notebook* computer.

LCD (liquid crystal display) A flat-screen display where images are created by light transmitted through a layer of liquid crystals.

library A kind of virtual folder that doesn't physically exist on your hard disk but instead points to files and folders placed within it.

M–N

megabyte (MB) One million bytes.

megahertz (MHz) A measure of microprocessing speed; 1MHz equals 1 million electrical cycles per second.

memory Temporary electronic storage for data and instructions, via electronic impulses on a chip.

microcomputer A computer based on a microprocessor chip. Also known as a *personal computer*.

microprocessor A complete central processing unit assembled on a single silicon chip.

modem (modulator demodulator) A device capable of converting a digital signal into an analog signal, which can be transmitted via a telephone line, reconverted, and then "read" by another computer.

monitor The display device on a computer, similar to a television screen.

motherboard Typically the largest printed circuit board in a computer, housing the CPU chip and controlling circuitry.

mouse A small handheld input device connected to a computer and featuring one or more button-style switches. When moved around on a flat surface, the mouse causes a symbol on the computer screen to make corresponding movements.

network An interconnected group of computers.

O–P

operating system A sequence of programming codes that instructs a computer about its various parts and peripherals and how to operate them. Operating systems, such as Windows, deal only with the workings of the hardware and are separate from software programs.

parallel A type of external port used to connect printers and other similar devices; typically not found on newer PCs.

path The collection of folders and subfolders (listed in order of hierarchy) that hold a particular file.

peripheral A device connected to the computer that provides communication or auxiliary functions.

phishing The act of trying to "fish" for personal information via means of a deliberately deceptive email or website.

pixel The individual picture elements that combine to create a video image.

Plug and Play (PnP) Hardware that includes its manufacturer and model information in its ROM, enabling Windows to recognize it immediately upon startup and install the necessary drivers if not already set up.

pop-up A small browser window, typically without menus or other navigational elements, that opens seemingly of its own accord when you visit or leave another website.

port An interface on a computer to which you can connect a device, either internally or externally.

printer The piece of computer hardware that creates hard copy printouts of documents.

Q–R

RAM (random access memory) A temporary storage space in which data can be held on a chip rather than being stored on disk or tape. The contents of RAM can be accessed or altered at any time during a session but will be lost when the computer is turned off.

resolution The degree of clarity an image displays, typically expressed by the number of horizontal and vertical pixels or the number of dots per inch (dpi).

ribbon A toolbar-like collection of action buttons, used in many newer Windows programs.

ROM (read-only memory) A type of chip memory, the contents of which have been permanently recorded in a computer by the manufacturer and cannot be altered by the user.

root The main directory or folder on a disk.

router A piece of hardware or software that handles the connection between two or more networks.

S

scanner A device that converts paper documents or photos into a format that can be viewed on a computer and manipulated by the user.

screensaver A display of moving designs on your computer screen when you haven't typed or moved the mouse for a while.

serial A type of external port used to connect communication devices; typically not found on newer PCs.

server The central computer in a network, providing a service or data access to client computers on the network.

shareware A software program distributed on the honor system; providers make their programs freely accessible over the Internet, with the understanding that those who use them will send payment to the provider after using them. See also ***freeware***.

software The programs and procedures, as opposed to the physical equipment, used in computing.

spam Junk email. As a verb, it means to send thousands of copies of a junk email message.

spreadsheet A program that performs mathematical operations on numbers arranged in large arrays; used mainly for accounting and other record keeping.

spyware Software used to surreptitiously monitor computer use (that is, spy on other users).

system unit The part of a desktop computer system that looks like a big beige or black box. The system unit typically contains the microprocessor, system memory, hard disk drive, floppy disk drives, and various cards.

T-U-V

terabyte (TB) One trillion bytes.

theme A combination of Windows color scheme, desktop background, sound scheme, and screensaver.

track pad The pointing device used on most notebook PCs, in lieu of an external mouse.

upgrade To add a new or improved peripheral or part to your system hardware. Also to install a newer version of an existing piece of software.

upload The act of copying a file from a personal computer to a website or Internet server. The opposite of *download*.

URL (uniform resource locator) The address that identifies a web page to a browser. Also known as a *web address*.

USB (universal serial bus) An external bus standard that supports data transfer rates of up to 480Mbps; an individual computer can connect up to 127 peripheral devices via USB.

User Account Control (UAC) A Windows security feature that requires administrator authorization before major operations are allowed to run.

virus A computer program segment or string of code that can attach itself to another program or file, reproduce itself, and spread from one computer to another. Viruses can destroy or change data and in other ways sabotage computer systems.

W-X-Y-Z

web page An HTML file, containing text, graphics, and/or mini-applications, viewed with a web browser.

website An organized, linked collection of web pages stored on an Internet server and read using a web browser. The opening page of a site is called a *home page*.

Wi-Fi The radio frequency (RF)-based technology used for home and small business wireless networks and for most public wireless Internet connections. It operates at 11Mbps (802.11b), 54Mbps (802.11g), or 248Mbps (802.11n). Short for "wireless fidelity."

window A portion of the screen display used to view simultaneously a different part of the file in use or a part of a different file than the one in use.

Windows The generic name for all versions of Microsoft's graphical operating system.

Windows Explorer The Windows folder used to navigate and display files and folders on your computer system.

Windows Flip The display of thumbnails for all open windows, used to cycle through and select programs in Windows 7 and Windows Vista; you enable Windows Flip by pressing Alt+Tab.

World Wide Web (WWW) A vast network of information, particularly business, commercial, and government resources, that uses a hypertext system for quickly transmitting graphics, sound, and video over the Internet.

Zip file A file that has been compressed for easier transmission.

Index

Symbols

A

B

C

D

G

H

J - K

L

M

N

O

P

Q - R

W

X-Y

Z